J. L. jun. Glasscock

The Records of St. Michael's Parish Church, Bishop's Stortford

J. L. jun. Glasscock

The Records of St. Michael's Parish Church, Bishop's Stortford

ISBN/EAN: 9783337007614

Printed in Europe, USA, Canada, Australia, Japan

Cover: Foto ©Lupo / pixelio.de

More available books at **www.hansebooks.com**

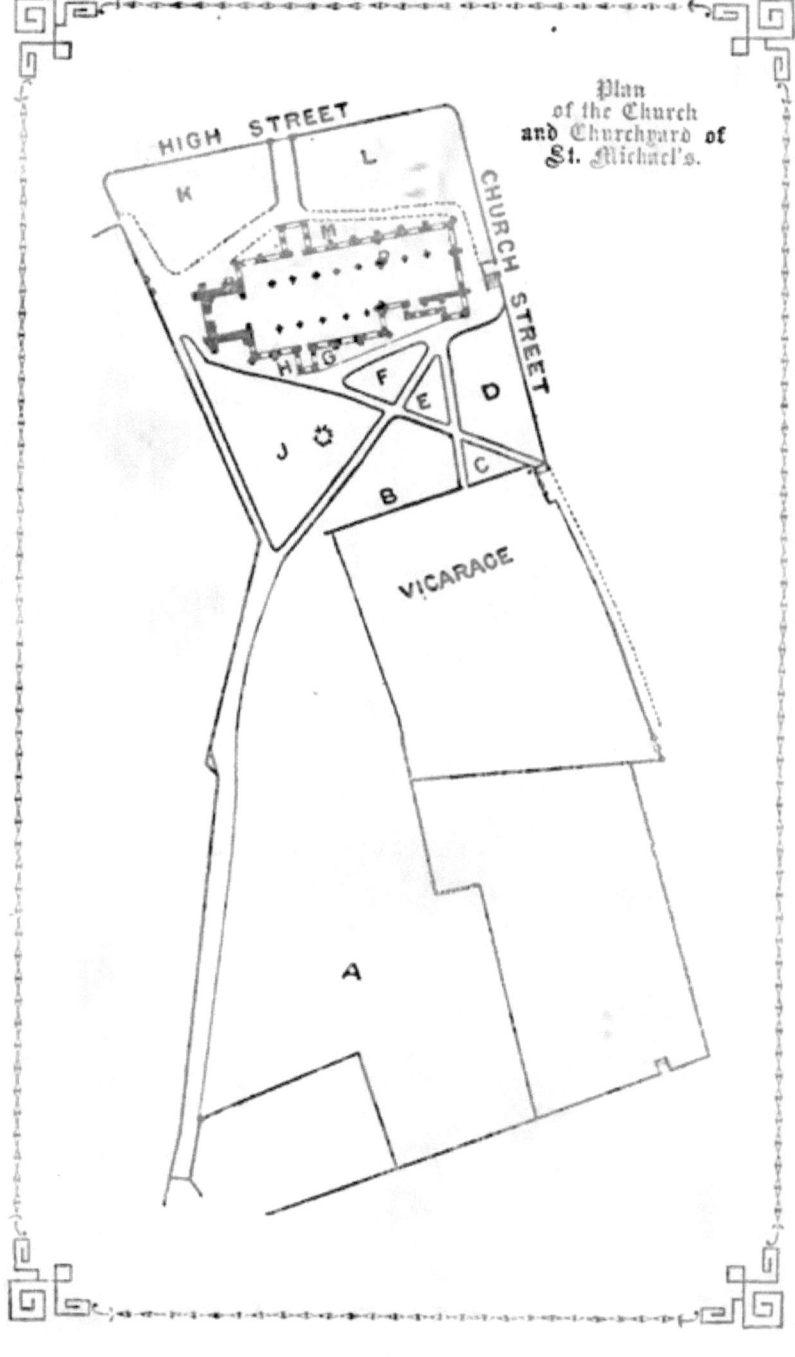

THE RECORDS

OF

St. Michael's Parish Church,

BISHOP'S STORTFORD.

EDITED BY
J. L. GLASSCOCK, Jun.

LONDON:
ELLIOT STOCK, 62, PATERNOSTER ROW.
BISHOP'S STORTFORD: A. BOARDMAN.
MDCCCLXXXII.

CONTENTS.

	PAGE
PREFACE	vii
CATALOGUE OF THE PAPERS	ix
THE ACCOUNTS OF THE CHURCHWARDENS	1
NOTES TO THE CHURCHWARDENS' ACCOUNTS	89
THE VICARS AND CHURCHWARDENS OF ST. MICHAEL'S	110
THE CHANTRY AND GUILD OF ST. JOHN THE BAPTIST	118
THE INVENTORIES OF THE CHURCH GOODS	124
CHURCH RENTALS	139
THE CHURCHWARDENS' BOOK, 1642	145
THE DESTRUCTION OF VERMIN	156
ACCOUNTS OF THE COLLECTORS FOR THE POOR	158
EXTRACTS FROM THE OVERSEERS' BOOK	163
THE NAMES OF THE COLLECTORS AND OVERSEERS OF THE POOR	168
THE FINDINGS OF THE CHARITIES' COMMISSION, 1692	174
SUBSCRIBERS TO THE SCHOOL-HOUSE	186
FROM THE MISCELLANEOUS PAPERS	189
MONUMENTAL INSCRIPTIONS	190
INDEX OF NAMES	221

PREFACE.

READERS of County Histories must be aware that the County Historian, as a rule, has neither time nor space to devote to what may be termed the more minute details of the domestic life and customs of each Parish in his County. He cannot, for instance, be expected to transcribe the Parish Register, or the accounts of Churchwardens; and yet these documents contain information which must be extremely interesting to all residents, and without which no Parochial History can be said to have been thoroughly and completely written.

Impressed with this idea, I have often wished, if it were possible, to add some little link in the chain of the history of my native town. An opportunity occurred a few years ago, when Mr. Speechly (one of the present Churchwardens) undertook the rearrangement of the Parish Papers. I had the pleasure of helping him in the work, and I found the papers contained so much interesting matter, that I determined, if possible, to publish a transcript of them, my only regret being that the work had not fallen into abler hands.

In the following pages I have endeavoured to put before the reader, without any unnecessary comment of my own, a transcript of all the interesting portions of the papers, in such a form as to enable him to realise for himself the details of the quaint life and curious customs which have surrounded the Church and its neighbourhood during the last 400 years. The Parish Register is not included, because I consider that extracts *only* are worse than useless, and a verbatim copy would be quite beyond the scope of a work like this.

No apology, I think, is needed for the introduction of the Monumental Inscriptions. Though they do not, strictly speaking, come under the head of Parish Papers, they certainly form an important part of the records of St. Michael's.

I would here call the attention of readers to this fact, that there is a large amount of information interesting alike to inhabitants of the parish, and to antiquaries generally, contained in the title deeds and writings of property; and I feel sure that the information to be obtained from them would amply repay any little trouble or inconvenience that a search might occasion. It will be noticed, for example, that in the transcript of receipts and rentals, several houses and streets are mentioned, the names of which have long since disappeared and been forgotten; these are doubtless mentioned in most cases in the writings, and the old names might by this means be identified with the existing houses or sites. I shall be very grateful for any information which may reach me from such reliable sources.

I take this opportunity of thanking the Vicar and the Churchwardens for their courtesy, and the facilities they have afforded me for the inspection of their papers; and also those ladies and gentlemen who by their subscriptions have helped me to carry out my work. As the work of leisure hours in winter evenings, I now modestly put this little book before my readers, trusting that they will not find its perusal altogether uninteresting, and that it may awaken a keener interest in the antiquities of our town.

BISHOP'S STORTFORD,
December, 1881.

CATALOGUE AND DESCRIPTION OF THE VARIOUS PAPERS AT PRESENT (1881) *IN THE CUSTODY OF THE VICAR AND CHURCHWARDENS OF ST. MICHAEL'S AND THE OVERSEERS OF THE POOR.*

The papers comprised in the following catalogue were, when I first saw them in 1877, tied up in small parcels and packed away in a chest in the vestry. In this condition they were practically useless, as any reference to them would have entailed great labour and loss of time.

The idea of cleaning and examining the papers having been suggested, Mr. Speechly, one of the present churchwardens, undertook the by no means easy task, and has now succeeded in arranging the whole of the parish papers in books in chronological order. I may mention here that the late Dr. Starling evidently had a somewhat similar idea in view, but his death prevented him making any progress in the work. I am indebted to his son, Dr. John Starling, of Kensington, for a perusal of his father's memoranda relating to the Churchwardens' Accounts.

The following is a complete list of the books and papers :—

BOOK No. 1 contains :

Churchwardens' Accounts from 1431 to 1440.
      „   „   „   1482 to 1582 (about 15 years missing).

Six rentals or portions of rentals :
(1) Date lost, but probably temp. Edw. IV. or Rich. III.
(2)   „   „   „   „   late Hen. VII. or early Hen. VIII.
(3) 21st of Hen. VIII.
(4) 31st of Hen. VIII.
(5) 38th of Hen. VIII. or 1st Edw. VI.
(6) 6th of Edward VI.

Two papers very much torn, no date, endorsed on the back "relating to the Chantry."

Nine papers of inventories and memoranda relating to the sale of the Church Goods.

Book No. 2 contains:

Churchwardens' Accounts from 1583 to 1661 (18 years missing).
,, ,, ,, 1680 to 1700 (7 ,, ,,
,, ,, ,, for the years 1701-3-4-6-9-10-12-13-14-15-16-17-18-20-21-42-43-85.

Six Rentals, dates 1600-2-5-70-76 and 1721.

Book No. 3 contains:

The Apprenticeship Orders and Indentures from 1693 to 1790.

Book No. 4 contains

The Original Vouchers or Bills which are referred to in the Accounts from 1663 to 1799. As a whole these are not worth transcribing, but they contain a few items which are interesting as examples of the rate of wages and the price of materials in various trades. The following are the charges of a master bricklayer in 1685:

for "a trouellman" 1s. 8d. per day.
,, "a laborer" 1s. 2d. ,,
,, "31 bus. lime" 18s. 1d.
,, "8 bus. hare" 5s. 4d.

In the same year a Glazier charged for:

"39 squares of glazing at 2d. ye square."
"4 great squares 1s. 2d. ye square."
"new leading 2d. per foot."

The following papers are arranged in parcels, and are endorsed on the covers:

The Overseers' Accounts from 1692 to 1749 . . 20 papers.
The Accounts of the Collectors for the Poor . . 9 ,,
Memoranda and letters relating to the Inquisition of 1692 about the Charities.

Under this head are preserved 43 papers consisting of minutes and memoranda; they contain no very interesting matter. In addition to these there are 14 letters from and to Dr. Yardley, Mr. Altham, etc., all relating to the same subject . . . . . 57 ,,
Miscellaneous Papers . . . . . . 32 ,,

Total 118

A small parcel containing particulars of the Rents belonging to the Church and Poor of Stortford from 1782 to 1794.

In addition to the above-mentioned papers there are the following books:

(1) A vellum bound book endorsed on the cover: " In this Booke is the decree of the High Court of Chancery concerning the Charities of the Church and Poor of B^p Stortford." From a letter pasted inside the cover it appears that this book was sent to the late vicar (Rev. F. W. Rhodes) in 1872 by a gentleman into whose hands it had come through an executorship, and who very properly considered that it ought to be again placed in the parish chest.

The contents of the book are as follows:

A discharge for Mr. Polhill's legacy of £50.
A Copy of the Will of the Rev^d. W^m. Polhill.
A Receipt from the Churchwardens and Overseers to Edward Denny and Cordelia his wife acknowledging the receipt of £20, the legacy of Rowland Hill; this is signed by William Bayford and William Barnes, Churchwardens, John Jennens and William Ely, Overseers.
A surrender by Rowland Hill of two half acres of land at Easton (C^o Huntingdon) to the Lord of the Manor of Spaldwick, dated 1671.
The Decree of the Commissioners concerning the Charities, 1692.
Minutes of a meeting of the Charity Trustees, 1693.
An additional order of the High Court of Chancery concerning the Charities, 1716.
An Inventory of Church Goods, 1537.
       "   "   "   "   1548.

NOTE.—These are copies of two of the Inventories in Book No. 1.

Inside the cover of this book a MSS. is placed entitled " An Ode to Science, recited by a chorus of Youths at Bishop Stortford School feast, August 13, 1754."

(2) The Churchwardens' minute book from 1712 to 1858.
(3) Another minute book from 1858 (in use in 1881).

The whole of the above-mentioned books and papers are kept in the vestry of St. Michael's Church.

The Assistant Overseer, Mr. Thomas Coote, has under his charge at his office:

(1) A large book bound in calf with a clasp, called " A Booke of the accompte of the Churchwardens, Overseers, and the Officers of the P'ishe of Stortford," date from 1656 to 1772.
(2) The Overseers' Book from 1772 (in use 1881).

In a room in the Corn Exchange are the Rate Books and

Overseers' accounts for the last eighty or ninety years, and some interesting old account books relating to the management of the old workhouse previous to the passing of the present Poor Law. These, however, must be considered inaccessible for reference in their present state. At the annual vestry meeting, March 25, 1881, it was "resolved that the Assistant Overseer should be empowered to remove all books belonging to the Parish from the Corn Exchange, and take charge of them at his own residence."

ERRATA.

Page 108 *for* "Mannden," *read* "Manuden."
Page 109 *for* "know," *read* "known.
Page 121 *for* "hampir," *read* "haniper" = Hanaper.

THE
ACCOUNTS OF THE CHURCHWARDENS.

No accounts previous to 1431 have been preserved, and of the 354 years over which the accounts extend, no less than 151 are missing. This is much to be regretted, as some of the missing years would in all probability have contained especially interesting items.

As a rule, the papers are dated according to the Regnal years, but for uniformity I have adopted the A.D. dating throughout.

The year over which the account extended was reckoned previous to 1504 from Michaelmas to Michaelmas; and from 1504 to 1611, from Palm Sunday to Palm Sunday; since the year 1611 the reckoning has been from Easter Monday to Easter Monday.

The writing of the accounts in most cases appears to have been the work of a Scribe, and is consequently good; a few years are indifferently written, and about three or four are very badly done.

The accounts for the following 17 years, viz., from 1431 to 1440, 1489, 1490, 1495, 1496, 1499, 1500, 1501, 1502, are written in Latin. As a fair specimen of the whole I give verbatim the parchment roll containing the accounts from 1431 to 1440 and in making this transcript I have extended the abbreviations of the Latin which occur in the original. The items in the remaining 8 years are very similar to those transcribed from the roll; I therefore thought it sufficient for the purpose to give the translation of the more interesting.

In making the extracts from the English accounts, while trying to avoid a needless repetition, I have endeavoured not to omit anything relating to the Service, Ornaments, Goods or Fabric of the Church, nor any item containing allusions to old customs, names of streets, houses or persons. I have throughout preserved the spelling of the original as far as possible, only deviating from it in cases where the abbreviations in the original might render the word obscure or unintelligible; in such cases I have supplied the missing letter or letters.

At first I thought of contenting myself with simply exhibiting the testimony of the records themselves, but it afterwards occurred to me that a few notes might possibly make them more interesting to the general reader.

TRANSCRIPT OF THE ACCOUNTS FROM 1431 TO 1440.

STORTEFORD'.

COMPOTUS JOHANNIS WOLVERSTON ET JOHANNIS BUSCH YCONOMORUM ECCLESIÆ IBIDEM A FESTO SANCTI THOMÆ MARTYRIS ANNO DOMINI MILLESIMO CCCC^{MO} TRICESIMO PRIMO USQUE IDEM FESTUM ANNO DOMINI MILLESIMO CCCC^{MO} XL° VIZ. PER IX ANNOS INTEGROS.

Arreragia.
Iidem receperunt de arreragiis ultimi compoti Thomæ Pygeon et Johannis Clapton existentibus super diversos debitores viz. super Johannem Flemyng vj*d.* Thomam . . . . vj*s.* vj*d.* Johannem Bryd iij*s.* vj*d.* Thomam Payn xviij*d.* et Johannem Thurkeld bocher viij*d. obolum.*
    Summa xij*s.* viij*d. ob.*

Redditus.
Et de xxxix*s.* vj*d.* redditus per annum existentis super diversos tenentes ut patet per unum Rentale videlicet pro ix annis infra tempus compoti xvij*li.* xv*s.* vj*d.*
    Summa xvij*li.* xv*s.* vj*d.*

Firmæ.
Et de xxj*s.* ij*d.* per annum pro diversis fermis dimissis certis tenentibus ut patet per idem Rentale videlicet pro dictis ix annis ix*li.* x*s.* vj*d.*
    Summa ix*li.* x*s.* vj*d.*

Wexsilver.

Et de wexsilver collecto in ecclesia in die Paschali anno Domini mccccxxxij viz. j^{mo} anno infra tempus hujus compoti	vij*s.*	viij*d.*
Et de eisdem denariis collectis in ij° anno infra tempus compoti viz. anno mccccxxxiij^{tio}	viij*s.*	vj*d.*
Et de eisdem denariis collectis in ecclesia eodem die iij^{tio} anno viz. anno mccccxxxiiij^{to}	viij*s.*	iv*d.*
Et de consimilibus denariis collectis eodem die in iiij^{to} anno infra tempus compoti viz. anno mccccxxxv^{to}	viij*s.*	iij*d.*
Et de eisdem denariis collectis in v^{to} anno viz. anno mccccvxxvj^{to}	ix*s.*	ij*d.*

Et de eisdem denariis collectis in vj⁺⁰ anno viz. anno
   mccccxxxvij^(mo) . . . . . . viijs.   vd.
Et de eisdem collectis in vij^(mo) anno viz. anno
   mccccxxxviij⁺⁰ . . . . . . ixs.
Et de eisdem collectis in viij⁺⁰ anno viz. anno
   mccccxxxix^(no) . . . . . . viijs.   ijd.
Et de eisdem collectis anno nono viz. anno mccccxl^(mo)   ixs.
   Summa lxxvjs. vjd.

Receptiones Forinsecæ.
Et de stationibus carectarum super solum ecclesiæ
   temporibus nundinorum infra tempus compoti .   iiijd.
Et de stationibus in le gatehouse cimiterii eisdem
   temporibus . . . . iijd.
Et de melle proveniente de ij hyvis apum infra tem-
   pus compoti ij lagenis pretii . . . ijs. viijd.
De cera proveniente de dictes hyvis nil quia expenditur
   in ecclesia et non exposita venditioni.
      Summa iijs. iijd.
De ij messuagiis ecclesiæ juxta cimiterium viz. le
   Scolehous et le gatehous nil hic quia ruinosa et
   stant vacua per defectus conductorum.
De stallis in piscaria nil quia non occupantur in
   mercato sed incumbuntur cum fimario ut patet etc
      Summa nil.

Summa totalis receptionum cum arreragiis xxxjli. xviijs. vd. ob.

Reparatio ecclesiæ.
De quibus solutum plumbatori de Hadham emendanti
   diversos defectus coopertura ecclesiæ .   . iijs.
Et pro soudura empta de eodem . . .   iiijd.
Et in clavis emptis pro eodem opere vocatis lednaylis
   et carbonibus . . . . . . iiijd.
Et pro iij tabulis emptis viz. ij pro gutteris supra le
   porche ex parte boreali ecclesiæ et j pro le
   cherchestyle . . . . . . vid.
Et solutum pro muris ecclesiæ et campanili coope-
   riendis cum stramine et plumbo ad ffestum
   Sancti Lucæ Evangelistæ in primo anno hujus
   compoti . . . . ijd.
Et circa cooperturam ejusdem operis in ij⁰ anno hujus
   compoti . . . . vd.
Et vitrario de Walden emendanti diversas fracturas
   fenestrarum ecclesiæ . . . . ijs.   ijd.

Et solutum plumbatori pro emendatione porticus borealis et plumbatione ejusdem ex conventione in grosso . . . . iiij$s$.
Et Johanni Everard pro emendatione et induratione unius teltis ferri pro lez spowtes ejusdem porticus dilatandis . . . . ij$d$.
Et Johanni Wrighte operanti per iij dies ad tascam cum   Bukberd factore horologii circa ordinationem et repositionem ejusdem horologii . xvj$d$.
Et in j planke de popler empta pro eodem horologio vd.
Et solutum Johanni Mason et duobus filiis suis pro relevatione et complanatione ariæ ecclesiæ ex parte occidentali juxta campanile . . . iiij$d$.
Et solutum plumbatori pro plumbatione de le Halywaterstoppe in porticu boreali viz. pro operatione . . . . . . iiij$d$.
Petra et x^{lb} plumbi . . . . . xviij$d$.
Et in iij petris et dimidio plumbi emptis pro eodem opere petra ad ix$d$. ob. plus in toto . . ii$s$. viij$d$.
   Summa xvij$s$. iiij$d$.

Reparatio domorum et stallorum ecclesiæ.

Et solutum Johanni Monkes pro reparatione stalli ecclesiæ in le mercerie juxta messuagium suum ex conventione secum facta per Thomam Pygeon et Johannem Clapton nuper custodes bonorum ecclesiæ . . . . . . xs.
Et solutum Johanni Wavell pro gruncellatione pro impositione unius stode pro splentatione et fissuris eorundum et pro ij novis fenestris pro le cherchehous apud le cherchestyle per iij dies capienti per diem ad tascam vj$d$. . . . . xviij$d$.
Et in una antica viz. j hacche de novo facta per Edwardum Webbe pro camera apud le Pultrihell viij$d$.
Et pro tabulis sive bordes emptis pro dictis fenestris . viij$d$.
Et in clavis pro eisdem fenestris faciendis . . iij$d$.
Et in j gruncelle j stode splentes et legges supra dictis emptis . . . . xv$d$.
Et pro daubatione fracturarum ejusdem domus apud le cherchestyle . . . . . . iij$d$.
Et solutum pro serura et clavi factis per Colyn pro domo ecclesiæ super le Pultrihell . . . iiij$d$.
Et in reparatione unius stalli in le Bocherie cum ij plankes quercus pretii vj$d$. . . . . ix$d$.
Et Johanni Wrighte conducto per vj dies ad reparan-

dum domum juxta cimiterium capienti per diem
v*d*. ad tascam . . . . . ij*s*. vj*d*.
Et Johanni Bargayn pro simili per v dies et dimidium ij*s*.iij*d*. *ob*.
Et in mæremio empto viz. gruncelles stodes gystes et
j coyseschyd . . . . . . iij*s*.
Et in ij braces emptis de Johanne Goos . . v*d*.
Et in ij ligamentis ferreis cum clavis pro eisdem . iiij*d*.
Et Johanni Wavell per ij dies circa facturam unius
pale cum hostio pro le Bellehous in Cimiterio
capienti per diem vj*d*. ad tascam . . xij*d*.
Et Johanni Bargayn pro eodem opere per ij dies
capienti ut supra. . . . . xij*d*.
Et Johanni Dane pro serura cum clavi pro eodem
hostio . . . . . . iiij*d*.
Et solutum pro sera cum clavi pro le Cherchehous
apud Pultrihell empta per Busch . . iiij*d*.
Et solutum pro reparatione messuagii ecclesiæ in le
Southstret ubi Thomas Andrew inhabitat ut in
allocatione firmæ suæ in principio termini sui . v*s*. vij*d*.
Summa xxxij*s*. v*d*. *ob*.

Reparatio Clausurarum et ornamentorum ecclesiæ.
Et solutum Johanni Sprynholt pro emendatione unius
bellerop . . . . . . *ob*.
Et Johanni Clerk pro filo ad consuendum vestimenta
ecclesiæ . . . . . . ij*d*.
Et Thomæ Beverley pro ligatione situlæ pro aqua
benedicta importanda . . . . ij*d*.
Et Adæ Drakelowe pro emendatione seruræ archæ
ecclesiæ . . . . . . ij*d*.
Et in custis circa elevationem et depositionem sepulcri
in primo anno hujus compoti cum obolo in clavis
pro eodem sepulcro . . . . iij*d*. *ob*.
Et pro clavis de latonia ad emendandum libros
ecclesiæ . . . . . . j*d*.
Et Johanni Sprynholt pro emendatione unius bellerop
alia vice . . . . . . *ob*.
Et Johanni Clokmaker de Walden conducto per vj
dies ad emendandum vetus horologium viz. in
ferro carbonibus stipendio et mensa . . ij*s*. vj*d*.
Et Johanni Wrighte pro factura cooperturæ libitinæ
cum le herse ejusdem et pro emendatione unius
portæ in ortum rectoris versus le Werkhous latomorum juxta cimiterium. . . . xv*d*.
Et pro tabulis emptis pro dicta coopertura et le herse xij*d*.

Et in clavis haspis et stapelles cum ij garnettes emptis
    pro feretro . . . . . . vij*d*.
Et in expensis circa elevationem et depositionem
    sepulcri ij° anno hujus compoti . . iij*d*.
Et in clavis emptis pro uno lectrino emendando . *ob*.
Et in filo pro vestimentis ecclesiæ emendandis alia
    vice . . . . *ob*.
Et Ricardo Cuttercote una vice pro emendatione
    veteris horologii . . . . . iiij*d*.
Et in rubis et dumis emptis de Johanne Cook pro
    cimiterio includendo . . . . viij*d*.
Et in cariagio eorundem . . . . xij*d*.
Et pro separatione et inclusione dicti cimiterii viz.
    ex parte occidentali . . . . x*d*.
Et in uno carpentario conducto per j diem ad facien-
    dum unam portam ibidem et pro emendatione
    lez steyles cimiterii simul cum c clavis et aliis
    ferramentis emptis pro eadem porta . . viij*d*. *ob*.
Et Johanni Wrighte pro opere suo circa campanas
    cum j tabula de popler empta pro eodem opere . vj*d*.
Et in filo empto pro emendatione vestimentorum alia
    vice . . . . *ob*.
Et Johanni Spryngholt pro emendatione de lez baude-
    rikes campanarum et pro emendatione de lez
    belleropes . . . . . . ij*d*.
Et Johanni Wavell pro una rota facta pro media
    campana . . . . . . xviij*d*.
Et Johanni Sparwe juniori pro emendatione unius
    bauderyke . . . . . . ij*d*.
Et Johanni Wrighte pro trussatione magnæ campanæ ij*d*. *ob*.
Et in clavis emptis pro eodem opere . . . ij*d*.
Et solutum Adæ Drakelowe pro serura cum clavi pro
    magna cista ecclesiæ . . . . v*d*.
Et Johanni Parker pro emendatione ij bauderikes
    cum corio albo empto pro eodem opere . . iij*d*.
Et solutum pro iij aubez viz. pro factura . . viij*d*.
Et in filo empto alia vice pro emendatione vestimen-
    torum ecclesiæ . . . . . j*d*. *ob*.
Et circa elevationem et depositionem sepulcri iij° anno
    hujus compoti . . . . . iij*d*.
Et solutum pro iiij^{or} bolstrers factis pro veteri horologio j*d*.
Et solutum Willielmo Rede pro factura unius muri
    terrei a gardino vicarii usque introitum de le
    cherchecroft ex conventione in grosso cum ij*d*.
    allocatis pro cariagio straminis . . . ixs. viij*d*.

Et in stramine empto de Johanne Trotte pro eodem
muro . . . . xxiij*d.*
Et in stramine empto de Thoma Mynot pro coopertura ejusdem muri . . . . ij*s.*
Et in stipula empta pro eodem cum ij*s.* pro calmatione
ejusdem stipulæ . . - . . vj*s.*
Et in cariagio eorundem in stipendio et mensa cum ij
hominibus euntibus cum carecta . . . ij*s.* x*d.*
Et Willielmo Rede pro stakyng ejusdem muri ex con-
ventione in grosso . . . . xvj*d.*
Et in virgis emptis pro watlyng sprendelles et ligamiri-
bus . . . . x*d.* *ob.*
Et tectori conducto per vij dies capienti per diem ij*d.*
ob. ob. plus in toto . . . . xviij*d.*
Et pro mensa ejusdem per idem tempus . . xiiij*d.*
Et in j operario sibi deserviente per v dies in stipendio
et mensa . . . . xx*d.*
Et Aliciæ filiæ Johannis Stonhard tractanti stramen
per iiij*or* dies in stipendio et mensa . . xiiij*d.*
Et Johanni Wrighte pro emendatione rotarum cam-
panarum per ij vices . . . . vj*d.*
Et solutum pro clavi cameræ Johannis Sprygholt apud
Potterscros . . . . . . ij*d.*
Et in filo pro vestimentis emendandis alia vice . j*d.*
Et Johanni Rose pro emendatione cathenæ aspersorii
ad hostium porticus ecclesiæ . . . j*d.*
Et Adæ Drakelowe pro emendatione seruræ portæ
cimiterii . . . . j*d.*
Et pro emendatione situlæ fontis apud Wyndhell pro
aqua latomorum haurienda . . . j*d.*
Et Johanni Wrighte pro emendatione rotarum cam-
panarum . . . . vj*d.*
Et pro emendatione unius boket pro aqua benedicta . j*d.*
Et pro emendatione unius rochet . . . vj*d.*
Et pro emendatione unius bellerope . . . *ob.*
Et circa elevationem et depositionem sepulcri iiij*to*
anno infra compotum cum clavis pro eodem . ij*d. ob.*
Et pro emendatione unius bellerop pro parva cam-
pana . . . . *ob.*
Et pro emendatione caparum et vestimentorum
ecclesiæ cuidam reparatori vestimentorum de
Coggeshale . . . . . . ij*s.*
Et circa erectionem et depositionem sepulcri v*to* anno
infra tempus compoti cum *ob.* in clavis et *ob.* in
filo . . . . iiij*d.*

Et solutum Adæ Drakelowe pro emendatione candelabri coram ymagine beatæ Mariæ de Pietate cum circulo ferri pro ridello circa ymaginem Trinitatis . . . . . xvj*d*.
Et eidem pro clavi hostii cancellæ et pro instrumento horologii vocato le flye pro clavi pro hostio domus latomorum et pro garnettes pro hostio in le rodeloft ij*s*. ix*d*.
Et pro emendatione seruræ pro porta cimiterii . ij*d*.
Et pro emendatione ij crucum ij candelabrorum magnorum unius thurribuli et unius canopæ . . iiij*s*.
Et in ære et stanno emptis pro eodem opere et in aliis expensis viz. pro mensa illius per j diem ex conventione . . . . . . vj*d*.
Et Johanni Wavell pro emendatione rotæ parvæ campanæ . . . . . . v*d*.
Et solutum pro emendatione iiij bauderikes . . iiij*d*.
Et in filo pro emendatione vestimentorum ecclesiæ . *ob*.
Et in uno ligno empto de Johanne Busch pro campanas trussandas . . . . j*d*.
Et Johanni Carpentario et socio suo per ij dies ad trussandas campanas pro stipendio et mensa . xxij*d*.
Et in expensis cooperantibus ad dependendum dictas campanas . . . . . j*d*.
Et Johanni Everard pro ferramentis dictarum campanarum . . . . . xj*d*.
Et pro emendatione et consolidatione unius aspersorii de latonia fracti . . . . . iiij*d*.
Et circa erectionem et depositionem sepulcri vj^{to} anno infra tempus compoti . . . ij*d*.
Et solutum factori vestimentorum pro factura ij chesiblis de worsted cum fraruris ex conventione . vj*s*. viij*d*.
Et pro iiij^{or} peciis de reban emptis Londoniæ pro eodem opere pretium peciæ xij*d*. cum iiij*d*. in expensis Londoniæ . . . iiij*s*. iiij*d*.
Et Johanni Ricard pro factura de le belleclaper magnæ campanæ simul cum cariagio usque Elmedon and recariagio ejusdem . . . ij*s*. viij*d*.
Et in filo pro vestimentis ecclesiæ consuendis . *ob*.
Et solutum uni carpentario conducto per iij dies ad v*d*. in die ad tascam pro clausura circa cimiterium et factura de les steyles . . . . xv*d*.
Et pro v stodis ij stulpis j gruncelle et diversis palis et clavis emptis pro eodem opere . . xij*d*. *ob*.
Et Johanni Wrighte pro suspensione et trussatione magnæ campanæ . . . . ij*d*.

Et Willielmo Hunte pro factura unius gojoun' cum
reparatione alterius et *ob.* pro clavis . . xij*d.*
Et pro consolidatione unius aspersorii de latonia . ij*d.*
Et circa elevationem et depositionem sepulcri anno
vij^mo infra tempus hujus compoti . . ij*d.*
Et solutum pro emendatione rotæ magnæ campanæ
cum clavis emptis pro eodem opere . . viij*d. ob.*
Et Margaretæ atte Lee pro emendatione unius super-
pellicii . . . . . . iij*d.*
Et Adæ Drakelowe pro serura clavis et aliis ferramen-
tis ecclesiæ . . . . . iiij*s.* vij*d.*
Et circa elevationem et depositionem sepulcri anno
viij^vo infra tempus compoti—cum *ob.* in filo . ij*d. ob.*
Et Johanni Ombler pro factura iij bauderikes pro cam-
panis . . . . . . vj*d.*
Et Johanni Janyn pro clavi pro magna cista ecclesiæ. iij*d.*
Et in expensis ad domum Willielmi Hunte circa
operationem ferramentorum campanarum . j*d.*
Et in j fraxino empta pro carpentario pendente campanas j*d.*
Et Johanni Cotiller pro . . novis bauderikes pro novis
campanis. . . . . . xviij*d.*
Et Johanni Marchaunt eunti usque Manewden pro
dictis bauderikes cum *ob.* pro emendatione unius
bellerope . . . . . . ij*d. ob.*
Et Johanni Dane pro sera cum ij clavibus pro porta
cimiterii et j hange pro dicta porta et clavi mag-
næ cistæ . . . . . . viij*d.*
Et circa erectionem et depositionem sepulcri ix^no anno
infra tempus hujus compoti cum ij*d.* sacristæ pro
custodia luminum . . . . v*d.*
Et solutum Willielmo Hunte pro factura de le fyrpanne xij*d.*
Et in emendatione unius bellerop . . . *ob.*
Et solutum ad picturam ymaginis sancti Michaelis
per manus Walteri Blank de redditu domus suæ
in Baysebollane . . . . . xij*d.*
Et in filo pro vestimentis ecclesiæ consuendis . *ob.*
Et Willielmo Hunte pro factura v bokelles pro v
bauderikes campanarum novarum . . v*d.*
Summa iiij*li.* xij*s.* vij*d. ob.*

Expensæ neccessariæ.

Et in j potello olei pro lampadibus ecclesiæ cum
cariagio . . . . . . vij*d.*
Et in j potello olei altera vice . . . viij*d.*
Et in viij lb. ceræ emptis Londoniæ pro luminaribus
ecclesiæ . . . . . . iij*s.* iiij*d.*

Et in uncto empto pro campanis primo anno hujus compoti quolibet quarterio ij*d*.	viij*d*.
Et in j lagena olei pro lampadibus cum olla empta pro eodem	xiij*d*.
Et in iiij lb. ceræ emptis	xix*d*.
Et x lb. di. ceræ emptis erga Pascha	iiij*s*. iiij*d*.
Et pro iij belleropis ponderis xiiij lb. pretium libræ j*d. ob.*	xxj*d*.
Et pro factura cereorum et luminis Paschalium primo anno infra tempus compoti	xx*d*.
Et in expensis istorum computantium cum aliis secum existentibus circa facturam ejusdem luminis	xj*d. ob.*
Et Johannæ Keteryng pro lotione de les kevercheris pro ymaginibus ecclesiæ et pro lotione de le rodecloth	iij*d*.
Et solutum Clerico et Sacristæ pro custodia luminarium ecclesiæ in tempore Paschæ	iiij*d*.
Et in iiij lb. candelarum de cotono tempore hiemali expendendarum in ecclesia	vj*d*.
Et pro falcatione stramenti ecclesiæ ad festum Sancti Johannis primo anno hujus compoti	iij*d*.
Et in j lagena olei lampadis	xij*d*.
Et in factura ij parium processionar[iorum]	iij*d*.
Et in j potello olei lampadis	vj*d*.
Et in uncto pro campanis ij° anno infra tempus compoti	viij*d*.
Et in iiij lb. candelarum de cotono eodem anno	vj*d*.
Et in xvj lb. ceræ emptis erga Pascha eodem anno	vj*s*. viij*d*.
Et in expensis eodem anno circa facturam cereorum Paschalium cum aliis luminaribus	xxiij*d. ob.*
Et Johannæ Keteryng pro lotione de les kevercheris in ecclesiæ	ij*d*.
Et Clerico et Sacristæ eodem anno pro custodia luminarium tempore Paschæ	iiij*d*.
Et in j potello olei lampadis	vj*d*.
Et in j sera pro porta cimiterii	v*d*.
Et pro falcatione stramenti ecclesiæ ad Nativitatem Sancti Johannis ij° anno infra tempus compoti	iij*d*.
Et Thomæ Barbor pro factura iiij^{or} cereorum processionalium cum candelis ad celebrandum et visitandum	iiij*d*.
Et in potello olei lampadis	vj*d*.
Et in wyre empto pro horologio	vj*d*.
Et in iiij^{or} lb. candelarum de cotono tempore hiemali a° iij° hujus compoti	vj*d*.

Et in factura ij parium processionalium cum candelis
ad celebrandum et visitandum . . . ij*d.*
Et pro vj lb. ceræ . . . . . ij*s.* vj*d.*
Et in uncto pro campanis iij° anno hujus compoti . viij*d.*
Et in xiij lb. ceræ erga Pascha eodem anno . v*s.* v*d.*
Et in factura ejusdem cum expensis circa facturam
ejusdem . . . . . . ij*s.*
Et Sacristæ pro custodia luminarium eodem anno . ij*d.*
Et in j lagena olei lampadis . . . . xij*d.*
Et Thomæ Barbor pro factura ij processionalium . ij*d.*
Et pro falcatione stramenti ecclesiæ iij° anno infra
tempus compoti ad Nativitatem Sancti Johannis iiij*d.*
Et in j lagena olei lampadis . . . . xiij*d.*
Et Thomæ Barbor pro candelis ad celebrandum et
visitandum . . . . . j*d.*
Et pro factura ij parium processionalium . iiij*d.*
Et in expensis circa cariagium stramenti ecclesiæ ad
Natale Domini . . . . . j*d.*
Et in j lagena olei lampadis . . . . xvj*d.*
Et pro vij lb. ceræ . . . . . iiij*s.* vj*d.*
Et in iij lb. candelarum de cotono iiij^{to} anno infra tem-
pus hujus compoti . . . iiij*d. ob.*
Et in x lb. ceræ erga Pascha eodem anno . iij*s.* xj*d. ob.*
Et pro factura ceræ Paschalis eodem anno cum
expensis istorum computantium circa facturam
ejusdem . . . . . . xxj*d.*
Et Sacristæ pro custodia luminarium hoc anno . ij*d.*
Et in uncto pro campanis eodem anno . . viij*d.*
Et in bellerop empto . . . . . vj*d. ob.*
Et in j potello olei lampadis . . . . viij*d.*
Et in vj lb. ceræ cum ij*d.* pro factura ij processionalium
et candelis ad celebrandum . . . ij*s.* viij*d.*
Et pro falcatione stramenti ecclesiæ ad Nativitatem
Johannis eodem anno . . . . iij*d.*
Et in j lagena olei lampadis . . . . xiiij*d.*
Et Thomæ Barbor pro factura cereorum procession-
alium et candelis ad celebrandum et visitandum . iiij*d.*
Et in j corda empta pro parva campana . . j*d. ob.*
Et in j pekke pro pane benedicta . . . ij*d. ob.*
Et solutum pro j bellerope . . . . vij*d.*
Et Thomæ Barbor pro factura candelarum ad cele-
brandum et visitandum . . . j*d. ob.*
Et circa cariagium iiij^m quercuum legatarum ecclesiæ
per Johannem Colyn . . . . iiij*d.*
Et in j lagena olei lampadis . . . . xiiij*d.*

Et in vj lb. candelarum de cotono tempore hiemali v⁽ᵗᵒ⁾
anno infra tempus hujus compoti . . ixd.
Et pro factura ij parium processionalium cum candelis
ad celebrandum et visitandum . . . iiijd.
Et in uncto pro campanis eodem anno v⁽ᵗᵒ⁾ . . viijd.
Et in j lampade vitrea empta . . . . jd.
Et in xviij lb. ceræ emptis erga Pascha eodem anno
et j lagena olei cum iiijd. pro cariagio . . viijs. ijd. ob.
Et pro factura ceræ Paschalis hoc anno cum expensis
circa facturam . . . . . xixd. ob.
Et Sacristæ pro custodia cereorum tempore Paschæ . ijd.
Et in j bellerop . . . . . vjd.
Et pro lotione de le rodeclothe et kevercheres ymagi-
num ecclesiæ . . . . . ijd.
Et pro falcatione stramenti ecclesiæ ad Nativitatem
Johannis eodem anno v⁽ᵗᵒ⁾ cum expensis circa
cariagium . . . . . iiijd.
Et in j potello olei lampadis . . . . viijd.
Et Thomæ Barbor pro factura ij processionalium cum
candelis ad celebrandum et visitandum . . ijd.
Et solutum   Bukberd pro arreragiis novi horo-
logii cum jd. in beveragio . . . ijd.
Et in j lagena olei lampadis . . . . xijd.
Et Sacristæ pro custodia luminarium ecclesiæ ad
Natale Domini . . . . . ijd.
Et pro vj lb. ceræ emptis . . . . ijs. iiijd.
Et in vj lb. candelarum de cotono tempore hiemali
vj⁽ᵗᵒ⁾ anno hujus compoti . . . . ixd.
Et in uncto pro campanis eodem anno . . viijd.
Et in iij cordis emptis pro   et pro parva cam-
pana . . . . . . vjd.
Et in j schovelle pro latomis . . . . jd. ob.
Et in clavis emptis diversis vicibus per Busch . iijd.
Et in j marra empta . . . . . viijd.
Et in xiiij lb. et di. ceræ emptis erga Pascha eodem
anno vj⁽ᵗᵒ⁾. . . . . . vs. ixd.
Et in una olla terrea pro aqua ad ministrandum in
ecclesia . . . . . . ob.
Et in j bellerop empto ponderis vj lb. et di. . . ixd.
Et pro factura ceræ Paschalis cum expensis circa
facturam ejusdem . . . . xxjd.
Et Sacristæ pro custodia luminarium ecclesiæ eodem
anno tempore Paschæ . . . . ijd.
Et in j lagena olei lampadis cum cariagio . . xiiijd.
Et in corio empto pro vexillo . . . jd.

Et   Bukberd pro horologio ab eo empto ut de
    xiij*s.* iiij*d.* aretro existentibus ultra prius solutum
    per Wardanos operis ecclesiæ   .   .   .   iij*s.* iiij*d.*
Et Willielmo Cokeyn pro falcatione stramenti ad Na-
    tivitatem Johannis eodem anno vj^{to} cum expensis
    cariagii .   .   .   .   .   .   iiij*d.*
Et in j lagena olei lampadis .   .   .   .   xiiij*d.*
Et Thomæ Barbour pro factura ij parium processiona-
    lium et candelis ad celebrandum et visitandum   vj*d.*
Et solutum filio Johannis Weldham pro ij paribus
    cruettes ab eo emptis .   .   .   .   xij*d.*
Et in una lagena olei lampadis   .   .   .   xij*d.*
Et solutum pro vj lb. ceræ .   .   .   .   xxviij*d.*
Et pro factura ij processionalium cum candelis ad
    celebrandum   .   .   .   .   .   ij*d.*
Et in lagena olei   .   .   .   .   .   xij*d.*
Et pro factura candelarum ad celebrandum   .   .   j*d.*
Et pro factura ij cereorum processionalium cum can-
    delis ad celebrandum .   .   .   .   ij*d.*
Et in uncto pro campanis anno vij° infra tempus
    compoti .   .   .   .   .   .   viij*d.*
Et in vj lb. candelarum de cotono tempore hiemali
    eodem anno vij^{mo} .   .   .   .   ix*d.*
Et pro factura ceræ Paschalis eodem anno vij^{mo} cum
    expensis circa facturam ejusdem .   .   .   xvj*d. ob.*
Et pro xiiij lb. ceræ emptis lb. ad iiij*d. ob.*   .   v*s.* iij*d.*
Et Sacristæ pro custodia luminarium eodem anno   .   ij*d.*
Et Johanni Belheme pro dimidio corio equino pro
    bauderikes   .   .   .   .   .   x*d.*
Et Johanni Colyn pro falcatione stramenti ecclesiæ ad
    Nativitatem Sancti Johannis cum expensis cariagii   iij*d.*
Et Johanni Thurkeld pro factura processionalium cum
    candelis ad celebrandum   .   .   .   ij*d.*
Et in j lagena olei   .   .   .   .   .   xij*d.*
Et pro factura j paris processionalium   .   .   ij*d.*
Et in j potello olei lampadis   .   .   .   .   vij*d.*
Et in j bellerop   .   .   .   .   .   .   vij*d.*
Et in ij lb. ceræ   .   .   .   .   .   ix*d. ob.*
Et in factura cereorum processionalium cum candelis
    ad celebrandum .   .   .   .   .   ij*d. ob.*
Et Johanni Algood pro uncto pro campanis anno viij^{vo}
    infra tempus compoti   .   .   .   .   viij*d.*
Et in j potello olei lampadis   .   .   .   .   viij*d.*
Et in iij lb. candelarum de cotono hoc anno viij^{vo}
    tempore hiemali .   .   .   .   .   iiij*d. ob.*

Et solutum pro xxiiij lb. et di. ceræ emptis erga Pascha eodem anno viij^{vo}	ix$s$.	vj$d$.
Et pro factura ij parium processionalium		iij$d$.
Et in factura ceræ Paschalis hoc anno viij^{vo} cum expensis circa facturam		xiiij$d$.
Et in j lagena olei lampadis		xij$d$.
Et in j potello olei lampadis		ix$d$.
Et pro factura ij cereorum processionalium cum candelis ad celebrandum		ij$d$.
Et solutum pro v belleropes emptis pro novis campanis	iij$s$.	viij$d$.
Et in j potello olei lampadis		ix$d$.
Et in uncto pro campanis anno ix^{no} infra tempus compoti		viij$d$.
Et pro factura ij parium processionalium		iij$d$.
Et in j bellerop		xj$d$.
Et in j potello olei lampadis		ix$d$.
Et in xij lb. ceræ erga Pascha hoc anno ix^{no} lb. ad vj$d$. ob.	vj$s$.	vj$d$.
Et in factura ceræ Paschalis cum expensis circa facturam		xvj$d$. ob.
Et in j lagena olei lampadis		xij$d$.
Et pro custodia luminarium		ij$d$.
Et solutum pro tribus ciliciis emptis pro tribus altaribus ultra viij$d$. solutum per Johannem Broun ex donatione		iij$s$.
Et pro lotione iij kevercheres pro ymaginibus		ob.
Et pro ij belleropis pro ij maximis campanis cum j lyne' pro horologio	ij$s$.	vj$d$.
Et Willielmo Cokeyn pro falcatione stramenti ecclesiæ ad Nativitatem Sancti Johannis hoc anno ix^{no} cum expensis cariagii		iij$d$. ob.
Et in iij lb. candelarum de cotono hoc anno ix^{no} tempore hiemali		iiij$d$. ob.
Et in iiij lb. ceræ	ij$s$.	ij$d$.
Et in j lagena olei lampadis		xij$d$.
Et in factura ij processionalium Thomæ Ber'		jd. ob.
Et executoribus Bukberd in plenam solutionem pro horologio ultra prius solutum		xs.

Summa viijli. xiiij$s$. xd. ob.

Expensæ forinsecæ.

Et in expensis circa collectionem reddituum diversis vicibus infra tempus compoti	ij$s$.	viij$d$.
Et pro factura unius indenturæ domus ecclesiæ in le Southstrete dimissæ Thomæ Andrew		iiij$d$.

Et pro cariagio unius carectæ arenæ pro statione
 juxta le cherchestall cum stokkatione ejusdem .   ij*d.*
Et pro denariis Sancti Petri pro iiij^{or} annis ad xviij*d.* per
 annum solutum ad ffestum Sancti Petri ad Vincula   vj*s.*
Et pro j indentura facta de stallo ecclesiæ juxta le
 pentys dimisso Johanni Belheme de Water-lane .   iiij*d.*
Et in papiro et pergameno emptis pro parcellis inser-
 endis et pro presenti compoto faciendo .   .   iij*s.* iiij*d.*
Et in expensis factis filio   Bukberd et uxori
 ejusdem et aliis venientibus diversis vicibus pro
 pecuniis sibi debitis pro horologio ab eo empto .   ij*s.*
Et in uno examine apum evolantium et iterum repor-
 tando . . . . .   iiij*d.*
Et in effugatione ij hyvis tempore hujus compoti .   iiij*d.*
Et in factura ceræ . . . . .   ij*d.*

Summa xv*s.* vij*d.*

Allocationes.

Et allocantur istis computantibus ut de iij*d.* redditus
 per annum de mesuagio Johannis Wrighte de
 Southstrete oneratis superius titulo de redditu et
 hic allocantur quia non solvit nisi ij*d.* per annum
 et sic allocatur pro quolibet anno j*d.* viz. pro ix
 annis . . . . .   ix*d.*
Et eisdem pro j waterwey Johannis Busch quondam
 Johannis Partrich oneratæ ut supra ij*d.* per annum
 ut patet per rentale et hic allocantur quia
 Johannes Busch dedicit viz. pro ix annis .   ix*d.*
Et eisdem ut de iiij*d.* per annum de redditu Willielmi
 Bysmer pro tenemento quondam Johannis Hogon
 senioris oneratis ut supra et hic allocantur quia
 dictus Willielmus Bysmer dedicit videlicet pro v
 annis et dimidio. . . .   xxij*d.*
Et de ij*d.* per annum pro j pecia terræ in Aptonfeld
 vocata le Speteleakre modo in manibus Johannis
 Cook ad firmam oneratis ut supra et hic allocantur
 quia Johannes Cook dedicit et solvit pro eadem
 pecia terræ Johanni Leventhorp iiij*d.* per annum
 viz. pro ix annis . . . .   xviij*d.*
Et de ij*d.* per annum oneratis ut supra pro mesuagio
 quondam Willielmi Belhos modo Johannis Cook
 et hic allocantur quia dictus Johannes Cook solvit
 domino Episcopo Londoniensi et dedicit redditum
 predictum viz. pro ix annis . . .   xviij*d.*
Et de ij*d.* redditus per annum oneratis ut supra de

tenemento Johannis Cook quondam Williemi Priour in le Northstret et allocantur quia dictus Johannes Cook dedicit viz. pro ix annis . xviij*d*.

Et de iij*d*. redditus per annum oneratis ut supra de tenemento Beveris et hic allocantur causa supradicta videlicet pro ix annis . . . ij*s*. iij*d*.

Et de iiij*s*. per annum oneratis ut supra de Williemo Barbour pro tenemento Blankes in le Northstrete et hic allocantur quia dictus Williemus dedicit viz. pro ix annis . . . . . xxxvj*s*.

Et de vj*d*. per annum de una pecia terræ nuper Johannis Flemyng in Hokerhillefeld oneratis ut supra viz. pro v annis quibus dicta terra fuit in manibus ipsius Johannis ij*s*. vj*d*. pro tempore hujus compoti modo tamen dicta terra seisita est per istos computantes et dimittitur ad firmam pro vj*d*. per annum Thomæ Andrew de Hokerhell .

Et de ij*d*. per annum oneratis ut supra de uno stallo sub porta tenementi quondam Johannis Ardent viz. pro ix annis et hic allocantur eo quod feodum ignoratur . . . . . . xviij*d*.

Et de j*d*. per annum onerato ut supra pro terra in le Nofeld juxta le Delle quondam Ricardi Blythewyn pro ix annis pro eo quod feodum ignoratur . ix*d*.

Et de iiij*d*. per annum pro terra in Lyghes quondam Johannis Chambre oneratis ut supra et hic allocantur ex causa predicta viz. pro ix annis . iij*s*.

Et de viij*d*. per annum pro stallis quondam Nicholai Warden in piscaria oneratis ut supra et hic allocantur quia non occupantur sed diruta sunt penitus et destructa viz. pro ix annis . . vj*s*.

Et de iiij*d*. per annum oneratis in rentali pro terra nuper Johannis Bryon senioris modo Hugonis Busch in le Downe et hic allocantur quia non solvit nisi iij*d*. per annum et sic petunt allocationem pro ix annis . . . . ix*d*.

Et allocatur ut de x*d*. per annum pro messuagio nuper Thomæ Pygeon ubi fuit una grangia ædificata et hic allocatur quia oneratæ in rentali ad x*d*. et non solvit nisi iiij*d*. per annum et dedicit vj*d*. ut apparet per unam cartam deberet reddere vj*d*. per annum viz. pro ix annis . . iiij*s*. vj*d*.

Et de ij*d*. per annum oneratis in rentali de Ricardo Takeley nec apparet unded eberet exigi viz. pro ix annis . . . . . . ij*s*. iij*d*.

Et de firma unius stalli in le Bocherye quod Johannes
Threscher de Buntyngford tenuit pro ij*s.* viij*d.* per
annum pro medietate anni quia condonatur eo
quod fuit in debato . . . . xvj*d.*
Et de xviij*d.* per annum oneratis in rentali pro j acra
terræ Walteri Blankes in Kythalescroft per cartam Willielmi Rodlon et hic allocantur quia
dictus Walterus non solvit nisi vj*d.* per annum
Ideo allocantur pro ix annis . . . ix*s.*
Et de viij*d.* per annum per aliam cartam sic oneratis
in rentali pro j pecia terræ dicti Walteri Blankes
in Aptonfeld juxta Goodwynestyle et hic allocantur quia non solvit istis computantibus nec debet
ut dicit sed invenit annuatim unum cereum
ardentem coram sepulcro pro eodem redditu
prout sibi fuit injunctum per Ricardum Bregge
nuper vicarium ut dicit Ideo allocantur pro ix
annis . . . . . . vj*s.*
Et de xij*d.* novi redditus donati per Johannem Busch
seniorem pro j lampade invenienda viz. pro j^{mo}
anno hujus compoti quia isto anno Alicia Trotte
relicta præfati Johannis Busch non solvit redditum prædictum sed invenit lampadem prædictam cum eodem redditu ideo hic allocantur . xij*d.*
Et de firma cameræ juxta Cherchestile pro j anno eo
quod stetit vacua pro defectu conductorum illo
anno præterquam senex presbiter occupavit
eandem cameram quasi per mensem pro iiij*d.*
ideo hic allocantur pro residuo illius anni . iij*s.* viij*d.*
Et allocantur de firma ejusdem cameræ anno iiij^{to}
infra tempus hujus compoti ut in expensis apud
Halyngbury Parvam circa recuparationem redditus illius anni . . . . . viij*d.*
Et de firma cameræ apud le Pultrihelle onerata ad iiij*s.*
in rentali et non dimissa per vij annos et dimidium nisi pro iij*s.* x*d.* ideo allocantur pro quolibet
anno ij*d.* . . . . . xv*d.*
Et de eadem camera hoc anno quia non dimittitur
pro defectu conductoris nisi pro iij*s.* vj*d.* ideo
allocantur . . . . . vj*d.*

Summa iiij*li.* x*s.* vij*d.*

Respectus.

Et respectuantur ut de vj*d.* per annum oneratis in
rentali pro j pecia terræ in Hokirhillefeld nuper

Aliciæ Frere nuper solutis per Thomam Mynot
et modo Ricardus Pygeon perquisivit de prædicto
Thoma Mynot omnia terras et tenementa quæ
fuerunt Johannis Frere sed dubitat utrum habeat
terram prædictam necne ideo non solvit redditum
prædictum sed respectuatur quousque melius
inquiratur per evidentiam videlicet pro vij annis
hujus compoti . . . . . iij*s*. vj*d*.
Et de vj*d*. per annum oneratis in rentali pro mesuagio
nuper Johannæ Panfeld et hic respectuantur quia
dubitatur de quo mesuagio dictæ Johannæ exi-
gantur eo quod duo habuit mesuagia ideo respectuantur quousque inquiratur. . . iiij*s*. vj*d*.

Summa viij*s*.

Vadia et Stipendia.
Et solutum Johanni Clee pro stipendio suo custodientis
horologii per iiij^{or} annos et dimidium ad iiij*s*. per
annum ex conventione . . . . xviij*s*.
Et uxori ejusdem pro lotione vestimentorum lineorum
ecclesiæ ad ij*s*. per annum ex conventione viz.
pro ix annis . . . . . xviij*s*.
Et Johanni Ombler pro custodia horologii per unum
annum et dimidium infra tempus hujus compoti
capienti per annum ut supradicitur de Johanne
Clee . . . . . . vj*s*.

Summa xlij*s*.

Summa totalis omnium expensarum et allocationum
xxiij*li*. xiij*s*. v*d*. ob.

Et debent viij*li*. v*s*.

Unde super diversos tenentes pro redditibus et firmis aretro
existentibus ut patet per unam cedulam huic compoto annexam
et consutam viij*li*. viij*s*. xj*d*. ob.

Et sic nil debent sed excedunt ij*s*. xj*d*. ob.

[*Endorsed.*]

Storteford. Compotus Johannis Wolverston et Johannis
Busch yconomorum ecclesiæ ibidem factus die
Dominica proxima post. . . . .
anno Domini millesimo cccc^{mo} quadragesimo et
anno regni regis Henrici sexti decimo nono.

1489 (?).—*From the "Receptiones Forinsecæ."*
Profit of the Hokkyng Ale	0	15	0
From two drinkings called May Ales	4	6	8
The Profit of one q^r of brass given to the Church by Sir William Say K^t	0	20	0
The donation of a woman of the town of Dunmow	0	3	4

Received towards the New Bells.
Of the collectors of the guild of the Blessed Mary in this Town for the renovation of the Bells this year	7	3	4
Of William London Vicar here of the legacy of William Newman (?) "Tayler"	0	6	8
The legacy of Thomas Turnor	0	6	8
From William Tayler of Birchanger the legacy of Margaret Sabbisford	0	6	8
The donation of Thomas Gyva	0	6	8
The donation of William Thurgoode of Morton by the hands of John Yve (?) of "Stansted Thele"	0	10	0
From William Colyn	0	6	8
From Thomas Akastr' in money from the Guild of the Blessed Mary	0	6	8
Received of the profit of a drinking made by Sir John the Chantry Priest here and William Morse	0	11	2
From divers persons of this Town	3	10	3

"Reparatio Ecclesiæ."
The Walden Plumber for mending some defects in the lead on the South side of the Church	0	3	4

"Expensæ Forinsecæ."
Peters Pence paid to the commissary of this diocese	0	1	3
Expenses at "Sabbisford May et lytill Hadham May"	0	3	0
Expenses at "Thorleigh May"	0	0	6

Expenses relating to the New Bells.
To Henry Spencer for taking down and hanging up again the five bells	0	36	8
Expenses of the Churchwardens in going to Bury St Edmunds to make the agreement about the Bells with Reginald Chirche Bellfounder	0	4	8
For taking the Bells from Stortford to Bury St Edmunds and bringing them home again	0	52	0
To a workman at Bury St Edmunds for renovating and renewing the five clappers	0	39	0

To John Thurkill for himself and 6 horses about the carriage of the said Bells as agreed	0	4	8
In money paid " pro sāfitatone " of the aforesaid bells this year	0	17	4

The agreement with Chirche appears to have been for £42 0s. 0d. of which sum the churchwardens this year paid him £10 0s. 0d.

1490. (?)

"*Receptiones Forinsecæ.*"

Of the Ex^{ors} of John Esgore, the gift of the said John Esgore	0	20	0
Of the profit of the Play	0	26	7
Of the issue of a drinking made in the Church here on Sunday last after the day of the aforesaid Play	0	6	1½
Money received towards the Bells this year from divers persons	0	10	2

Repairs to the Church.

Paid to Robert called "litill Robyn" for mending the palings	0	0	3
Paid to William Willey "harnez maker" for necessaries (probably baldricks) about the mending of the Bells	0	2	6
For one Cord " pro le wathe "	0	0	9

"*Expensæ Necessariæ.*"

Paid for two new cruetts	0	0	7
P^d to John Grace "pro stipendo armature erga diem de le pley"	0	2	0
P^d the aforesaid John Grace for his expenses to London about the aforesaid business	0	0	6
P^d for 8 "pullis" against the same day	0	0	8
P^d to Thomas Short for his labour the same day "pro turnyng of the broche"	0	0	2
P^d William Warner for his labour on the same day "circa carnes assand"	0	0	2
P^d to Robert Harris "pro bosco die de le pley"	0	0	5
" Et pro falcatione bladorum pro ecclesia pro sternend ad Festum S^{ti} Johannis Baptiste "			

1495.

"*Receptiones Forinsecæ.*"

6s. 8d. in part payment of 13s. 4d. received of the

profit of a certain drinking called "Luntis yelde" by the hands of Thomas Grace.

The receipts towards the Bells this year amounted to £7 0s. 5d. of which sum £2 6s. 8d. was received from the Guardians of the Guild of the Blessed Mary.

Repairs to the Church and Churchyard.

Paid to Robert Carpenter and William Cooke for making "lez Rayles et Steyres" at the East Gate of the Churchyard	0	1	4

"*Expensæ Necessariæ.*"

Expenses about the obit of William Roose . .	0	1	5
Expenses about the obit of Reginald Baldewyn Priest	0	1	4
P^d for two new clasps "cum burden ad librum voč. the Cowcher jač. ante crucem in ecclesia " .	0	0	8

"*Expensæ Forinsecæ.*"

Paid for the carriage of brass from the house of John Stone of Thorley to this Town . . .	0	0	2
Paid for the expenses of John Sadde at London about a new Cross	0	2	8

This year the Churchwardens went to Bury St. Edmunds and paid Reginald Chirche another instalment of £4 0s. 0d. on account of the Bells; their expenses for two days amounted to 3s. 4d.

1496.

"*Receptiones Forinsecæ.*"

Received of the Bachelors of the said Town of the profit of a certain drinking called the May Ale	0	35	4
Received of the wife of Thomas Feld for the burial of her mother within the Church . .	0	6	8

The receipts towards the Bells this year amounted to £6 4s. 11d. of which £3 2s. 6d. came from the Collectors of the Guild of the Blessed Mary.

From an item in this year's account it appears that the names of the parishioners who subscribed towards the Bells were entered into a book; the book, however, is not among the Churchwardens' papers.

A new "Bertilment" to the Church was made this year.

"*Expensæ Necessariæ.*"

Paid to John Fraunces for mending the lantern	0	0	4
For "Estriche bordis" used for mending a bell wheel	0	0	4

"*Expensæ Forinsecæ.*"

For removing lime and sand which lay in the Gatehouse of the Churchyard to the Church House	0	0	1
In expenses at the time of the visitation at Hatfield this year when the Bishop of London was there	0	0	6

This year the Churchwardens went to Bury St. Edmunds again and paid Reginald Chirche a further instalment of £10 0s. 0d.; their expenses for three days were 5s. 6½d.

1499.

Receipts.

"de John Dane apud le Wrestlers xx*d.*"

The issues of drinkings made for a new sepulchre	0	14	0
For waste of Torches at the obit of the wife of John Payn	0	0	6
Collected of various parishioners for the new Sepulchre	0	11	5

Repairs and General Expenses.

"Et iij*s.* iiij*d.* pro factura de la mudde wall in grosso."
This is followed by items for laths, tiles, and straw for the same wall.

Paid to Henry Spenser for making a frame for the torches in the Church			
Paid to the Parish Priest for washing the surplices and other vestments	0	2	4
For making the new sepulchre	0	46	8

1500.

Receptiones Forinsecæ.

The donation of S^r. John Wylkynson Chantry Priest here for the reparation of the "Batylment" of the Church	0	6	8
The profit of 1 q^r. of brass and one measure of corn given by the said S^r. John Wylkynson towards the repairs of the Church	0	5	10
Received from a certain drinking made here called "Iuntys Gylde" (1)	0	9	0

Received from S^r. William Swafeham "monaco prioratus de Hatfeld Regis" by the hands of the

Parish Priest towards mending the vestments of
the Church . . . . .

Repairs and General Expenses.
Paid to one of Dunmow and his three servants for
making the new " batylment " on the north part
of the Church 0 9 4
Paid to little Robyn the carpenter for mending a de-
fect in the Canapy 0 0 1
Paid to one of Walden a "Glasyer" for mending defects in the windows of the Church . . 0 12 9
Paid to John Stacy of Walden Ropemaker for bell-
ropes bought of him 0 2 6

1501.
Repairs and General Expenses.
Paid to William Glascok for mending a lantern in the
Church 0 0 4
" Et iiij$d$. solutum Clerico parochialis pro factura unius
panni qui jacet super tumba cujusdam (?) puelle
in ecclesia vocatæ mayden Olyve.
Received of Thomas . . . . . one of the ex^{ors} of S^r
John Wylkynson Chantry Priest here for the
burial of the said John in the Church . . 0 6 8

1502. (?)
Received of the profit of two standings under the
Church House on Michælmas day . . 0 0 8
. . . for making a Bannercloth against the Rogation
days (1) . . . . .
Paid for mending the Herse 0 0 8

EXTRACTS FROM THE ENGLISH ACCOUNTS.

1482.
Rec. of Richard Masson for Elisabet Spicers dette (1) ij$s$. iiij$d$.
payd for settyng up of the sepulcur and takyng
downe (2) . . . . . iij$s$. vj$d$.
payed in exsepences for the quarrymen at makyng of
the Bargeyne for the stone . . . xd.
. . . to John Pettford for fettyng (? fetching) of Wyll^m
Masson at Hadham the same tyme . . ij$d$.
Item payed to Wyll^m Masson for lettyng wyth the
quarrymen wyth mending of the stepyll dore . xd.
Item payd to John Munday for v day worke in the
flore ovur the bells takyng by the day vj$d$. . ij$s$. vj$d$.
Item payed to John Marchaunt and to herry Sckeppe
to helpe John Munday in the same worke . iij$d$.

Item payd to John Strong for ij day werke to draw up the tymbir in to the stepill takyng by the day iiij*d*.	viij*d*.
Item payd to Wyll^m Masson for settyng in of the candilsteke before the Brune Rode	x*d*.
Item payed to Wyll^m Masson for mending of the South Porch	iiij*d*.
Item payed to the same Wyll^m for makyng of the Wyndowys on the north syde of the cherch in grete (3)	viij*s*. ij*d*.
Item payed to John Tinkker for Sowdyng of the ledde on the south syde of the cherche	ij*s*. viij*d*.
Item payed to John Stone for iij stapills to the bare and for a cheyne of yern to the Boke and for nayle and for claspis to the bellyn	xx*d*.
Item payed to John Strong for helping of John Munday in makyng of the stepyll fflore	ix*d*.
Item payed to the same Munday and his ffelerscheppe for swepping of the cherch walls	ij*d*.
Item payed to John Marchaunt for keping of the Clokke the same yere	vj*s*. viij*d*.
. . . for a claspe to the boke	
Item payed to John Munday for makyng of the leyturne at seynte Jones Aulter	vj*d*.
Item payed in exsepences on Corpis day xpī at the pr'essin (procession ?)	xij*d*.
Item payed in exsepences at diverse tymyse w^t beryng of ye hokkyng ale	vj*d*.
Item payed to John Strong on Corpys Xpī day for helping of pr'essin (procession) (4)	xij*d*.
Item payd to Wyll^m Northach for mending of dragon and for his labur (4)	iiij*d*.
Item payd to the petyr pensse	xvj*d*.
Item payd to John Jardevill for fettyng of j lode stone from Assewelle	iiij*s*.
Item payed to Wyll^m Schepperd for makyng of owir bills	xij*d*.

1484.

Item pd for a roppe to the West gate of the cherch and for trenddelys to the cherchgates	iij*d*. *ob*.
Item pd for nayle to the Sparrefete of the cherch howse	*ob*.
Item pd to John Tyler and to his man for tylyng of the cherch howsse (1)	ij*s*. vj*d*.

Item pd for ix bᶻ malte to the hoke ale	vjs.	iiijd.
Item pd for iiij bᶻ whete to the hoke ale	iijs.	iiijd.
Item pd for makyng of the key to the vestrie dore		iiijd.
Item pd for makyng of the key to Sir Roberds Chest		iiijd.
Item pd for bakyng of the brede at hoketyde (2)		vd.
Item pd for brewyng of the hokyng ale xvj bᶻ		xvjd.
Item pd to John Clerke of Takeley for makyng of a booke of the service of the visitacion of ouure lady	iijs.	iiijd.
Item pd in exsepences of mʳ Vicar and for Willᵐ Schepperd to Takeley to speke wᵗ John Clerke for the same boke		iiijd.
Item pd to Thomas Dane for makyng of a lokke to the Chest in the stepill		iiijd.
Item pd for mowyng of the Cherchyerde		iijd.
Item pd for v li. wexe for prosessinaries and for singyng candell and for lygts in the cherch		iiijs.(?)
Item pd to John Smyth for mendyng of the Coppis and vestements ther as it was ffrayed		xd.
Item pd to John Tynkker for mending of the lede on the stepell		viijd.
Item pd for leying of Bawdwyn Victors stone to John Marchaunt (3)		xd.
Item pd for iij bᶻ lyme to ley Bawdwyn stone and for to mende the pavement in the cherch		vjd.
Item pd for mending of a Sawterbooke		xiiijd.
Item pd for mowyng of the gresse at midsomer wᵗ brede and ale		iiijd.
Item pd to mʳ lowesse keper for makyng of a booke of Prikkyd songge (4)	ijs.	viijd.
Item pd to Thomas Cotterotte for Cariage of the wyne from london	iijs.	
Item pd to the Glasser for mending of the Glasse Wyndowys	iiijs.	ijd.
Item pd for ij Capon to geffe Reynold Rottoʳ of london		xd.
Item pd to John Tynker for Shettyng of the lede		iiijd.
Item pd in exsepences at dressyng of the bells		iijd.
Item pd in exsepences to Wydford to speke wᵗ mʳ Brawghing for the yevedens in Kent and for his labor		iiijd.
Item pd for a lyne to seynte Jones belle		iiijd.
Item pd for iij li. wex for tapirs to Joh(ns) messe the price the li. viijd.	ijs.	
Item pd for a pece of lede (r?) to make pypis for the belle roppis		vjd.

Item pd for a halywater styke to John Mathew		j*d*.
Item pd to John Stone for mending of the chyme and for mending of the clokke and for makyng of nayle to the cherch and for makyng a cheyne to Wyndehull gate and for mending of the mattoke and for othir things done in the cherch	ij*s*.	j*d*.
Item pd for S*r* Reynolds obyte day to Prests and Clerks and in brede and ale	ij*s*.	iiij*d*.

1491.

Item of the playe silver	xiij*s*.	iiij*d*.
Item of John Esgore of hokerell the whiche he gafe to the use of the peyntyng of the tabernacle of seint Mighell (1).	xx*s*.	
Item of diverse gaderyngs in the church	iiij*s*.	ij*d*.
Item of the gifte of Robert Bardney to the said tabernacle		xij*d*.
Item of the gifte of Edmund Davy to the same tabernacle		iiij*d*.
Item of the execut*ors* of John Algore of the bequest of the same John	xiij*s*.	iiij*d*.
Item of the bequest of John Smyth ffanwryght	vj*s*.	viij*d*.
Item of the bequest of John Nobill	iij*s*.	iiij*d*.
Item of the bequest of John Smyth moder (?) of hokerell	iij*s*.	iiij*d*.
Item of the bequest of John Monk		xx*d*.
Item of the bequest of Jone Tailor	iij*s*.	iiij*d*.
Item of the gifte of Thomas Gyva	iij*s*.	iiij*d*.
Item of Jone Mason of sutche money as she had of the yelde of seint mighell	iij*s*.	iiij*d*.
Item of Jone Jardvilde of sutche money as her husbond hadde of the may money	v*s*.	vj*d*.
Item of Richard Prior of the bequest of his fader	vj*s*.	viij*d*.
Item of puylle Palmer in parte of payment of suche money as she had of the yelde of seint mighell	ij*s*.	
Item of Thomas Denys for a horse	vj*s*.	
Item of a chirch ale which was made to the use of the tabernacle	vj*s*.	viij*d*.
Item of potte of the same ale which was afterwards lefte		ix*d*.
Item of the wyfe of John Jenyns of in parte payment of suche money as was owyng for the buryyng of her other husbondis (2)	iiij*s*.	vj*d*.
Item paide agenst Ester for x li. wex for the pascall for the harow the basyn in the chaunsell the standards and for syngyng candell price the pounde vij*d*.	v*s*.	x*d*.

Item paide for makyng of the same lyghtis to John Trotte	xij*d*. ob.
Item paide to Willm Mason for makyng of the standyng for the pascall in the chaunsell (3)	iiij*d*.
Item paide for wire for the Chyme	vj*d*.
Item to John Cosyn for pleyyng at the orgens at Ester	v*d*.
. . . . . for pleyying at the organs ad fest^m pentecost^m and corpis xpī	vj*d*. (?)
Item to John Cosyn for playng at the organs at Cristmas	vj*d*.
Item for mending of an awbe	j*d*.
Item paide to Willm Mason at another tyme for the werkmanship of the batilment	xx*s*.
Item to the Plomer at one tyme	x*s*. iij*d*.
Item to John Newman for lede	vj*s*. viij*d*.
Item for a borde to make w^t the gutteris	iiij*d*.
Item to Willm Clerke (?) for makyng of the same gutteris	iij*d*.
Item to Willm Monke for caryyng of the lede	viij*d*.
Item in expens aboute the drawyng uppe of the lede	ij*d*.
Item paide to the plomer for sowder and for layyng of the sowder	vij*s*. iiij*d*.
Item to John Marion for his horse and hymselfe to sheryng	iiij*d*.
Item to Willm Mason for settyng of seynt Jonys candillstik in the walle (1)	ij*d*.
Item for a rope for the sanctus bell	ij*d*.
Item to John Cosyn for pleyyng at the organs agenst mighelmas	j*d*.
Item to John Cosyn for pleyyng at the organs at alhalowntide	j*d*.
Item paide to maister ffuller of Dunmow for the peter pens	xv*d*.
Item for makyng of stage afore seynt mighellis tabernacle and for nayles therfor (1)	iiij*d*.
Item to the paynter in parte of paiment of viij*li*.	vj*s*. viij*d*.
Item to George Bolyngton for the wasshyng of the kerchirs for the Images	ij*d*.

1503.

Item payde to thomase norman for makeyn of the (?) Chyrche howse (1)	xxvj*s*. j*d*.
Item for takeyn downe of the howlde howse	ij*d*.
Item payde to Wyll^m masen for laying (?) the stone at the chawnsell dore	ij*d*.

Item payde for the fremasenys dynare		vj*d*.
Item payde for the new service bokeys	xxv*s*.	
Item for a payer of latyn sensarys	iiij*s*.	iiij*d*.

1504

Item ress. of the dragun to brawyng playe (1)		iiij*d*.
Item ress. of my lady of wyldecherys sarfauntys whane her bonys cam thorow the towne that thay mase to (? at) the cherche		xij*d*.
Item pd for making the iiij belclapare to parle (?) of hatfelde	iij*s*.	iiij*d*.
Item pd. to Sybthorpe for a loge sawyng that my lord gafe to the cherche stayerys		x*d*.
Item to Stoke of hellysnam for v belropys	iiij*s*.	iij*d*.
Item to Wylliam Masen for mending the crose and the cherche flowere		x*d*.

1505.

Item of John Noble for his messuage callid Savages (?) in South strete		iij*d*.
Item of S*r* John london for the Chauntry londe	ij*s*.	vj*d*.
Item of Edmonde Davy for the Crane		j*d*.
John Bolyngton for his tenement in Baysbollane		
Item of Robert flleccher for his tenement wt the gret chamber in the chirche yerde	ij*s*.	v*d*.
Item Res*d* of John marchaunt oone of the executors of Kateyn Kokyñ (?) late of Braughing of her bequest	vj*s*.	viij*d*.
Item of the issues and profite of the hokkinge ale	xij*s*.	
Item of the issues and profite of a drinking made for the chirche pale before cristmas	ix*s*. (?)	
Item for iij broken surpleys and a torren Awter cloth.		vj*d*.
Item Resceyved of the collectors of luntes yelde (1)	xviij*s*.	
Item resceyved of Richard Pelham and William Crowe late chirchwardens for a pott of peuter		iij*d*.
Item Resceyved of diverse persones for the chirch ferme as herafter ensuyth that is to say first of John Bussh		iiij*d*.
Item of John Cok Tayler for his half yere ferme	ij*s*.	
Item of John Turnor for his Chamber	ij*s*.	
Item for cariage of strawe to the chirch		j*d*.
Item for settyng up and taking downe the sepulcre and nayles to the same		v*d*.

Item for wood and coles ayenst Ester eve (2).	
Item for mendyng of the best Sensor.	vj*d*.
Item for vij ells of holland cloth for a slevid surpleys to the parysh prest the ell at viij*d*.	iiij*s*. viij*d*.
Item for iij ells of lynnen cloth for a Rocchet	xviij*d*.
Item for mowyng of grasse for the chirch agenst midsomer w^t drinke to the carters of the same	iiij*d*.
Item for makyng and strikeng of the standerds and other lights agenst the seid midsomer	iij*d*.
Item for felling of iij okes to the Chirch pale	iiij*d*.
Item to Thomas Norman carpenter for makyng the new pale in the cherch yerde.	xxj*s*.
Item for ij yerdes and iij quarters of rede Satten of Sypres for the couvryng of the canapye over the high Awter the yerde at ix*d*.	xxiij*d*.
Item for frenges to the same canapye	vj*d*.
Item to the parish clerk for skoryng and makyng of the said Canapie	xx*d*.
Item payd to mast' officiall for petyrpennes	xv*d*.
Item in expences at the visitacion at Ware	xvj*d*.
Item to the sexton for keping the chyme and the clokke all the yere	vj*s*. viij*d*.
Item for v lb. candyll in the wynter season for the qwier	v*d*.
Item for ij lb. wex to the standerds and other lights agenst o^r ladys day th' anunciacon	xij*d*.
Item for the obyte of Sr Baldewyn prest and the bedroll	xvj*d*.
Item payed to Sr lewes for the bedroll of the seid Sr Baldewyn for the last yere that was not content (?).	iiij*d*.
Item to the kerver for iiij angells kervyd and peynted	iiij*s*.

1506.

Item of Sr John london chauntry priest v^s for olde arreiags resceyved of John payne for the stall in the bochery	xij*d*.
John Turnor in parte of this yeris ferme for his in the chirchyerd	xij*d*.
Also resceyved of dyverse persones for the seid chirch Rente whoes names herafter ensuyth ffyrst resceyved of John Bush of haseley	iij*d*.
John Dane att Southstret ende.	j*d*.
Thomas Clerk for marions	ix*d*.

The Chirchwardens of Farnham for godyngs tenement	xij*d*.
Thomas Clerk for sabbisfords . . .	iij*d*.
for the paskalsylver at Ester eve (1) . . . viij*s*.	viij*d*.
Rec. of Thomas Whepyll for the waste of torches at his wife's burieng (2)	iiij*d*.
Rec. on michelmas day for stonding of bowers w^tn the chirchyerde (3)	ix*d*.
Resceyved of John Marchaunt executors for his bequest to the reparacion of the chirch . .	ij*s*.
Also resceyved of the collectores of seynt mighells yelde for this yere and the last . . .	xv*s*.
Item in brede and drink to the carters for the chirch strowyng	j*d*.
Item in bred and ale at the takyng downe the broken bell	iij*d*.
Item to John Dane ffyrher (3) for hiering of ij horses in ledyng up the bells (5) to london . .	xij*d*.
Item for richard Newmans expences at the cariage of the seid bells (5) to london . . ij*s*.	viij*d*.
Item expences of the seid Rychard at the fetching home the seid bells (5) . . .	xvj*d*.
Item for tolle of the same bells (5) at Stansted thele (4)	viij*d*.
Item to the belfounder . . . . viij*s*.	
Item in mete and drinke to Spencer and vj other persones helping up the seid bells (5) in to the stepyll	xvj*d*.
Item for serching the chirch evydencs for the rente of seid chirch	ij*d*.
Item in rewarde to my lorde of london^s servunte at the halowing of a chaleys and v awterclothes .	xij*d*.
Item for a corde to the sauntes bell . . .	ij*d*.
Item for Sr Reynolde baldewyn obyte . .	xviij*d*.

1509.

Item resseyvid for a stondyng undernethe the Chirche wall on mighelmas day	vj*d*.
Item ressived ffor wastyng of torchis when that jenyns wyfe was beryed and at her monthe mynde (1) .	ij*d*.

1510.

Item of Rychard wood for a watercorse (1) . .	j*d*.
Item of Rychard Jardfeld for the farme of his Tanhouse in Warter lane	ij*s*.
Imprimis receyved of the profite of the playe above all Charge . . . . . xvj*s*.(?)	viij*d*.

Item receyved of herry cok of ffarnham of the gyft of Elizabeth Sparow	iij*s*.	iiij*d*.
Item recayved of the profyte of the hokkyng ale	xxiij*s*.	
Item receyved of the collectours of Seynt mighells yelde for the profite of the same yelde	xix*s*.	x*d*.
Item To Thomas Josselyn for payntyng of the tabernakell of sen Joone (2)	xiij*s*.	iiij*d*.
Item payd for iij precesshiners (3)	iij*s*.	
Item payd for v foote of tymber to make a porche over the Saunsebell		v*d*.
Item payd for werkmanship of the lectorns in the chaunsell and on in the chirch and the stuff of them	iij*s*.	iiij*d*.
Item payd for skoryng of the latten agenst Ester		vij*d*.
Item payd to Thomas Josselyn and to Thomas Whepille for peterpens which they payd the last yere and axte not alowaunce thereof		xv*d*.
Item for makyng of a plate afore seynt Jame and mendyng of the clok		iiij*d*.
Item payde to the collecturs for the kepyng of the lyght before seynt mighell	iij*s*.	iiij*d*.

1513.

Item of Richard Jardfeld for rente of his messuage in Northstrete		vj*d*.
Item of the wyfe late of Edmond Davy for rente of her messuage in highstrete		j*d*.
Item of Willm Sturdy for rente of his gardyn in Waterlane		vj*d*.
Item of Thomas Chamberleyn for arerage of his messuage at the Cornehell		viij*d*.
Item of the Collecturs of Seynt Johns yelde	ij*s*.	vj*d*.
Item of John maryon for rente of his gatewey		viij*d*.
Imprimis receyved of Willm Butteler for farme of his tenement at potters crosse (1)	iij*s*.	
Item of Rychard Woode for farme of his gardyn lying next to paradise called Thorleywyke		iiij*d*.
Item of Roberd ffuller for farme of his messuage at Teyntor hille	ij*s*.	
Item of Willm Butler for rerage of his forge at pottershell	iij*s*.	
Item of Thomas Chamberleyn for arerage of his stalle in Highe strete		x*d*.
Item of the profite of the pascalsilver	viij*s*.	vij*d*.

Item for the stondyngs at the cherche gate letyn on mighilmas day		viijd.
Item pd for makyng of the cherche walle letyn a grete (2)		xls.
Item for iiij lode and an halfe of tymber redy hewen for the same walle the lode ijs. viijd.		xijs.
Item pd for ij m of tyle with the cariage for the same walle the m iijs. viijd.	vijs.	iiijd.
Item pd for a hundred of Roofe tyle for the same walle	iijs.	viijd.
Item pd to Rafe the Sexten for havyng awey of the old cherche walle		xxd.
Item pd for a staffe for the crosse (3)		jd.
Item pd for iiij cruetts (4)		xijd.
Item pd for iiij lb. of wex for the bason and Standards ayenst Candilmas the li vjd. ob. (5)	ijs.	ijd.
Item pd to Roberd Grey for Tylyng of the Cherche walle	ijs.	iiijd.
Item pd for mendyny of the halywater potte		iijd.
Item pd to old John Prene for somonyng of John maryon to the Bysshoppis Courte		iiijd.
Item pd for the obite of Syr Reynold Baldwyn to the parish prest for Dirige Messe and the bedrolle		ixd.
Item pd to the clerke and sexten for the same obite		vjd.
Item pd for bred and ale abowte the same obite	ijs.	vijd.
Item to almes to iiij pore pepell		iiijd.
Item pd to William Langham for paper and ink and for writing of this accompte	ijs.	iiijd.
Item pd to William Shepperd and Robard Water for wrytyng of ther parcells for remembrance.		

1514.

Item of John Bolyngton for rente and arrerage of his berne in Wyndhille	iiijs.	
Item of Syr Roberd Savill Chauntrie preest for rent	ijs.	vjd.
Item of Stracy of Reyston for Ryngyng at his buryyng		xijd.
Item of Syr John London at the obite of Syr Edward Haward knyght (1)	iijs.	
Item of Thomas Chaundeler for waste of Torchis at the buryyng of his wyfe		xvjd.
Item of John Wylley of London for the wast of torches at the buryyng of his mother	ijs.	
Item receyved of the gyfte of Syr Nicolas Baryngton Knyght	iijs.	
Item of Jocne ap ricæ wydowe for brekyng of Ground in the cherche at the buryyng of her husband	iijs.	iiijd.

Item to Redwood for settyng of iij bees at Sabryches-worth (2)	ij*d*.
Item pd to the scrivener (?) for mendyng of the cherch bokis	xx*s*.
Item pd to the clerke for mendyng of auterclothis obis amessis towellis and diverse other thyngs (3)	xij*d*.
Item to Willm Chaundeler for ij betyng candilles for the Standardis (4)	ij*d*.

1515.

Item for rente of the howse perteyning to the cherch of (? at) Farnham	xij*d*.
Item resseyvyd of the may ale above alle charge (1)	l*s*.
Item pd for brede and ale the same day that Sabbysford may was whan they of Sabysford did come rydyng to the towne to sett ther may	ix*d*.
Item pd for lxxxxiij li. of wex to make w^t alle ij torchis price of every li vij*d*. *ob*. summa	lviij*s*. j*d*.
Item pd for Rosen and goldfoyle and for the makyng of the same torches (2)	xv*s*. iiij*d*.
Item paid to Willm Chaundeler for takyng downe of the pascall & tryyng of the wex thereof	j*d*.
Item pd to the bokemaker and his servaunt at ij tymes	xxxiij*s*. iiij*d*.
Item pd to the scorers for scoryng of the branche before the roode	viij*d*.
Item pd to them for scoryng of the laton in the chaunsell	iiij*s*. viij*d*.
Item pd for the herts skynne to Sr Roberd Savyll (3)	viij*d*.
Item pd to Dewgard for tawyng of the same skynne (4)	xvj*d*.
Item pd for wex candills for the childern in the Queer on all halowen day	j*d*.

1516.

Item of old mother bate for rent	iij*d*.
Item of Collecturs of o^r lady yeld of farnham for a tenement in southstrete	xij*d*.
Item receyved of dyvers persons of ther devocions at the cherch reconsilyng and halowyng	xix*s*.
Item pd for peyntyng of a baner clothe (1)	j*d*.
Item pd for strykyng of viij li. wex for the bason lyght and the standards agenst Trinite sonday (2)	iiij*d*.
Item pd to John hopkyn for hymselfe and his horse and ther cost at the fetching (?) of the boks at Bassyngborn	
Item pd to the bokebynder for his costs comyng heer	xij*d*.

Item pd for stokyng and caryyng of ij lode of clay for
the tenauntries in the cherch yerde . . viij*d*.
Item pd for a key to Sr Johns chamber dore in the
chirch yerd . . . . . ij*d*.
Item pd for the rewards and costs of the Suffricane and
of the Comyssarie and diverse other weyting upon
them at the tyme of the cherch halowyng as appe-
rith by a bille . . . . . lj*s*. xj*d*.
Item for writyng of new rentall for the chirche . xij*d*.

At the foot of the above account is written
m^d that the issues and profits of seynt mighells yeld
did not come to the hands of the above seid accomptaunts the yere aboveseyd but was leyd owte
by the hands of the Collecturs of the said yeld by
the advise of the seid parishioners
m^d that the issues and profits of the may ale the yere
above seid did not come to the hands of the seid
accomptaunts but was bestowed upon the Cawsy
by the advise of the seid parishioners.

1517.

Item to John Pilleston John Josselyn Syr Roberd Savyll
and Thomas Jegon for the tenemente that old
mother harryes dwellith in . . . iiij*s*.
Item of the may ale above all charge . . . xl*s*.
Item pd to the bookebynder at on tyme for his bargyn
takyn a grete . . . . . xliij*s*. iiij*d*.
Item pd for flower and woode for the byndyng of the
books . . . . . . ij*d*.
Item pd to the same bookbynder for mendyng and
coveryng of the grete booke . . . x*s*.
Item pd for a skeyn to kefer w^talle the same booke . xij*d*.
Item pd for x bolyens and claspis . . . viij*d*.
Item pd for iiij red Skynnes for to lyne withall the
keferyngs of the same books . . . xvj*d*.
Item pd for small naylis for the same books . . j*d*.
Item pd to the same bookbynder for his reward
assigned by the parishioners . . . x*s*.
Item pd for charcole on Ester evyn . . . j*d*.
Item pd for brede wyne and ale at the comyng of
Sabrichesworth may . . . . x*d*.
Item pd to the Tynker for mendyng of the silver sensers
and for the crosse and canstikis and the brassis of
the bellis . . . . . vij*s*.

1518.

Item pd for a new lather bag to bere in the chirch keyes . . . . . . ij*d*.

Item delyverd to Andrew Clyfton and Thomas Chaundeler for to fynde w'alle a lyght before seynt myghell for a hole yere . . . . v*s*.

1519.

recyved at dyverse Bonfyers whereof the summe is (1) vij*s*. ij*d*. *ob*.

Item of soche mony as was delyverd to kepe seynt Mighillis light at the last accompte and was spared and the lyght found . . . . xij*d*.

Item to master knyghtton's clerke for a copye of clerkis supplicacon . . . . . viij*d*.

Item pd to John ap Rice for caryyng of a letter to master Vyker agenst Clerke . . . xij*d*.

Item pd for wyne at Jegyns at soche tyme as master Knyghton and other gentilmen were ther for the same besynes . . . . . vj*d*.

Item pd for the examinacon in the White Hall at Westmester . . . . . ij*s*.

Item pd to Peter Baron for his counsell and helpe agenst the seid Clerke . . . . . iij*s*. iiij*d*.

Item pd for makyng of an obligacon at Westminster for the same besynes (2) . . . . ij*d*.

Item pd to gray and his server for pathyng of the seid chirche and chirche porche and mendyng of the crosse in the chirche yarde by the space of vij dayes takyng by the day for mete drynke and wages x*d*. (3) . . . . . v*s*. x*d*.

Item pd to Rafe Thomas for going to Walden for the Clokmaker and to Pukriche for Richard Bryan for to make the bell whelis . . . . iiij*d*.

Item to Rafe Thomas for dygyng of the holis for the grate (4) . . . . . iiij*d*.

Item for a silken rebend to mend w'all the best vestment . . . . . . ij*d*.

Item to Jardefeld for tymber for the chirche grate (4) . xiiij*d*.

Item to John Josselyn for tymber for the same grates (4) . . . . . xx*d*.

Item to John Dane Smyth for on of the grates for the chirche yerd weyyng xij score li. and v li. (4) . xxv*s*. vj*d*.

Item to Hothe the Carponter for makyng of the tymber werke at the south gate and grate of the chirche yerd . . . . . iiij*s*.

At the foot of this account is the following

M^d that the parishioners at this day have chosyn John Josselyn and Nicholas Redwood to be gyders and rulers of the Comon light for the yere folowyng.

1520.

Receyved of John Dane pulter for rent		j*d*.
Item of William Jenyn		iij*d*.
Item of Richard Tebold		j*d*.
Item of Julyan Eton		vj*d*.
Item of Richard Glascok for the tenement late old Bardeneys		vj*d*.
Item of John Luke		j*d*.
Item of Thomas Parys for his ten^te	ij*s*.	
Item of Wallers wife for the Ten^te that old Spycer dwellid in	ij*s*.	
Item of Richard Duddesbury for rerage		xij*d*.
Receyved of the pascall selver at Ester	viij*s*.	x*d*.
Item rec. of Water the begger toward the reparacone of the bellis (1)		xx*d*.
Item of the Bonfyers at hoktyde	vj*s*.	iij*d*.
Item for the stondyngs on mighilmas day		xij*d*.
Item of the executurs of Willm Bardeney for waste of torchis at the Buryall and month day of the seid Willm and of Elizabeth his wyfe	v*s*.	iiij*d*.
Item of the parissheners for the makyng of the bells (bells)	iiij*li*. iiij*s*.	ix*d*.
pd to a glasyer for mendyng of the stepyll wyndowe		xvj*d*.
pd to John Dane Smyth in full contentacon and payment for the fyrst grate (2)	v*s*.	
Item pd to John Dane Smyth for the other grate	xx*s*.	
Item pd for stavys and pynnakyllis for the canapye		xiiij*d*.
Item pd for settyng on of the frenge of the canapye		j*d*.
Item for brede and ale at the bryngyng of the gras at mydsomer to strewe w^tall the chirche		ij*d*.
Item pd for the costs of a man that dide come to se the brokyn bell		vj*d*.
Item pd to John Hoth Carponter for makyng of the tymber werke of the grate to wyndhillward	ij*s*.	
Item pd to Ric. Gybbe for burds for the same grate		iiij*d*.
Item pd for makyng of the pett at the same grate		iiij*d*.
Item pd Richard Jardefeld for tymber for the seyd grate (2)	iij*s*.	iij*d*.
Item pd for makyng the wrytynges bytwene the parisshe and the belfounder		xx*d*.

Item pd to the belfounder in parte of payment	xljs. jd. ob.
Item pd for settyng (?) of herry Spencers Tryce at Ware for to take downe with alle the bells (bellC)	iijd.
Item pd to herry Spenser for takyng downe and havyng up agen of the seid bells (bellC)	viijs.
Item pd for mete and drynke for them that dide helpe downe and up the seid bells (bellC)	ijs. vd.
Item pd to Crabbe for Irenwerke and naylis for the said bellis	xd.
Item pd for a staff for the new strem' (streamer) of seynt mighell	xiiijd.
Item pd for the seid Strem' byside the iiij nobillis that was pd by the colecturs (3)	xxd.
Item pd to on for rydyng to Ware for to have herry Spencer to hang up the bellis	iiijd.
Item pd to Crowcheman for somonyng of Willm Schepperd and John John to the Bysshoppis Courte	ijd.
Item pd to the scrybe for enteryng of ther names	iijd.
Item pd to the belfounders servaunt in reward at his comyng to the towne for to have knowledge of the grement and cordyng of the bellis	xijd.
Item pd for the costs of John Hawkyn and of his horse at his rydyng to london to se the bell cast	xxijd.
Item pd in reward to the belfounders servaunts at the castyng of the seid bell	iiijd.
Item pd for the costs of John Hawkyn at another at his goyng to london to speke wt the belfounder for to take downe agen the seid bell	xd.
Item pd to Crab for mendyng of the cherche mattok and for Irenwerke for the new tabernakyll	viijd.
Item pd toward the gildyng of the tabernakill	vjs. viijd.
Item pd to Blancheflower for pathyng in the cherche	xd.
Item pd for mendyng of on of o{r} lady Canstykes	ijd.
Item pd for makyng of a bare ayenst that old Bardeney and his wife was buryed	iiijd.
Item pd toward the gildyng of the new tabernakyll (4)	vjs. viijd.
Item pd for a frenge of sylke for the Canapye	xijs.

1521.

Item of Syr Roberd Sale Chauntrye preest	ijs. vjd.
Item of the ffurbussher for rente of the schoppe at the chirche gate (1)	ixd.
Item of John Hawkyn for a peyer of beds wt ryngs on the seyd beds late in the hands and kepyng of olde bardeney	iijs.

Item receyved on the feyer dayes for stondyngs	xvij*d*.
Item pd to the peynter for gyldyng of a crowne for oure lady in the cherche	ij*s*. iiij*d*.
Item pd for scoryng of the bason and standards and rubbyng of the George agenst Ester	viij*d*.
Item pd to a furbussher for scoryng of the same George	ix*d*.
Item pd to John Kemp for makyng of the gret bell claper and for the caryyng of the seyd claper to and froo	vij*s*. viij*d*.
and the seid Kemp doth promyse that if the seyd claper do breke w^tin the time of vj yeris next after this accompte that then he to make yt agen and to have alowed for his labur but	iiij*d*.
Item pd to John Graye for makyng of the Irenwerke for the new Tabernakyll (2)	xvij*d*.

1523.

Receyved of the profite of the pley	xxxiij*s*.
Item pd to the schot of hatfeld may (1)	xij*d*.
Item pd for the caryyng of ij loods of free stoone and for horse mete and mannysmete comyth with the seid carts	xv*s*. viij*d*.
Item paid to the mason and his servaunts for the seid ij loods of stoon and for ther werkyng at the seid cherche by the space of a month	iij*li*. ij*s*.
Item pd for the caryyng of a loode of grete stonys	viij*d*.
Item pd to a man for mendyng of iiij coopis and for the makyng of ij awter clothis and for mendyng of the Canapye over the pyx at the hye awter and for makyng of a myghtter for the bisshop	v*s*.

1525.

Item pd for sowdyng of the old crosse	iiij*d*.
Item pd for the peyntyng of ix new baner clothis and for peyntyng of the cloth at the scryvng howse	vij*s*.
Item pd for mendyng of the cherche bare	viij*d*.
Item pd for a quarter of lyme to set up w^talle the palme crosse and to pathe w^talle in the cherche	xvj*d*.
Item pd for bryke for the seid palme crosse ... and for the werkmanship of the seid cros (1)	
Item pd for ij li. of wex for seynt mighills lyght ayenst Ester last past	xiiij*d*.
Item pd for ij li. of wex for Seynte Mighills lyghts ayenst Mighilmas	xiij*d*.
Item pd for the scoryng of the bason and standards and the facon and the branche before seynt mighill	xiiij*d*.

Item for wrytyng of the inventorye of the cherch
  goods (2) . . . . . . xijd.

1526 or 1527.

Item rec. of Henry Musgrave for rerage of rent of the
  tenement in Southstrete belonging to o^r lady
  yeld in ffarneham . . . . . xijd.
Item of Syr Edward Pye chauntree preest . . ijs. vjd.
Item of Gyfferey Thurgood for the rent of his gardyn by
  the mylle . . . . . . ijd.
Item pd to a broyderer for mendyng of the best coope vjs. viijd.
Item pd for halowyng of the cherche cloothis . ijs.

1529.

Item of Master Wylleys bonfyer . . . xxijd.
Item of Thomas Clerks bonfyer . . . viijd.
Item pd to John Hawkyn for mony that he paid for the
  orgons (1) . . . . . . vs. vjd.
Item pd to a Tynker for sowdyng of the cros and for
  mendyng of ij cansticks . . . . xvjd.
Item pd for the obyte of Syr Rafe baldewyn . . iiijs.
Item pd for starchyne of Seints lawnys . . ijd. ob.

1530.

Item of George Thomson gentilman . . . xviijd.
receyved of the yeveste of Sir Wylliam Say Knight (1) vjs. viijd.
also receyved of the hokynge ale at dyverse bone-
  flyers . . . . xvjs. xd.
Item pd for mendyng of the cros att ij tymes . . vd.
Item pd to Roberd Hothe and laurence for mendynge
  the iij gayts and makyng of the poste for the
  cherche doore . . . . . . ijs. iiijd.
Item for makyng a key to an hangynge loke for the
  cherche gate . . . . . . ijd.
Also paid for a messe boke . . . . iiijs. iiijd.

1531.

Of Willm Butler for ffarme of his tenement att the
  letherstalls (1) . . . . . . iijs.
Of the Scryvener for the Scole howse . . . vjd.
Item pd for v new torchis by the collectors of Seint
  Mighells yeld . . . . . xxvijs. vijd.
Item pd for payntynge the grene crosse for lent (2) . ijd.

1532.

Item pd for tymber for the portall at the queer dore and for the ffont and for certen palis . . ij*s.* vij*d.*
Item pd to Joob for makyng of the seid portall . iiij*s.*
Item pd to Joobe for makyng of the ffunt and sepulker x*s.*
Item pd to Roger Trenham for makyng of the seynt Joones bell wheele . . . . viij*d.*
Item pd for lyne to drawe with all the cloth in the roodeloft . . . . . . ij*d.*
Item pd to Whyte of London for mendyng of the orgons . . . . . . v*s.*

1533.

Item of Cowley the Capper for rerage of rent of his howse in Wyndehill . . .
Item of Syr John Petche for rent . . . ij*s.* vj*d.*
Item pd to Brancheflower for tylyng of the stalle that John Peyn bocher holdyth . . . v*d.*
Item pd to the mason for iij week and ij dayes werkyng upon the steepill and on the vyse by the rood loft xiij*s.* iiij*d.*
Item pd to a laborer to helpe to sawe ston . . viij*d.*
Item pd to Roger Trenham for makyng of the stages and takyng downe of them and for helpyng to set the stoones . . . . . xij*d.*
Item pd to the seyd mason for another dayes werke . viij*d.*
Item pd to John Barell for ij dayes werke at another tyme for helping of the seid mason and beryng home of the same stage tymber . . . viij*d.*
Item for makyng of a releece and dede indented for the sale of Walchis howse to laye . . xiiij*d.*

1534.

Item rec. for the stondyngs of Corpus Cristi day and myghilmas day . . . . . ij*s.* v*d.*
Item pd for a lok for the clok howse doore . . iiij*d.*
Item pd for ij new surplecs for the childern (1) . ij*s.* vj*d.*

1535.

Item of Thomas mede for rent of his kechyn in North-strete . . . . . . j*d.*
Item of Andrew Clyfton for rent of his schop in the ffyschrowe (1) . . . . . j*d.*
Item of Richard Jardefeld for Banstrets howse in Sowthstrete . . . . . j*d.*

Item of master Vyker for rent of parcell of the towne
dyche on the west parte of the Vykerage . iij*d*.
Item rec. of Barret for rent of the schop at the cherche
gate . . . . . . ix*d*.
Item rec. clerely for the cherch clerkis mede and lond
bysyde the fyndyng of the lampe and kepyng of
the obyte . . . . . iij*s*. xj*d*.
Item pd for makyng of a bill at the vysitacon . ij*d*.
Item geve to the cherch Clerke for his reward at his
fyrst comyng to Stortford . . . xij*d*.
Item pd for a new surples for the sexten . .
Item for a quarter and an halfe of lyme for to mend w*t* all
the cherch howsis and the well at the cherche
gate . . . . . . ij*s*.
Item for ij bourds to ley on bookis . . . ij*d*.
Item pd for xliiij foote of bourde for to mend with all
the flower of the scoole howse . . . xvj*d*.
Item for fetching (?) and caryng of the Cherch Clerks
stuff from Chesterford to Stortford . . ij*s*.

1538.

Item of Will*m* Thurgood of Birchanger for rent of his
water wey in Southstrete . . . j*d*.
Item of m*r* pyleston for his stondyng at the George gate viij*d*.
Item pd to Roberd water for helpyng to gather the
grene wex and for the makyng of this account (1) ij*s*. viij*d*.
Item pd to m*r* pyleston for rent of the chirche yarde . iiij*d*.
Item for mendyng of the grete lantern in the cherche iij*d*.

1539.

Item to the pursers wyfe for mendyng of the surplecs v*d*.
Item to Web and John Rafe for beryng of the cros at
gangtyde (1) . . . . . iij*d*.
Item to Ederiche for a stapill for the kyngs chest .
Item pd for the Obyte of Syr Reynold preest . iiij*s*.
Item for mendyng of the hand at the Dyall . . j*d*.

1540.

Item of an old woman and her daughter for halfe yere
rent of the tenemente that they dwell in by the
cherche yard . . . . . xij*d*.
receyved of John myller and John Smyth for the stok
of oure lady yeld (1) . . . iij*li*. viij*d*.
Item pd to Richard Gib for rent resolute (2) . ij*d*.

Item pd to m^r bayly for ij yere rent for the bysshop of london for the cherch yard (3)	viij*d*.
Item pd for a lyne for the lampe	iij*d*.
Item for naylis for the lowpe doore unto the leeds	*ob*.

1541.

Item of W^{ill}m Sybthorp for rent of his gatewey	viij*d*.
Item rec. for a crowne that was brought from ffarneham	ij*s*.
Item pd to stonard for bartlyng of the cherche howse that Roger Trenham holdyth	vj*d*.
Item pd at stansted pley to make up the sume ther w^t all	ij*s*.
Item pd to the kyngs xv for the cherch clerks mede	vj*d*.

1542.

Item pd for naylis for the orgons and Sepulker	j*d*.
Item for three new rollis for the orgons and for irenwerke to them	v*d*.
Item for lyne for the same orgens	j*d*.
Item to Trenham for tendyng of the comon light	ij*d*.
Item to barett for iij dayes beryng of the Cros at gangtyde	iij*d*.
Item for settyng on of a pipe on the Ewer	j*d*. *ob*.
Item for rosyn for the belfounder	*ob*.
Item for a new bybill and the bryngyng home of it (1)	vj*s*. j*d*.
Item pd for new settyng and tewnyng of the orgons	viij*s*.
Item for ij schepekynnes to amend w^tall the bellis for the orgons	vij*d*.
Items for lynes nayles and pakthrede for the seid orgons	iij*d*.
Item for browne paper for the seid orgons	*ob*.
Item pd for j b^z of charle colis at the mendyng of the seid orgons	j*d*.
Item to Th. South for ij dayes blowyng of the same orgons at the settyng of them	iiij*d*.
Item pd for mete and drynke of the seid Th. Southe the seid ij dayes and of the orgon maker for a hole weeke	xx*d*.
Item to Calydays boy for helpyng of the orgon maker	ij*d*.
Item paid for Irenwerke for the seid bellis	j*d*.
Item j li. of glewe	iii*d*. *ob*.
Item for fetching (?) of the orgon makers toolis from Baldok	viij*d*.
Item pd to the Sexten for his hole yeris wages	vj*s*. viij*d*.

Item for a new stoode for the Clok . . . iijd.
Item pd to Roberd Water for wrytyng of a new rentall
for helpyng to gather the cherche rent and for
makyng of this account . . . . ijs. viijd.
Item for lynyng for the care cloth (2) . . iiijd.
Item to hokley for emtyyng of on of the grats and for
drawing of a lood of claye (3) . . . iijd.

1545.

Item pd to the tynker for mendyng of a chalyse . vd.
Item pd to Scharpe at on tyme for kepyng of the
cherche booke . . . . . iiijd.
Item pd for ij procession books . . . vd.
Item pd for a lok for the chapell doore (1) . . iiijd.
Item pd for iij dayes beryng of the cros at Gangtyde. iijd.

1546.

Item of old John Jacob for ij yeres rent of the
Chauntrye londs . . . . . vs.
Item rec. of the parissheners then toward the cherche
clerks wages for vij quarters of ij yeris endyd at
the ffest of the Anunciacon of oure lady in anno
primo Reg^{is} Edwardi Sexti . . iiij*li*. viijs. ijd.
Item of mostres Glascok for brekyng of ground in the
cherche at the buryall of her husbond (1) . vjs. viijd.
Item pd to master Josselyns servaunt that was the
orgon pleyer for his reward at his ffyrst comyng . iiijd.
Item pd for lenyn cloth for the clok . . . jd.
Item pd to hym that mendyd the Clok and the chyme xs.
Item pd to John Whepyll for Colys and for occupyyng
of his toolys at the makyng of the seyd clok and
chyme . . . . . . xxd.
Item pd for a rope for seynt Joonys bell . . iiijd.
Item pd to yong Scharpe for his servyce and attendaunce
gyvyng heer while that ther was no cherche
Clerke . . . . . . vs.
Item pd to William that was at mast^r Carrowes for
pleyyng upon the Orgons . . . vjs. viijd.
Item pd for iiij processioners . . . vijd.
Item to Roger Trenham for makyng of a bell wheele
ayenst All haluntyde . . . . iiijs.
Item pd for gyrdells to the vestments . . jd. ob.
Item pd to the clerke of Clare for a rewarde . . ijs.
Item pd to him in yernest . . . . iiijd.
Item pd for the caryyng of the same Clerks stuff . xs.

Item pd for brede and ale for the carters at the same tyme		j*d*.
Item pd to one of Plesschy on the dedycacion day (2)		xij*d*.
Item pd to Potter for pleyyng on mighilmas day		iiij*d*.
Item pd to Peercy the cherche clerke that now is for the caryyng of his stuff	x*s*.	
Item pd to Browne the Smyth for mendyng of a bell claper and for makyng of the nepill of the same claper	viij*s*.	
Item pd to Roberd hothe for makyng of the Clok howse and for tymber for the same	iiij*s*.	v*d*.
Item pd to mather Calyday for bourde for to cover the lytill sched over the clok (3)		xx*d*.
Item to the seid Trenham for helpyng of hym that made the Clok and chyme by the space of vj dayes	iij*s*.	

Written at the foot of this account

m^d that ther remayneth in mastres Glascokks hands of her husbands bequest to the use of the cherche. xx*s*.

m^d that John Skyllyngham the elder owith xiij*s*. iiij*d*. wherof the parissh hath forgeve him x*d*. and other xl*d*. he promysith to pay at Whytsontide next comyng and the other vj*s*. viij*d*. the seid John Skyllyngham promysith to pay to Wyll^m Crab for his peyn taking before the makyng hereof.

1547.

Item of Grace Glascok widow		vj*d*.
Item of Roger Jenyn for Cowleys		vj*d*.
Item of Wyll^m Norfolke for the Almes howse gardyn for halfe a yere (1)		iiij*d*.
Item of John Dowsehed for his tenement at Teyntor hyll	ij*s*.	
Item of master Carrowe for his parte of the Tanhowse		viij*d*.
Item for the rent of the iiij tenements in the cherche yarde for a hole yere endyd now at this present sonday beyng Palme sonday and also oure lady day	viij*s*.	
Item of Thomas Papys for the schop at the cherche gate		xvj*d*.

The following is a verbatim transcript of the "Receptiones Forinsecæ" for this year (1 of Edw. VI.)

Also the seyd accountants yeld account of dyverce foren receyts by them receyved w^tin the tyme of

ther seid account as foloweth ffyrst of the parisheners ther at Ester for the Pascall sylver . . viijs. viijd.
Item rec. of John Dowsede as in full payment of his
old dett . . . . xxs.
Item rec. of dyverce persons at midsomer mighilmas
and cristmas towards the cherche clerks wagys . xls.
Item rec. of Roger Trenham for the stondyngs on
mighilmas day . . . . . iijs. iiijd.
Item rec. of the seid Roger Trenham for the rent of
the chamber in the cherch yard that the
chauntrye preest dide lye in . . . iijs. iiijd.
Item for a cros of sylver and gylte w^t a foote to the
same a chaleys of sylver gylte w^t a paten to the
same a pax of sylver and gylte ij payer of sensers
of sylver w^t the toppis beyng gylte a schip of
sylver ij crewetts of sylver weyyng together seven
score and xiij unces and was sold at vs. jd. the
unce sume (2) . . . xxxviij*li*. xvijs. ixd.
Item for a brokyn chalys and other brokyn sylver that
was sold by weyght and dide wey xxxiiij unces
and di. and a halfe quarter of an unce at vs. the
unce sume (2) . . . . viij*li*. xiijs. ob.
Item for a Tabernakyll that was sold to Richard Jardefeld (2) . . . . . . vjs. viijd.
Item for an old Tabernakyll sold to Willm Pygott (2). xijd.

Summa lj*li*. xiiijs. viijd. ob.

Item pd to the cherche clerke for his hole yeris wages
endyd at the seyd ffest of the anunciacion of oure
lady . . . . . iiij*li*.
Item pd to Roger Trenham for settyng up and takyng
downe of the sepulker at Ester . . . iiijd.
Item pd to hym for naylis and charcolis on Ester
evyn . . . . . . jd.
Item pd to Wyll^m Crabbe by the comaundment of the
parisshoners at the last account for soche peyne
as he had takyn before that tyme in the cherche
and for ryngyng . . . . . iijs. iiijd.
Item pd to Roger Trenham for tendyng of the comon
lightts at Ester . . . . . ijd.
Item pd to Syr Rafe for mendyng of the Orgons . vs.
Item for mendyng of an ovyn and a chymnye at the
tenemente that the cherche clerke dwellith in . viijd.
Item pd to Ransewold for whytyng and wasshyng of
the cherche wallys (3) . . . . xls. iiijd.(?)

CHURCHWARDENS' ACCOUNTS.   47

Item pd to Wyll^m Crab for makyng clene of the cherche and for beryng of the stonys and rubbrusshe forthe of the same,	xv*d*.
Item pd to old John Patryk in almes at the request of the parisshoners ther	xx*d*.
Item pd to John Turn(er ?) for peyntyng of an awter clothe	x*d*.
Item pd to harry marvell for makyng of ij round irens for the curtens in the queer and for the makyng of a new key	xj*d*.
Item pd for paper for the cherche boke (4)	ij*d*.
Item pd for wrytyng of the same boke agenst the vysytacon	viij*d*.
Item pd to on of the vysyturs clerks for makyng of a certyficat for the parisshe at the vysyters beyng heer	viij*d*.
Item pd to their scrybe for the receyvyng of the seid certyficat	iiij*d*.
Item to them for an injuncon (5)	iij*d*.
Item for brede and ale for them of the parisshe that was sworn at the seyd vysytacon	iij*d*.
Item pd for ij li. of fflokks to stop w^tall the new velvett kusshyn	iiij*d*.
Item pd for the costis of the cherche wardens and other of this parisshe beyng at the vysytacon at Ware and of ther horsis	xvj*d*.
Item pd for makyng of a byll ther of the cherche plate and other of the cherche goodis	vij*d*.
Item payd to Burle the joyner for a chest to set in the chaunsell (6)	v*s*.
Item payd for iij lokks and keyes and garnettis for the same chest	iiij*s*.
Item payd for the deñ (dinner ?) and other costs of John Laxton the peynter at his fyrst comyng	x*d*. *ob*.
Item pd to hym in yernest	xij*d*.
Item pd to the same John Laxton for xxj dayes	xvij*s*. vj*d*.
Item pd to Thomas Wulman peynter for x dayes peyntyng at x*d*. the day	viij*s*. iiij*d*.
Item payd to the same Wulman in rewarde for his goyng and comyng	viij*d*.
Item pd for the seid John Laxtons horse hyer and for the costs of hym and his horse at his rydyng to london for to vew and se other cherchis ther	iij*s*. iiij*d*.
Item pd to John Turn(er ?) for ij dayes helpyng of the seyd paynters	xx*d*.

Item pd for syse for the clothe in the roode loft		viijd.
Item pd for wood for the same paynters	ijs.	iiijd.
Item pd for grene byse for them to Burle		xijd.
Item pd for cottun for them		ijd.
Item pd for brede and ale for the same peynters		iiijd.
Item for the peyntyng of ij curtens for the queer	ijs.	viijd.
Item pd to Burle for ij dayes takyng downe of the thyngs in the Roodeloft		xvjd.
Item pd to the aboveseid Edward Wylley for grene byse a quarter of a pound		xxd.
Item pd for sap grene		vjd.
Item pd for varnys		iiijd.
Item for blew byse	iiijs.	
Item pd for spalt		iiijd.
Item pd for blak cerus and marbyll		viijd.
Item pd for vermylyon		ixd.
Item pd for fflorye		xvd.
Item for fyne gyldyng guld	xs.	
Item for sanguadragonys		iiijd.
Item for lynsed yolle		iiijd.

(The above mentioned colours were used as I find by a marginal note in this account "to peynt and gyld w'all in the cherch")

Item payd to Wyll^m Crab for ryngyng of the day bell and Curfew	iijs.	iiijd.
Item pd for the costs of the seid accountants at Hertford w^t dyverse other of the parysshe before the kyngs Comyssioners at ij tymes (7)	vjs.	
Item pd for ou^r seyng of the cherche evydense and for makyng of a paper rentall and a certyficat for to certefye unto the kyngs commyssioners of the obite londs and light londs (8)	ijs.	

	£	s.	d.
The receipts from all sources this year amounted to	55	19	8¼
And the expenditure to	14	2	5½

The balance £41 17s. 3d. is thus accounted for at the foot of the account:

In the hands of Sr Henry Parker K^t £32 4s. 5d.
Lord Henry Morley has *without* the consent of the Parishioners £4 0s. 0d.
In the hands of the Churchwardens £5 12s. 10d.

1548.

Item ffyrste receyved of m^r Bayley ffor festements v*li*.
receyved of m^r Patmer . . . vij*li*. xiiij*s*.
receyved of certeyn other men as apperethe by the Inventory . . . . . xiij*li*. vj*s*. viij*d*.
receyved of m^r Bayley and Certeyn other for lvij unces of plate . . . . xxvij*li*. viij*s*. vij*d*. *ob*.
Rec. of Thom^s Stok for wexe . . . xxix*s*. ij*d*.
Rec. of m^r Carowes executors . . . vj*s*. viij*d*.
Rec. of the rents of the Churche . . liiij*s*. ij*d*.
Rec. of the rents in the Churche yerd . xxiij*s*.
Rec. of the goodman Whyppylle . . xx*s*.
Rec. of m^r Elyot . . . iij*li*. v*s*.
Rec. of Bedwelle for a portaylle . . vj*s*. viij*d*.

Some, lxiij*li*. xiij*s*. xj*d*. *ob*.

Layde owte of thys
Item ffyrste delyvered to Roger Waren . x*li*.
delyvered to John Jacobbe . . . viij*li*.
delyvered to Rychard Roberts (?) . . v*li*.
delyvered to waren the smythe . . x*li*.
pd to the Glasyer iij*li*. vj*s*. viij*d*. w^h was . iiij*li*. iij*s*. iiij*d*.
payd to the Glasyer for mendyng alle the holes abowte the Churche . . . . . iiij*s*.
Item delyvered to Raphe Smythe alias (?) Clarke viij*li*. ix*s*. viij*d*. w^h was . . xvj*li*. xix*s*. iiij*d*.
pd ffor the Charges Rydyng to the kyngs Comysseners at iij tymes the ffyrste tyme to Ware viij*s*. v*d*. *ob*., at the second tyme at Ware agen iij*s*. ix*d*., the thyrd to Welwyn viij*s*. vj*d* . . . xx*s*. viij*d*. *ob*.
Layd owt ffor reparacons of the Churche and Church yerd as apperethe after . . . v*li*. xv*s*. v*d*. *ob*.
And so Remaynethe in my hands Thom^s Chaundeler lij*s*. j*d*.
Rec. of thes men agen ffyrste of Raphe Smythe alias (?) Clarke . . . . viij*li*. xvij*s*.
of John Jacobbe . . . . iiij*li*.
of Warren smythe . . . . viij*li*.
of Rychard Roberts (?) . . . x*s*. (?)
Then I payd to the kyngs Justyces . xxx*li*.

And so ther remaynethe dew unto me Thom^s Chaundeler by thys myne accomte . v*li*. x*s*.

Item for takyng down of the aulters . . . x*d*.
pd to whyte lyme borner for di (half) a q^t (quarter) of lyme . . . . . x*d*.

pd to Wyll^m balam and hys son for makyng the places
  where the alters dyd stond . . . xiiijd.
pd to hym for tylyng Churche howsse and Chappelle (1) viijd.
pd to Henry Morwyll and hys men for dygyng up of
  the brycke in the Churche yerde . . iijd.
pd for plonkes for the table . . . . xxijd.
pd for quarters for the table . . . . ijs.
pd to Cornelys for makyng the table (2) . iijs. viijd.
pd to the Chancelers Clarke for notyng of a bylle . ijd.
pd to the Comysary for a sytacyon . . viijd.
pd to the scrybe for hys fees . . . . xviijd.
pd to Sr Thomas for rehersyng ye sytacyon . . iiijd.
pd to Wede (?) Coler maker for makyng the baderyckes
  for the belles . . . . . xxd.
pd to the Wever for sernyng (? serving) . . xijd.
pd to Water the tanner for servyng Certeyne . ijs. vjd.
pd to Mowton for makyng the bare . . vijs. ijd.
pd to Clarke for a shette of parchement to make a new
  rentalle . . . . . . vd.
pd to the Glasyer for mendyng the hole y^t the dogge
  brake . . . . . . vd.
pd for ij bokes for the new servys . . . viijs.
pd for lyme to the hy aulter . . . . xvjd.
pd to Clarke for a spade for to make Graves . vjd.

1549 and 1550.

Item I charge me Edward Wylley Rec. at the hands
  of Sir Henry Parkare Knyt for the reparasions of
  the churche and hother nesarys in the chyrche vli. xijs. xd.
Item I charge me w^t ij holle yers Reynt of the teny-
  ments in the chyrche yarde be longyng to the
  chyrche of stortffourde . . . . xixs. iiijd.

Item payd at bowntyngfourde for the Exspences of the
  Vykare S^r thomas chantary prest holde Jardivylde
  John Jacobe the holdere m^r waton (?) thomas
  Pykat (?) Edward Wylley chirchewardyne for
  mans meyt and horse meyt beyng ther a foure
  the kyngs comyssenares . . . . ijs. iiijd.
pd moure there for paper . . . . ob.
pd to the paynter of walden calleyd laxsame for the
  payntyng of a clothe a longes the Rowde loft . xiijs. iiijd.
pd for naylles for the stranyng of the sayd clothe
  appone the Rowde loft . . . . ijd.

CHURCHWARDENS' ACCOUNTS.

pd to persy clarke for the altrynge of the servys hought of lattyne in to ynglys by the conseynt of the Vykar m^r carow m^r John helyat w^t other . . ij*s*.

pd for a quoyre of whyt paper for hyme . . iij*d*.

pd to persy clarke at the seconde tyme by the comandement of m^r tomsone m^r helyat m^r Vykar Rychard pylstone Rayffe Clarke w^t other for ye transposyng vons agayne of the servys hought of lattyne in to ynglys . . . . . . iij*s*. iiij*d*.

pd agayne to persy clark for the last chandge of servys in to ynglys aganst trenyte sonday (1) . . xvj*d*.

pd for the vone halff of a boke calleyd the parafrasys of Eraysmous wyche the paryshe (?) y^s chargeyd at v*s*. vj*d*.

pd to the glasyere of donemowe for iij fout and do (half) of glase at iij*d*. *ob*. the fout wyche was seyt houppe over the Comysarys hede . . x*d*. *ob*.

pd to persy clarke for the makyng houppe of all the vestery twys at the . . . to make a playne sytyffycathe to the kynges majesty . . . viij*d*.

pd the xix day of marche an^o 1549 at warre when . . . (? we) weynt afour masto^r barley vone of the comysenares to make sytyfycathe of all the chyrche goods as shall apeyre by the kyngs hynvenetory Indentyd under thees namys that ffollos. Jhon helyat, Thomas Patmer, George Thomsone, Wyll^m Pygat, Sr Thomas Symsone prest and Edward Wyllay now chyrchewardyne. All thees be sworne to ye kyngs hynvenytory. vone Jhon Helyat was not sworne. the charges of all . . . and horse meyt in the company of m^r barley dyd cost was that I Edward Wylley dyd pay the some of (2) . . . . viij*s*. vj*d*.

pd at londone for a bowke of the last servys (?) seyt fourthe bounde in parchment calleyd the kyngs boke (3) . . . . iij*s*. viij*d*.

pd moure for the sayd chyrche for ij sawtors at x*d*. a pece . . . . xx*d*.

pd for ij newe bokys to m^r wylcoks calleyd the kyngs boke of the last settyng fourthe both at (3) for the comunyone . . . } vj*s*. iiij*d*.

pd by the comandement of . . . (? certain) of the parysh as by m^r tomsone, my ffather Jhon Wyllay, holde maryone and goodmane chandlere w^t others to persy clarke for the makyng of iiij

bowkys for to haff in the queyre w^t a queare of whyt paper	vs. iij$d$.
pd to Jhon bayfourde schowmakare for vj bourdes .	iij$s$.
Item payd hought by me moure to the clarke for hys wagys moure then the bowke of the gatheryng come to for the spaces of thys ij yere endyng at o^r lady day in leynt as schalle appeyre . . wyche I axe alowans of w^t the washyng and skowryng of the chyrche . . .	xlviij$s$. ij$d$.
Item moure I axe a lowans for dyverse warre y^t remayns unepayd In my bowk wyche was delyvered to the howse (?) of my lorde of myseru(?w)lle (Qy. misrule) y^t dyde reymayne behynde unep^d at the hands of Rayff Clark . . .	vs. ix$d$. ob.

1553.   [I. of Q. Mary.]

Item for making up of the aulter . . .	xiiij$d$.
Item for meat and drynk to his servante that wrought y^t	vj$d$.
Item to m^r Vicar for a mas bok . . .	xij$s$.
Item for vij ells of holond for the prysts surples	vij$s$. jd. ob. q^r.
Item for iij bokes more to the vicar . .	xxij$s$.
Item for a Manuell and a proossesioner . .	iiij$s$. vj$d$.
Item paid for a Pyx	vs.
Item paid for a holye water stope (1) . .	iij$s$. ij$d$.
Item for an elle of cloth for the pixe . .	xviij$d$.
Item paid for making of y^t w^t the sylke .	vj$d$.
Item for iiij yards of frynge blewe . . . . (? and red) silke and the sowing of y^t apon the sacrament cloth	vj$d$.
Item paid for the bysshopp boke of artycles . .	iiij$d$.
Item paid to Tyse for the Table where the sacrament y^s	ij$s$.
Item paid to the Screvenor for making the booke of artycles	ij$s$.
Item to the Scrybe when y^t was delyvered . .	iiij$d$.
Item paid to John Turnor for paynting of the crosse staff	iiij$d$.
Item to Burle for making of the Rood . .	xx$s$.
Item paid unto hym for coloring of the walle .	vj$d$.
Item paid to Burle for a crosse . . .	viij$d$.
Item paid to Thomas Barbore for a shippe for franckencence (2)	xvj$d$.
Item paid to crabe for rynging the day bell .	xij$d$.
Item payd to Tyse for two staunds (? standards) at the highe aulter	xij$d$.

Item paid to the vicar for half a pound beting
 candell (3) . . . . . . v*d*.
Item paid to Tyse for the crose . . . iiij*d*.

1554.

Item of John Busshe for a water course downe to the
 Ryver owte of Sowth strete . . . j*d*.
Item of John Savyll for a peece of lond in Comon
 downe . . . . . . iij*d*.
Of the parissheners ther at Ester for the pascall Sylver vij*s*. ix*d*.
Item of mysterys Glascoke for the gyft of here husband
 for the bells . . . . . xx*s*.
Item of Wyll^m Pylleston for the arrerages of the towne
 dyche . . . . . . ij*s*. iiij*d*.
Item Receyvyd of leacys and ffyns . . . xiij*s*. viij*d*.
Item of John Schrymp for arrerages . . . vj*d*.
Item pd for Ryngs for the Vayle (1) . . iiij*d*.
Item pd to Torner for payntyng of the cherche clothys vij*s*. viij*d*.
Item pd to Thomas mathew for making of the holy
 water stoke . . . . . x*d*.
Item pd for a cloth for the pryst hed . . . ix*d*.
pd for a sencer that was unpayd for at the last
 Rekenyng . . . . . ij*s*. viij*d*.

1557.

Item of Wyll^m Newman and John his sonne for a fyne
 for his house . . . . iij*li*. vj*s*. viij*d*.
Item for settynge up the wethercocke (1) . . xxj*s*.

1558.

Item payd to John Torner for payntyng the alters . ij*s*.
Item payed at the brynging of the pestrawe into the
 churche . . . . . . iij*d*.
Item pd unto John torner for payntyng the rode clothe iij*s*. iiij*d*.

This account contains the following:

Recepts of the Assessemente. (1)

Item of Edmond Browne	vj*d*.	Item of John Whippelle	ij*s*. vj*d*.
,, John Sprygge	iiij*d*.	,, Thoms Barbor	iiij*d*.
,, Richard Bedwell	ij*s*.	,, Thoms Chaundeler	xij*d*.
,, Richard Wood	iiij*d*.	,, George Hawkins	xx*d*.
,, Raffe Starkyn	iij*d*.	,, Grace Glascock	vj*d*.
,, John Ton' (Torner or Turner ?)	iij*d*.	,, Robt Chaundeler	x*d*.
		,, Willm Barnard	x*d*.
,, Phillippe Marchalle	iij*d*.	,, John Picke	ij*d*.

Item of Robt Hothe		vjd.
,, Thoms Jurningham		vjd.
,, John Bayford		ijs.
,, John Skingle		iiijd.
,, Richard Pilston		xd.
,, John Grene		iiijd.
,, John Wyfeeld Barnes		iiijd.
,, Andrew Cawton		ixd.
,, John Albert		vjd.
,, Robt Meade		ijd.
,, John Hilletam' (?)		vjd.
,, Nycholas Mardon		nihill
,, Thomas Mathew bricklayer		iiijd.
,, Thomas Crabbe		xviijd.
,, Richard Master		iijd.
,, John Newman		xxd.
,, George Jacobbe		xijd.
,, John Willey		xxd.
,, Henry parseley		xd.
,, Thoms Snowe		xxd.
,, John Smythe		vjd.
,, Raffe Smythe als Clarke		ijs. vjd.
,, John Chaynye		xviijd.
,, John Myller		xvd.
,, Willm Myller		xxd.
,, Willm Northsocke		vjd.
,, John Jardfeald		xijd.
,, Thoms Colborne		ijs. vjd.
Item of Willm Abbat		xijd.
,, Richard Calyday		iijd.
,, Thoms parsons Gent		iijs. iiijd.
,, John Sherwood Gent		vjd.
,, John Marion the elder		ijs.
,, Edward Gybson		xijd.
,, John Sowth		vjd.
,, John Ramsey		iijd.
,, John Maryon junr.		xijd.
,, John Graye junr.		iiijd.
,, Raynold myller		iijd.
,, John Elyot yoman		xxd.
,, John harlow		xvjd.
,, Richard Grave		xd.
,, Richard marion		xijd.
,, John Bowyer senr.		xvd.
,, George Eliot		xijd.
,, John Davy		vjd.
,, John Soles		iiijd.
,, James fraunces		iiijd.
,, Robt Goodday		xviijd.
,, Edward Davy		vjd.
,, James Bulle (?)		xd.
,, Peter Daw		vjd.
,, Wyllm Pylston		xijd.
,, John Boly' (? Bolyngton)		iiijd.

Summa totalis vjli. vijs. viijd.

1559.

Rec. of Edward Wylley of a obligacon (1)	xls.
Item payd for takyng downe ye hygh aulter stone	xxiijd.
Item payd for makyng and receyvyng your byll to the comyssyoners	xd.
Item pd to mr parson for ij yers Rent for ye churche	viijd.
Item payd to Willm Crab for baryng away ye bryk and yearth of ye awlters	viijd.
Item payd to Cornelyus for makyng the frame to ye table	xvjd.

1560.

rec. of ye paryshs for ye communion sylver	xiijs. xd.
Item rec. of tyes for ye pyllers of the rode loft	xix½d.
Item rec. of Edward Gybsonne for bords of ye roode loft (1)	ijs. vjd.
Item recd. of Mr. Crathorne for a freeston	viijd.
Item payd for ye boke of homelyes	
Item payd for ye boke of paraphraces of erasmy (2)	xxs.
Item payd for takyng downe of ye Roode loft	xxd.

Item payd for yᵉ table of yᵉ ten comandements and yᵉ
  table of the servyce . . . . xvj*d*.

1561.

Item receyvyd of John meller for yᵉ fyne of hys stale xiiij*s.* ij*d. ob.*
of John Spryg for yᵉ chappell (1) . . . xxviij*s.* iiij*d.*
Item rec. of mʳ Elyot for ye parson for halfe ye boke of
  ye parafracys . . . . x*s.*
Item payd to John Tornor for payntyng the cloth at
  yᵉ quere dore . . . . xiij*s.* iiij*d.*
Item payd for bread and alle for ye ryngers at the
  Quenes comyng through yᵉ towne (2) . . iiij*s.*
Item payd for a regester boke . . . xx*d.*

1562.

Receyvyd for a challys weyng xv onces dᵒ at iiij*s.* viij*d.*
  ye once . . . . . iij*li.* xij*s.* iij*d.*
Item receyvyd of Thomas Chaundeler for wood of ye
  pytell called thorley wyk (1) . . . v*s.*
Item payd for the communion cupe weyng x oncs halfe
  a quarter at vj*s.* iiij*d.* ye once . . iij*li.* iiij*s.*

1563.

Item recayvyd of Andrew Can(? w)ton for a mantyll
  pece . . . . . . ij*s.* x*d.*
Item for a boke of ye second omyles (1) . . ij*s.* viij*d.*
Item for a boke of prayers . . . iij*d.*
Item for hangyng of a bell . . . . ij*s.* ij*d.*
for a deaske for ye polpett . . . . vj*s.*

At the foot of this account is the following:

Mᵈ that Thomˢ Chaundeler ys contented and payed
the some of xxxvj*s.* vij*d.* in considertion that the
churchewardens hath lett unto the said Thomˢ
an Indenture of a meade called sextens and a pece
of lond (? in) Hockerellfeld for xxj yeres for the
Rent of xij*s.* a yere.

1564.

Rec. of John Bayford for the fowerth bell for hys
  mother (1) . . . . . viij*d.*
Rec. of Robᵗ Lewis for a pece of the Rode loft
  tymber (2) . . . . . xx*d.*

1565.

Item of John Parsmith senr. for the grett bell		xij*d*.
Item for Isabells knell the iiijth bell .		xij*d*.
Item of John Bayford for a fyne in consideracon of a lease made out unto him of a pece of lond in Apton feild	xiij*s*.	iiij*d*.
Item pd for iij yardds of Buckeram for ye comunion table	iij*s*.	iiij*d*.
Item pd to Willm Balam for paving of the churche and ij porches	ij*s*.	iiij*d*.
Item pd to Balam for making Townesends chym^y hearth and mending the arche by the well		
Item at the visitacion for the questmens byll making and their diners (1)	ij*s*.	viij*d*.
Item pd for ij smalle bokes . . .		iiij*d*.
Item pd to Mathew Barnes for mending of the steple leade	ij*s*.	ij*d*.

1566.

For the buriall of Ralfe Clarke in ye churche	vj*s*.	viij*d*.
pd for ij bokes of prayer agaynst ye turke (1)		iiij*d*.

1567.

Of the honorable lord morley for ye knell of Tho Crabbs child (1).		viij*d*.
paid for the cover to the comunion cupp .	xix*s*.	
pd to the Jyners for makyng the lecterne and deske	xj*s*.	iiij*d*.
pd for mending the mydle churche gate w^h was broke at ye fayer tyme borde and nayles . .		vj*d*.

1569.

pd for a new byble	xxx*s*.	
pd for a communion boke . . .	iiij*s*.	viij*d*.
pd for brennging them home ffrom Cambridge .		iiij*d*.

1570.

Receyved of diverse of the parisshe for the old bookes aulter clothes crosse clothes and suche other stuffe as we sold at the comandement of my lord of london	xliiij*s*.	vj*d*.
rec. for breaking the ground in the churche for burieng m^r Barley	vj*s*.	viij*d*.
pd for a bok of sermons concerning agaynst rebellion (1)		viij*d*.

pd for straw and Thetching ye howse at north gate	vjs.	xd.
pd for the bok of marters and moluments (?) (2)	xljs.	
pd for wryting a byll to my lord of london in testy-fieng howe we sold the old bokes and alter clothes and suche stuffe.		iiijd.

1571.

Rec. of mr Halshed for a C leade	xs.	
Rec. of Thomas Wylsemer for cccc li. of lead lacking viiij li	xxxvjs.	viijd.
pd to ffrancis Mathewe and his man for iiij dayes worke and to henry Mathewe and his man xij dayes worke in whyting the churche	xvijs.	viijd.
pd for xlv fott of plonke xl fott of quarters and liiij fott of bord to skyngle for ye Scole lofte	viijs.	xd.
pd to John hille carpenter and his man for reparing the scole lofte	iijs.	iiijd.
pd to James Stracy and his father for viij dayes worke in glasing ye church and xij fott of glasse	xviijs.	

1572.

Item pd for carrieng ye gret bell clapper to preslons of hadham		iiijd.
Item pd to preslond for mending ye said clapper	vjs.	viijd.
Item pd to Whit for trussing the seconde bell		xijd.
Item pd to Hills for trussing the great bell		xvjd.
pd for a bonche of lathe to George Mathewe		xijd.
pd to Antony Bayford for carrieng ye great bell clapper to preslonds to hadham		iiijd.
pd to preslond for mending ye clapper agayne	iijs.	iiijd.
pd to warren for mending ye gret bell clapper	xijs.	viijd.
pd to Tyes for making the clock fframe and tymber	vs.	
pd for making ye chyme frame and certayne tymber	ijs.	
pd to tyes for making the chyme wheale and for stuffe and borde to ye same	iiijs.	
pd to ye Clock maker for making the clock and chymes	xls.	
pd for putting in of bayle for Robt smith concerning ye stale in ye butchery . xviijd.		
pd for iij attorneies fees . xs.		
pd for ye copie of ye declaration . xvjd.		
pd for putting in of answer . xvjd.	xxvjs.	viijd.
pd to ye counceller at Hertford for his fee vjs. viijd.		
pd to the atterney for his fee ther . iijs. iiijd.		
pd to ye box ther . iiijd.		
Item in charge of ye churche warden for looking to ye sute . ijs. ijd.		

At the foot of this account is the following:

Soe the churche is found detted to m^r Pilston   iiij*li.* xiij*s.* viij*d. ob.*

W^ch some of iiij*li.* xiij*s.* viij*d. ob.* was paid unto the same Willm Pylston by Thomas Chaundeler collector for the market howse out of ye same the xxix^th daye of marche a^o d^i 1573 by the consent of the parisheners ther then present and the said Willm Pilston hath to y^e . . . . of the market howse subscribed his name for ye discharge thereof as it appereth by the same accompt for ye market howse.

1573.

pd to mathew for a quarter for the diall	iiij*d.*
pd to John kyng for wyre for ye diall	iiij*d.*
pd for iij bowstrings for the diall	iij*d.*
pd for making the diall	xiij*s.* iiij*d.*
pd for hokes for the diall	vij*d.*
pd for defacing of the Images in the glasse wyndowes to alsopp (1)	viij*d.*
pd for glasing and glasse to the glasier	viij*s.*
pd to Hylls for dressing and trussing the gret bell	ij*s.* iij*d.*
pd to tyes for bords nayles and making of the deske in the scole	xviij*d.*

1574.

Of the shoppe over the well (1)	
pd for the Gayle	xvij*s.* iiij*d.*

1575.

Of Bayford for the Round howse (1)	iij*s.*
pd for bred drinck and chesse for Ringing of St Hewes daye in reioysing of the quenes prosperous Range (2)	ij*s.* viij*d.*
pd to the gayle of Hertford	xxij*s.* iiij*d.*
pd for a boke for the clarke being a doble salter w^t other service	iij*s.* vj*d.*

1576.

of the howse at north gate end—vj*d.* widowe Evered shold have paid ij*d.* more but she is dedd.	
pd for wryting of the presentm^t (1)	iiij*d.*

1577.
pd for a catechesm . . . . . . j*d*.
pd toward the reparyng of the welle . . . xij*d*.
pd for a booke of articles and for ye byll when the
busshoppe was here . . . . xvj*d*.
pd to the hye constable for ye Gayle . . . xvij*s*. iiij*d*.
pd for ij bookes of ye quenes Injouncions . . xij*d*.

1578.
pd for ij bowstrings . . . . . . j*d*.
pd for Ringing to the Ringers when the Quenes ma^{tie}
came to m^r Capells and from m^r Capells thorrowe
the towne (1) . . . . . . x*s*.
pd for the hower glassis . . . . xvj*d*.
pd for a booke for the plage . . . . iij*d*.
pd for showing of an horse when m^r Jardfeld went to
london to se wether it was our byble that was
lost or no and for his charges . . . ij*s*. vj*d*.
pd to tyes for making of Jacks hamm' (Qy. hammer) (2) ij*d*. ob.
pd for ye making of ij bylls Indented one for collington
haven and j for Thomas Browne . . viij*d*.
pd to Tho Water for digging awaye the dong from the
corner wher ye fence was made . . . j*d*. ob.

1579 (? 1580).
pd to Harvie of Walden for a rope for the bell . ij*s*. iij*d*.
paied for x bookes of prayers at the comaundem^t of
the comissary for and concernyng the Earth-
quake and delivered to diverse of the parisshe . iij*s*. iiij*d*.
paied for one booke concerning the same for the
minister (1) . . . . . . vj*d*.
pd for a booke of Injounction at ye busshoppes vizi-
tacion . . . . xij*d*.
pd for bread drinck and other vittall for the Ringers
at the busshoppes vizitacon . . . ij*s*. viij*d*.
pd for a pint of Salatt oyle for the bells chymes and
clock . . . . viij*d*.
pd to Ties for mending of the Seates when my lord
was here . . . . . . vj*d*.
pd to fountayne for staynyng of the covering (?) of y^e
comunion table . . . . . viij*d*.
pd for Silke lace for stringes for the byble and comunion
book . . . . ix*d*. ob.
pd for mending the comunion booke and setting in
the leafes agayne . . . . . vj*d*

pd for bossing of the byble and stringing (?) of the
    same byble and comunion booke . . xij*d*.
pd to the Roper of Stansted for a rope for the great
    bell and for a stropp for the same . iiij*s*.
pd for mending of m^r parsons stole and bracketts . iiij*d*.
pd for a lock for the Lofte dore over the Barley
    market . . . . . . x*d*.
pd for mending of Seates in the same Loft (2) . iiij*d*.
pd for a li of caundell upon the crownacion daye . iij*d*.
pd to gennyngs for givinng his attendaunce ye same
    daye . . . . . vj*d*.
pd to the Ringers the same daye being St Hewes
    daye xj*s*. wherof we gathered vj*s*. iij*d*. and so
    we laied out more then we gathered . . iiij*s*. ix*d*.
pd for wryting the names for the seates and a remem-
    beraunce to laye in ye chest . . . ij*s*.
pd and layed out at Sabridworth for making of our
    byll and other charges when we enquired for
    papystes . . . . . . x*d*.
pd and laied out another tyme at Sabridgworth for
    Mr. Cory and booth of us being charged to goe
    thether before the comyssieners to enquire for
    suche as were gone out of the Reame as well for
    our charges as making of our byll . . iij*s*. iij*d*.
pd to Skyngell the Joyner for enlargm^t of the deske . v*s*.
pd to the Clock maker for and in ernest at his first
    comyng . . . . . vj*d*.
pd to Barnard for makyng a paier of bylls Indented
    betweene the Clockmaker and us . . xij*d*.

1581.

pd to tyes for a torned pyller to sett ye hower glass
    upon (1) . . . . . . viij*d*.
pd for mending of mother allens stayers . . viij*d*.
pd for making the booke to gather the churche rentes
    and the churche clarkes wages by (2) . . viij*d*.
pd for Steppes for the Styles next the Lane . . vj*d*.
pd to Taylor for mending of chenyes stole . . iiij*d*.

1582.

The following is a verbatim transcript of the Receipts
    of this year's account.

Receytes.
Item of Momford late Comfret . . xxiij*d*.

CHURCHWARDENS' ACCOUNTS.

Item for parcell of Bores House late Hylls and now Bridges .	
Of John Smyth for the other parte of the same howse	xij*d*.
Of Braugwyn .	j*d*.
Of Andrewe Cawton .	iiij*d*.
Of him for Jaxsons howse	j*d*.
Of Momford late Crowe	iiij*d*.
Of George Eliott late Best	j*d*.
Of Roger Jenning	iij*d*.
Of John Coller	iiij*d*.
Of Richard Burges .	ix*d*.
Of Cawbeck late Bushes	j*d*.
Of M^{ris} Crawthorne .	xiiij*d*.
Of George Hawkyn for a peece of lond late Hoothes .	ob.
Of Edward Gybson for spittle lond	ij*d*.
Of the howse where shepp' (Qy. Shepherd) dwell in hockerell	ob.
Of John Marryon	x*d*.
Of John Miller	ij*d*.
Of Willm Skyngell	j*d*.
Of George Abbott	j*d*.
Of Henry Parsely	viij*d*.
Of Thomas Chaundeler late Smithes	iij*d*.
Of George Jacobbe .	xv*d*.
Of John Parsmith alias Cheny	vj*d*.
Of John Gostelyn Saddeler .	iij*d*.
Of the howse where noone dwelleth .	vj*d*.
Of Wood late Wall .	xxiij*d*.
Of Edward Meade	j*d*.
Of him for that late Whippells	iij*d*.
Of Alsoppe for parcell of naylors howse	ij*d*.
Of Bartillmew Bedwell for the other parcell	vj*d*.
Of John Denyson	ix*d*.
Of Palmer .	xxiij*d*.
Of Willm Snowe late fraunces .	vj*d*.
Of Mr Jernegan late Tompsons	xiiij*d*.
Of Mathewe Ramsey .	iij*d*.
Of Thomas Chaundeler	iiij*d*.
Of Edward Gybson .	ij*s*.
Of Raynold Sumpner	x*d*.
Of Thomas Bowyere for the Chauntery	ij*s*. vj*d*.
Of Byllam for Savell .	
Of Henry Grene	ij*d*.
Of Thomas Hodgekyn late meade	iij*d*.

Of George Santon		vj*d*.
Of Thomas Crabbe		iiij*d*.
Of Browne late noke		vj*d*.
Of Gower late Pecocke		j*d*.
Of Rob*t* Dane	iij*s*.	iiij*d*.
Of Thomas Carrowe		iij*d*.
Of Rob*t* Shrimpe		vj*d*.
Of John Hoothe		vij*d*.

Rentes of the ferme landes and Tenements.

Item of Henry Eve		iiij*d*.
Of Edward Wylley		vj*d*.
Of Bayford for the round howse	iij*s*.	
Of him for ye Ten*te* at sowth streat ende and a peece of lond	vij*s*.	vj*d*.
Of George Hawkyn		viij*d*.
Of John Culverhowse late Callidaye	ij*s*.	
Of John Miller for the stall	ij*s*.	
Of Thomas Carrowe		viij*d*.
Of John Jardfeld for the Tanne howse		
Of Oswald Carton		xx*d*.
Of John Bowyere sen*r*		xvj*d*.
Of Thomas Wilsemer	iij*s*.	
Of the howse at north gate	} Geven back for his	
Of arrerages	} diligence (? at) the vizitacon	
Of Browne late noke	ij*s*.	
Of Thomas Chaundeler		iiij*d*.
Of Mendams wiffe	ij*s*.	
Of Will*m* Payne		
Of Mother Allen	v*s*.	
Of M*ris* Dane	ij*s*.	
Of Rob*t* Smithe for the stalle	iij*s*.	iiij*d*.
Of Thomas Chaundeler	xij*s*.	
Of John Gates	ij*s*.	
Of Percye	v*s*.	
Of Widow Hales (?)	ij*s*.	

Receytes of ye Parishe.

Item receyved for comunion silver	xviij*s*.	iij*d*.
Receyved for the churche clarkes wages	iij*li*. vij*s*.	xj*d*.

Layed out [*extracts only*].

pd to Will*m* Barnard for making of O Lord have mercy upon us to set upon the doores (1)	vj*d*.
pd to Rob*t* Plomer for going to m*r* Leventhorpes twyse for carryeng of Billes	iiij*d*.

pd to Taylor for making of a stoole to put in the
    Vicars deske . . . . . . iij*d*.
Layed out for delivereng of a byll to Doctor Byngham   ij*s*.
Layed out for wyne to George Hawkyn . . xvj*s*. iiij*d*.

1583.

Receyved for a little Bell w^h layd in the vestry waying
    xlj li. sold for v*d*. ye pounde . . . xvij*s*. j*d*.
pd for nayles to nayle up the carpet . . .   j*d*.
pd and layed out for expences when we ware before y^e
    Chanceler after y^e . . . . (? visitation) . iij*s*.
pd for charges upon the crownacion daye to the
    Ringers . . . . viij*s*. viij*d*.
pd for candelles for them to ryng by . . .   iiij*d*.
pd for a rope for the tenor . . . . iiij*s*.
pd for a pessock for m^r Bysshoppe . . .   iij*d*.
pd for making of two formes one before m^r parsons
    sete and m^r Jenegans . . . . xvj*d*.
pd for mending the Deske ye orgaynes and seates . xiij*d*.
pd for charges at Stortford at the comissaries court . viij*d*.
pd for the exchannge of the bell for Jack (1) . . vj*s*.

1585.

pd to Richard Taylor for mending the seates . . vj*d*.
pd to Michell for writing of the prayer set out by my
    lord . . . . xij*d*.
pd afterward for the same prayer in prynt . . iiij*d*.
pd when we brought in to the court the byble and
    comunion booke to shewe before the comysary . viij*d*.
pd to Barnes for the Injunction booke . . iiij*d*.
pd to Crabbe the high constable for ye gayle . . xiij*s*.
pd for a locke and chene for the booke of marters . xij*d*.

1586.

P^d to John Jeffery the Clock maker . . . xiij*s*.
pd to Reade for fire coles and Rome for the said
    Jeffery . . . . xij*d*.
pd for a plat and staple for the booke of marters to
    Reade . . . . ij*d*.
pd for the Latche to the chauncell dore . . ij*d*.
pd to Reade for making a key to the Cofer or Deske
    wher the regester book lieth (1) . . . vj*d*.
Item pd for mending the Byble and comunion booke
    being torne and rent and for clasping of them and
    for mending the pulpit clothe and poynts . xij*d*.

pd in repairing of the churche when my lord Busshop came in vizitacon	ix*d*.
pd for blacking the comunion clothe	vj*d*.
pd for the book of articles and the injoncions at ye vizitacion (2)	xij*d*.
pd for making of our byll to my lords man	viij*d*.
pd at the delyvering in of our byll	iiij*d*.
pd for the new booke of homylies and prayer	vj*d*.
pd to Richard Taylor for 39 foote of quarters for mending the Clock bell howse	

1587.

Rec. of George Bird for burieng of mr newman in the churche	vj*s*. viij*d*.
pd to Bretten for makyng the grett bell clapper and the fowerth bell clapper	xxxj*s*. viij*d*.
pd for red lether for the pulpet Chusshion	ix*d*.
pd for fethers to stopp the same	xxiij*d*.
pd for making thereof	vj*d*.
pd to rede for mending the lock and key to the churche chest in ye chaunsell	iiij*d*.
pd to Taylor for mending of the forme before mr Jurnegans stoole	iiij*d*.
pd for putting in of our byll at donmowe	viij*d*.
pd for a chene for the booke of marters and fastening ye same	viij*d*.
pd for the table that the wayght be proscribed by proclamacion (1)	ij*d*.

At the foot of this account is written:

Rec. of defaultes for absence.

Of Timothie Archer	iij*s*.	Of Richard Colt	xij*d*.
Of John King	xij*d*.	Of Edward Wood	xij*d*.
Of mr howe	xij*d*.	Of Edward Towneend	xij*d*.
Of Andrewe Cawlton	xij*d*.	Of Richard Shepperd	xij*d*.
	Of John molton	xij*d*.	

wherof delyvered to mr parsons to the use of the poore	ix*s*.
paied unto old shepperde	vj*d*.
pd to widowe moulton	viij*d*.
pd to . . . . (Qy. Hayes) for the pore	x*d*.

1588.

pd for ringing upon St James daye in rejoysing of ye victory (1)	xv*s*.

pd for ringing upon the crownacion daye in rejoysing of the Queenes prosperous Raigne in meate and drinck . . . . xj*s.* viij*d.*

pd for Ringing the tewsedaye after and for j li. of candell in rejoysing of our delyveraunce from the spaynnyardes (1). . . . . viij*s.* x*d.*

1589.

Of Philologus Bushe for parcelle of the howse some-tyme Bores . . . . . vj*d.*

Item spent in my jorneye to Cambrydge . . xxij*d.*

Item pd for fetchinge and carryenge from Belchanger a surples for a paterne to make one by for m^r Sandye unto Sckyngle . . . . iiij*d.*

Item pd for a borde to sette on an artycle . . ij*d.*

Item pd for one other borde to sette on an Injunction ij*d.*

Item pd for rynginge at the visitation and on the Coronation daye . . . . . xvj*s.* iiij*d.*

Item pd unto John Jynninges for halfe a hyde of whyt leather and halfe a calves skyn . . iiij*s.* x*d.*

At the foot of this account:

m^d rec. for a .... of Thom^s Grigges . . xij*d.*

The same gyven to Roger and morleye in ye tyme of ye trouble (1).

1590.

pd to tayler for halfe ynche bord and for mending the frame to the Queene armes . . . xiiij*d.*

pd to Braugwyn for the Queenes armes . . vij*s.* vj*d.*

pd to Rede for mending the jack to the chymes . iij*d. ob.*

pd for a paper (?) article of prayer for ye good successe of the king of ffraunce (1) . . . iiij*d.*

pd to Gace the highe constable for the gayle . . xiiij*s.*

1591.

pd for iiij li. of leade to dog the stones together of ye steple wyndowe . . . . . vj*d.*

pd for a newe Ladder to the clocke howse . . xij*d.*

pd to Taylor for mending of the diall in the churche. iiij*d.*

pd for newe paynting of the same . . . vj*d.*

pd for mending the saunce bell wheele being broken. viij*d.*

pd for mending of the formes wher the boyes sit . ij*d.*

1592.

pd for an hower glasse to Chaundeler . . iiij*d.*

pd for the Gret prynted paper for Tything . . ij*s.*

pd to fountayne for coloring the buckerom to the
    comunion table . . . . . . viij*d*.
pd for Glasing the Schole lofte . . . vj*s*. v*d*. *ob*.
pd for a Jack for the chymes . . . . iij*d*.

1595.

Item for breaking the ground in the Churche for y^e
    buryeng of m^r Edmund Parsons. . . vj*s*. viij*d*.
pd for a sermon booke to be reed in the tyme of
    dearthe . . . . viij*d*.

1596.

pd to Ward for the orders concerning the fast and
    releeve of the poore . . . . viij*d*.

1598.

pd for a Salter for the Clark . . . . iij*s*. viij*d*.
pd to Bennett for fetching of flaggs to strewe the
    churche agaynst the visitacon . . . x*d*.
pd for the regester booke in parchment wth my
    charges caring for it . . . . xviij*s*.
pd for wryting and Regestering in the same booke all
    the christenings marriages and buryalls (1) . xj*s*.

1600.

Item for the churche clarkes wages and gayle mony iij*li*. xiij*s*. v*d*.
Item sold the mettall of the little Broken Bell w^{ch}
    Garyes man broke . . . . iij*s*.
Item Receyved of Garies man towards the same Bell . ij*s*. vj*d*.
pd for a Roope for the Saunsebell . . . ij*s*. iiij*d*.
pd for a little bell wch is also broken . . . ij*s*. vj*d*.
pd to the highe constable for halfe a yere for the
    gayole and for maymed souldiers . . xij*s*.

1601.

Of Andrewe Calton for his Ten^{te} wherin he dwelleth iiij*d*.
Of him for his Ten^{te} nowe his Barke howse on the
    other side ye strett . . . . j*d*.
Of Abell for the Ten^{te} called the Crowne in hockerell viij*d*.
Of the howse agaynst the malt . . . wher whight
    dwelleth now (1) . . . . . j*d*.
Item Receyved for the mettall of a little bell that was
    broken . . . . viij*d*.
Item pd to Phillipe of Haseley for making the bell
    wheele and mending the certayne wheele . x*s*. viij*d*.

CHURCHWARDENS' ACCOUNTS.

pd to Brooke at the request of the Townemen wth
    Teasor's boye (2) . . . . xs.
pd for strawe . . . . . . vs.
pd for yelmyng . . . . . . xd.
pd to the thatcher and fixer . . . . iiijs. ijd.
pd for casting and layeng of yearth to the churche
    Rayle agaynst the lane to kepe out the hodgs
    (? hoggs) . . . . . iijd.
pd to docter standhope at his last being here (3) . xvjd.
pd for ij formes stonding in the myddell alye . iiijs. xd.

1602.

Item Receyved of a butcher for one daye stondyng in
    the butchers stall . . . . iijd.
Item pd to Doctor Stanhoops deputie to receyve bylls xvjd.
pd to whalle for Rynging sondayes and hollidaies . iijs. iiijd.
pd for a bill in manner of a proclamacon to be pub-
    lisshed in the churche for waights (1) . iiijd.
pd for mending of the houses in the churche yard . xviijd.
pd for 3 fyve article bylls wryting and a certificate for
    the reparacions of the churche . . . xiiijd.
pd for sommonyng of the quest men to take ther othe viijd.

1603.

pd to reade for a payer of hangs to a pewe dore . iiijd.
pd to the Ryngers of St James' daye (1) . . ijs. viijd.
pd for an hower glasse and for the Iron to set it in . ijs. ijd.
pd for copieng out the busshoppes Letter for the col-
    lection for the citie Geneva (2) . . . viijd.
pd for canvas to paynt the kyngs armes upon agaynst
    the assises (3) . . . . . xvd.
pd to Ayley for paynting the armes and mending the
    clothe . . . . . . xs.
pd to Whall for his worke at the assises (3) . . xijd.
pd and layed out for meat and drink for the Ryngers
    the 24 daye of marche as we accompte for the
    crownacon daye (1) . . . . xxvjs. xd.

1607.

pd to Cooke the smyth for making the hammer of the
    Clocke to strike upon the Gret Bell . . iijs.
pd to Tayler for mending the Clock and chymes and
    making the clocke to strick upon the great bell . xiijs.
pd to John Kensey for deliveryng a transcript into
    m^r blackwells office . . . . xijd.
pd for setting up the wether cock . . . xxxiijs. iiijd.

1608.

Of Henry Bowyere for the peece on Chalkecrofte hill   vj*s.* viij*d.*

1609.

Pd to Wm Tayler for altering the clocke to the litle
bell   .   .   .   .   .   .   v*s.*

1611.

pd for the oathes of the churchwardens and sydemen   ij*s.*
pd to the highe Constable for the Gayle and maymed
soldiers [see note]   .   .   .   .   vj*d.*

1612.

Of lands belonging to the Chantry ij*s.* vj*d.* viz. for a
peece in moche halfacres called Shortland otherwise the chauntry land, sometime Walter Blancks
iiij*d.* for an acre of land in Lithallcrofte behind
a garden sometime of John Clerks xviij*d.* and
for an acre at Goodwyn style some time William
Blanks viij*d.*   .   .   .   .   .
Item pd by John Miller to Mr Haynes for procuring
a certificate under seale for the death of M^{rs}
Veysie beyond Cambridge   .   .   .   v*s.* iiij*d.*
pd for a new Bible and the cariage of it from
London (1)   .   .   .   .   . xlviij*s.* viij*d.*

At the foot of this acct.

We elect and apoint that Robt Bowyere shall con-
tinewe another yere according to ye auncient
custome and we also apoint and chuse againe the
said Robt Colt as new churchwarden for that he
came in in the steed of John Miller who died
lately.

1614.

pd for charges of the Ringers the v of August and
coronation day (1)   .   .   .   . xij*s.*
pd to Mary Jackson and another for to s'che (? stretch)
Henry Pryce when he was dead .   .   . iiij*d.*
pd to Bowyere for a plank to lay over the skull
hole (2) .   .   .   .   .   . viij*d.*
pd to the Highe Constable for the Gaole Hospitall
and maymed souldiers .   .   .   . xij*s.*

1616.

Lithallcrofte is the crofte Mr Hawkyn holdeth behind
 sowth streate where his folke useth to hang
 clothes to dry . . . .
Gathered by the fortie shillings Rate .   xiij*li*. xviij*s*. viij*d*.
pd for 2 flagons for the comunion . . xiiij*s*. iiij*d*.
pd to Mowtens man for worke about the lowe seats
 for the comunicants in the Chancell . . xxj*d*.

1617.

Received for comunion silver and church clarks
 wages . . . . . v*li*. ij*d*.
Gathered by the fortie shillings Rate. . vj*li*. vij*s*. x*d*.
Rec^d of George Cheany for the Rate for the Church
 Rayles for the last yere . . . . iiij*s*. viij*d*.
Gathered at the comunions to the use of the poore iij*li*. ij*s*. xj*d*.
pd for mending the Butchers stall where old Sweeting
 doth sell flesh on Market dayes . . . xvij*d*.
(This year occur items of relief to poor people when
 sick—among them the following :)
given to a gretian by the consent of Mr Bendish . ij*s*.
given to a muscovian likewise . . . ij*s*.
given to another gretian by the consent of Mr
 Bendish . . . . . . xij*d*.

1619.

Of William Smith for the ten^{te} in Highe streate late
 skingles called the flower de luie . . j*d*.
Of Francis Abell Junr for the white horse in north
 streat wher he dwelth . . . . vj*d*.
Ther was collected in o^r Church wthin theis ij yeres
 past upon breifes and for fires by request xx*li*. xj*s*. ij*d*.
and the last yere for mathew Barnes when his leg was
 broken (1) . . . . j*li*. 12*s*. 6*d*.
pd for Junyper to burne in the church this yeare . ij*s*.
pd for a peece of timber to mend the little house on
 the Bartlement (2) . . . . xviij*d*.
pd for a key for the Martir booke . . . iij*d*.

1620.

pd for mending the sancebellhowse and hanging up
 the bell . . . . . . ij*s*. vj*d*.
pd for opening the spowts when they were frozen and
 for taking downe the kings armes . . vj*d*.

1622.

Of John Bull for the stalls on the Barley hill for halfe a yere . . . . ijs. vjd.
pd to Ringers on the v of November . . iijs.
Pd for wrighting a bill of presentments (1) . . vjd.
pd for the directions for ministers and for mending of o, bill . . . . ijs. xd.

1623.

pd for the prohibited degrees to hange in the Church (1) . . . . . ixd.
pd for Ringing at the Princes coming home (2) . iijs. ijd.
pd for the churchwardens dinner at ij corts j at Stansted and th'other at Sabridgworth . . ijs

1624.

Of Elizabeth Russell for her loft in the church howses for a yere at midsomer 1624 . . . viijs.
Gathered by the Towne rate for the making of the fframe for the Bells . . . xxixli. js. vjd.
Payd to Thomas Allis for making the frame for the bells and some other worke . . xiijli. xvjs. viijd.
pd for carting Timber out of Goosemeade to the Church . . . . . . viijs.
pd for making of the Diall on the south side of the church . . . . . . vjs. viijd.

1625.

Of Edward Chandler for Lowemeade sometime Mr Tompsons . . . . . iiijd.
Of Thomas Barnard the elder for his peece in Shepho alias windhillfeild next Vicars acre . . vjd.
Of Thomas Barnard Junr for a crofte called grovecroft now parte of Redcrofte . . . iiijd.
Of Tho. Milton for a peece in hockerhillfeild neere Tyegreene being now inclosed called Hallecrofte late Mr Jernegans sometime Joan Ingrams . iiijd.
Of Sir Edward Boteler knight for the Tanhowses for a yere . . . . xxs.
Layd out at the court at Sabridgworth . . iijs. ijd.
pd for pitch and ffrancuncence to burn in the church xiijd.
Given to the Ringers on the xxvijth of March last (1) vs.
pd for ij books for the generall ffast . . ijs.
pd for ij books of thanksgiving after the sickness (2) vjd.

1627.

pd to Warmans wife for Juniper and things to perfume the church . . . . .
pd for stakes to stake out the poores land . . xij*d.*
pd for going to Hertford about sending away of Sara Chandler . . . . ij*s.*

1629.

Of Mr Slater for his ten^te in Sowthstreat late M^ris Staverd of old John Sadds . . . iiij*d.*
pd for making a transcript of the Cristnings mariages and burialls . . . . . ij*s.*
pd for carieng it to London and putting of it into the Office (1) . . . . . xij*d.*
pd to Gryces wife for yelming strawe for her house . xviij*d.*
pd for a prayer booke for the Queene . . ij*d.*
pd for Ringing the day that the Kings Matie dyned at the George . . . . . iij*s.*

1630.

Of a peece of land in Comon downe in the holding of John Torrington sometime Mr Billams of old John Bushes now Mr Henry Glascocks (1) . . iij*d.*
Of . . . Wall for the stalls in the Barley hill nothing because ther were no fayers last yere.
Received of John Miller out of the Market House Rents for the purchase of the house in hockerell iiij*li.*
Rec. more of him out of the said Rents towards the paving of the seats and other works . iiij*li.*
Layd out to John Dayne for the purchase of hockerell house (2) . . . . iiij*li.*
pd to old Warman for mending the third Bell when it fell downe . . . . . iij*s.* iiij*d.*
pd to the Courtiers for o^r warning about the view of the ornaments and the church . . . xvj*d.*
pd for a note of the defects and for o^r order for time to provide . . . . . iiij*d*
pd for Ringing when the Kings Matie came to the George . . . . . iiij*s.*

1631.

pd for bread and beere for the Ringers at the Bishops vizitacon . . . . . iij*s.*

pd to Warman for sweeping downe the Copwebbs and making cleane the church against the Bishops coming (1)		ij*s*.	vj*d*.
pd to Aylie for paynting the Church	iij*li*.	x*s*.	viij*d*.
pd to John Tyler for enlarging the Pulpitt		xv*s*.	
pd to Haynes for taking down the organ case and setting up a shelfe			viij*d*.
pd to Warmans wife for making cleane the vestry and the lofte over it			iiij*d*.
pd for a certificate to put into the court and for a prayer for the Queenes ma^{tie}			xvj*d*.
pd to Warman to increase his wages and for Ringing the bell at ix of the clocke			x*s*.
pd for a q^t (? quarter) to mend the great Bell Wheele to Orde and for glewing the names of the seats and for paper			xvj*d*.
Gathered this yere at comunions to Charitable uses iiij*li*.		xiiij*s*.	vj*d*.

1632.

pd for paynting of the Jyces in the church porch	x*d*.

1633.

Item pd to old haynes for a cover for the ffonte and for ye formes and other work	xij*s*.	vj*d*.
Item pd to Aylie for paynting of the deske	iij*s*.	
pd for half a hyde and dressing it at the Curryers for the bucketts	v*s*.	
pd to old Warman for mending the deske wher the bookes lye and for the boyes seates	ij*s*.	iiij*d*.
pd to old Haynes for making M^{ris} Butlers Pewe	xiij*s*.	
pd to John Warman for a key to M^{ris} Leighes Pewe (1)		iiij*d*.
pd for a homylie booke and a new Service booke and for the cariage of them	xv*s*.	vj*d*.
pd to Hayward the aparitor for the Kings booke (2)		vj*d*.

1634.

Of James Archer for Momfords land at Maplecross sometime Alberts (1)		xx*d*.
pd for mending the Ministers Gowne		x*d*.
pd at twice to old Haynes for making Seats about the Comissaries Table and lower end there	x*s*.	
pd for not ringing the 9 of September when the Chancellor came (2)	v*s*.	
pd for ringing on the morrow at his going away (2)	ij*s*.	ij*d*.

At the foot of this account:

Item, it is agreed that the churchwardens shall not

hereafter be allowed for their charges at monethly meetings before the Justice.

1635.

pd for ringing when the Palsgrave came to Towne (1)		xijd.
pd for ringing at the King's coming and at his Maties retourne	ixs.	
pd to James Hastler for playstering up of the church windows		vjd.
pd to John Eve for 36 foote of new glasse in the sowth windowe to give more light to the minister at vd. the foote (2)	xijs.	vjd.

1636.

Layd out for mending the church houses after the great winde for lyme bricke tyles and worke	xxiijs.	iiijd.
pd for two bookes for the ffast	ijs.	iiijd.
pd for fetching Cusheons at the Lady Dennyes and carieng them home againe at the visitacon		iijd.

There was gathered at the ffasts 7li. 5s. 7d. whereof there was layd out for the poore in bread and given them 4li. 15s. and 50s. was agreed by the Townsmen that Ezechiell Aylie should have it for a yere giving his bond for repaying it w^h he hath done and the other 7d. that remayned was given to the widow Gurnard.

Layd out of the money gathered at the comunions as oppeereth by a bill of particulars 3li. 12s. 9d. to diverse poore people visited wth the Poxe and others sicke and lame.

1637.

Of John Glascocks house in hockerell sometime Archers		
pd to the Ringers when the Chancellor was here	3s.	0d.
pd for putting in the bill of Terrary for the Glebe lands	2s.	6d.
pd for ringing at the Kings coming and at his retourne	8s.	8d.
pd for putting in of the bill of presentment to the Chancellor	2s.	10d.

1639.

Item rec. for a peece of bras 3s. 6d. and for a litle Bell waying 5 pound 1s. 8d. and for farthings a chayne and leade 9d.	5s.	11d.
pd for laying the strawe in the stooles	1s.	0d.

1640.

Item given to an Irish man	1s.	
pd for a booke against the ffaste		xijd.
pd for 2 fast books the 8 of December (1)		
pd to the church clarks for their wages the whole yeare ended 25 march 1641		iij*li*.

1641.

Item for Wm Barnards charges and his horse to Hoddesdon to deliver up the names of them that subscribed to the protestation the 18 of ffebruary last	3s.	0d.
pd for Rafe Bull and his horse charges to Hoddesdon when he received the protestation	3s.	0d.
pd for writing the names of those that did subscribe and for the protestacon and for paper (1)	2s.	3d.
pd to John Eve for taking downe the glasse in the church windowes by comand and setting up new (A)	18s.	0d.
pd for my charges to Ware and for my horse at the monethly meeting 16 of November		

1642.

pd for the acte to gather the mony for Ireland		4d.
pd to old Eve for a horse to Hoddesdon about Ireland busynesse (1)	1s.	6d.
pd to Eve for making up the glasse windowes wch was broken downe by comand (A)	8s.	9d.
pd to the ringers on the powder treason day 5 of November	2s.	6d.

1643.

Of Mr Anthony Denny his howse in Water lane sometime Carrowes		iiijd.
Of John Eve for 126 li. of leade (A)	11s.	6d.
Of James Dorrington for 65 li. of Iron (A)	8s.	1d.
Of John Jones for 22 li. of Brasse (A)	7s.	4d.
pd for o' charges when we went to take the Covenaunt	6s.	0d.
pd for taking downe the Crosse and for setting the weathercocke upright and for Ironworke (A) 3*li*.	3s.	4d.
pd to the Earle of Manchester his officer (1)	1s.	6d.

1644.

Received for the hood	7s.	0d.
pd for setling a minister here after Mr. Butlers decease and for two Petitions and the Sequestration and a copie of an order and 4 journeys to London 5*li*.	2s.	9d.

pd to Mr Archer for preaching here 3 Saboaths when the place was voyd	1*li*. 10*s*.	0*d*.
pd for fetching a lode of Bricke and pavem{ts} from Hadham Kell	4*s*.	6*d*.

1647.

for registring the Christinings mariags and burialls in the parchment byoke for ten yeres ended 9 yeres agoe (1)	1*li*. 00*s*.	0*d*.
pd to John Eve for glazing the wyndowes wch were taken downe and for banding them (A)	1*li*. 03*s*.	0*d*.
pd more to Sam Knight for a great rayle and bords by the stayres going into the churchyard, etc.		

1648.

Rec. of the Iron taken out of the Church windowes 106 li. at 1½*d* the li. (A) (1)	14*s*.	11*d*.
for taking out of the old glasse and banding of it and setting it up againe	12*s*.	0*d*.
pd to Tho Warman for clensing the church and for sweeting it and washing the seats after the soldiers	13*s*.	4*d*.
pd to him for mending the chymes and wyres that the soldiers broke (2)	3*s*.	0*d*.
pd to George Read for taking downe the old Pewe and enlarging the old deske	1*s*.	0*d*.

1649.

pd to Thos Barnard for writing into the Register booke the names of those that have been married Christned and buried in this Towne w{th}in 11 or 12 yeares last past (1)	12*s*.	0*d*.
pd for paynting of the Sundiall	6*s*.	

1650.

pd to John Pegrome for blurring of the Kings arms in the church and making up of M{ris} Harts childs grave	3*s*.	8*d*.

1652.

Given the 12th of may given to Eliazor Jaxon and other poore poore people who had lost and consumed to the value of 700*li*. per an{m}	2*s*.	6*d*.
given to Goldsmith towards the Millers losse of Newport	2*s*.	0*d*.
given to Mary Williamson who had a certificate for collection	1*s*.	0*d*.

1654.

given to John Gray on the 18 of Aprill 1654	2s.	0d.
„ to two Irishwomen by a briefe		6d.
„ to a poore woman on the 10th of may		3d.
„ to Willm Samford and one Bayer a seaman by a briefe	2s.	6d.
„ to ffrancis Cortney by breeife	1s.	0d.
„ to a Dutch merchant	1s.	0d.
„ to two men that came out of Ireland by breeife	1s.	6d.
„ to a woman		6d.
„ to a souldier that came out of Scotland by breeife	1s.	0d.
„ to a woman that came out of Ireland by breeife	1s.	2d.
„ to two Irishwomen by breeife (1)		8d.

1655.

payd to William Bennet for paynting and setting of the Deyall . . . . . . 12s. 0d.

1656.

given to one with a letter of request	1s.	0d.
given to a minister on the ffirst day of July w^{ch} (? came) out of Chestsheire	1s.	8d.
given to a man that came from the barth on the 2 day of March	1s.	0d.
pd for 2 paires of Duftayles Joysts for the bellofte windows	1s.	0d.
pd to the clarke at Ware for the decree on the 26 of December	6s.	0d.
and for the paper wch was sett on the church dore	1s.	0d.
payd to m^r payne by the consent of the parishioners 3*li*.	0s.	0d.
payd to Humfrey Dixon for the booke on the 30th of December	10s.	0d.
payd for 20 yards of Jacklyn		10d.

1658.

Sept 4 Received of M^{ris} Hignall for breaking up the ground in the Church to bury one of her borders		6s.	8d.
payd for the pulpitt 5*li*.	0s.	0d.	
payd for the cushin to it 1*li*.	18s.	6d.	
7 payd to Samuell Knight for Board posts and other timber and worke in setting up of the Pulpitt and mending the seates 2*li*.	3s.	7d.	

CHURCHWARDENS' ACCOUNTS.

payd to Goodman Cramphorne for bringing downe the Pulpitt	8s.	0d.
payd to Samuell Knight for timber and worke about the Barley hiil	2s.	6d.

1661.

Given to the Ringers at the Kings crownation	5s.	0d.

NOTE.—The accounts from 1661 to 1679 are missing.

1680.—The receipts for this year are transcribed verbatim.

Receipts of the Church Rents due the 25th March 1681.

	£	s.	d.
Imprimis Received of Thomas Browne for Bulls	00	00	01
Of Thomas Clayton for the Red Lyon	00	02	00
of Jon Pynn for White's Lands			4
of Mathew Ramsey for his House			3
of Mr Cooke for the Crowne in Hockerell			8
of John Osborne for Anne Browne and Ramseys house in North street			6
of Richard ffeast for his house			1
of Mrs. Godfrey			2
of Mr. Aylmers house			1
of Mrs. Ashbyes house			8
of Thos Balaams house			6
of Tho Barnard for Kithall Croft			6
of Mr. Lay for Land in Apton Feild late Palmers			5
of Mrs. Read for Specialls house 1d.			
of Wid Binghams house 3d.			
of Tho Wheatly for Maplecroft		1	8
of Wid Laycock for Eves tenement			1
of Symon Curtis for Mr. Godfreys lands in Hockerell feild			2
of Jon Humfreys for the Catterne wheele in Basbo Lane			9
of Eliz. Phillips for the White Lyon in North Street			1
of Edwd Thurgood for the White Horse in North Street			6
of Thos Markwell for the halfe Moone in North Street			3
of Edwd Darnells house		1	3
of Mrs. Banson for Langhams Lands			3
of ffrancis Wynns house in Water Lane			6
of John Barrons house in Water Lane			3
of Mr. Maplesdens house in Water Lane			1

CHURCHWARDENS' ACCOUNTS.

	£	s.	d.
of Roger Banks for his house in South Street			9
of Henry Wallis for the Castle in the ffish markett (1)			6
of Wm Lucks house in the ffishmarkett			1
of Mrs. Aynsworths house (2)			6
of Mr. Manister for his house			8
of Mr. Dixon for his house		1	2
of Joⁿ Chalk for the Boares head in ye high street			2
of George Adams house in Windhill			2
of Mrs. Leigh for her house			6
of Tho Barnard for his house 1d. ffor Groves Croft 4d. and Spittle Acre 2d.			
of Mr. Sedgewicks house late Dr. Sparks 10d.			
of Joⁿ Payne for his house			1
of Mr. Hastler for his house			4
of John Mardens house Blew Anchor in South Street			4
of Ed Ashbys house at ye ffeathers in ye Leather markett 1d. (3)			
of Mr. Reynolds for ffremans house 4d. for Jer Gardners Land 6d. Halls Croft 4d.			
of Matt^h Bush for his house		1	0
of Wm Wright for his house			3
of Jer Gardner for knights			10
of Mr. Holgate for ffockinghams (4)			3
of Henry Chambers for his house			6
of Peter Sandford for Barnes Lands in Windle feilds			6
of Richard Bawcock for Palmers house in South Street			6
of George Chandler for his house and yard in South street			4
of Edwd Ellis house			3

Total gathered this year £1 5s. 6d.

Lease Rents.

	£	s.	d.
Received of Mr. Denny for Bark barne in Water Lane	2	0	0
of John Dugoods house (5)	3	0	0
of Wm Hastlers house	4	0	0
of Wm Gladwyn for a peece of land near Paradise (6) and for two houses and peece of land in South street late Mr. Woolleys	4	5	0
of Henry Wallis for a stall next the George	1	6	8
and for an house in South Street	1	5	0
of Tho Clayton for Sextons mead and Land in Hockerell feilds (7)	2	2	6
of Wid Waters house		10	0
of Tho Jones for Chalk Croft (8)	1	10	0

	£	s.	d.
of Jo^n Knight and Edwd Ramshaw for Butchers stall		7	0
of Nath Jones for the Barly Hill		17	0
of Willm Chandlers house	1	10	0
of Robert Bonns house, stall, and shopp	2	18	0
of Tho Scott for a shop		16	0
of Tho Barnard for a chamber	1	0	0
and for land in Apton feild		6	8
of Wid Nicholls for land in Comon Downe (9)		18	0
of John Graves for a stall in the Butcher Row		10	0
of Mr. Ray for a chamber		14	0
of John ffinshes house		4	0
of Tho Pryor house		10	0
of Harmans house			
pd for passocks for the church		2	0
pd for mending the pendalum of the clock		2	6
pd for an order for the Chimes		6	8
pd at Procession		2	0
pd Mr. Osborne for ringing Kings birth Coronation and going and coming from Newmarkett	2	16	4
pd Mrs. Aynsworths Bill for bread and wine (10)	2	3	5

1681.

	£	s.	d.
P^d Ringers ye Kings going to Newmarket and returne twice	1	6	8
Going to Ware and to Hartford and Sr Tho Clutterbucks and Sr Thomas ffeilds severall times about Butlers bastard child		9	0
and going to London about it 6s. 8d. and carrying it to Hasle end		7	8
Going to the Sessions about ye pump on ye markett hill		3	0
P^d Mr. Chancey for the fyne and charges	1	0	8
P^d Wm Jordan the booksellers bill	1	3	6

1682.

	£	s.	d.
P^d Ringers for King's going and returne from Newmarkett		13	4
P^d Ringers for returne from Newmarkett		6	8
P^d Ringers for Kings going and returne from Newmarkett last		13	4
P^d Wm Hastlers bill for work at ye schoole		5	0

	£	s.	d.
ffor 3 new ffeoffments drawing and ingrossing	1	10	0
Pd Jordan for new binding a book of Erasmus		3	6
Pd for wine for ye ministers that preached for Mr Leigh		10	3

1683.

	£	s.	d.
pd for 2 Tables of marriages		1	0
Mending the hood		1	6
pd for silk to new line ye old hood and new mending it		8	0
pd for a new silk hood	1	4	6
pd for a silver patten for ye communion bread	3	16	10
Pd Ringers 29 May 1683		6	8
pd at ye procession		2	0
Going to ye Petty Sessions		3	0
pd for 2 acres of land John Johnsons towards mending Aptonfield Lane		14	0

1684.

Of Willm Barnes for the Doggs head in the Pott (1).

	£	s.	d.
Aprill 13th payd to William Morrice for reading the Verdict in the Church	0	0	6
23 payd to the Ringers for Ringing that day		6	8
May 6th payd to Robert Bonns for Beere for those that went a prossessioning (2)		2	0
11th payd to Mris Aynsworth for a bottle of wyne when Mr Cooper pretcht		2	0
29 pd to the Ringers for ringing that day		6	8
30th pd for a rope for the saints bell		2	0
for fetching of a warrant from Justice Allen for Mary Lumly, Mary Bayly and severall others to make them goe to service		1	6
August 13th ffor Releiving of Mris Mary Hartly late wife of Mr William Hartly minester of Hamptonshall (?) in York		1	0
September 9th pd to the Ringers for wringing that day		10	0
October 4th pd to the Ringers for ringing when the King went to Newmarkett		6	8
19th pd to John Gray for singing the two psalms		4	0
23rd pd to the Ringers for wringing when the Kinge came from Newmarkett		6	8
November 6th pd to Symon ffranklin for Killing a bitch ffox (3)		3	4

CHURCHWARDENS' ACCOUNTS.

December 10th pd Edward Gardner for his sons reading and singing the psalmes 3 quarters of a yeare	15	0
ffebruary 8th ffor going to Stansted Abbott to the Speciall Sessions	3	0
,, 12th given to the Ringers when Kinge James was proclaymed	10	0
April 4th pd to Robert Bonns for his yeares wages	3 9	0
viz. fforty shillings a yeare to ring the Bell		
Twenty shillings a yeare to looke after the chymes		
ffive shillings a yeare to looke after the clocke		
and ffower shillings a yeare for oyle for the Bells, clock, and chymes.		
,, 15th pd to William Barnes for Beere for the workemen in the church and church howses viz. for all the Bricklayers, Carpinters and plumbers	9	8
,, 19th pd to Mr. Manister for cloath silke and other things for the churche clarkes coat as appeeres by bill	1 6	0

1685.

April 23rd given to the ringers when Kinge James was crowned	10	0
May 26th given to Mr. Waynckfords mayd when wee were a possessioning (1)	2	0
and spent of those that went a possessioning at Robert Bonns (?)	2	0
June 11th pd to Edward Matthew for mending the windowes in the Library	3	0
,, 14th pd to Mr. Meade for a bottle of Hock when Mr. Ward pretcht	1	6
July 2nd pd to the chimney men for John Wyberds house for 4 halfe yeares due at Lady day last (2)	4	0
,, 8th given to the ringers for wringing that the Duke of Mulmore was taken or fled (3)	7	0
,, 23rd pd to the parritor for the Kings proclamation and the booke of prayers for his ma^{ties} late victories over the Rebells	1	0
,, 26th given to the Ringers on the Thanksgiving day	10	0
September 21st for going to Hadham to the Justices about sending Mary the wife of Robt More to Sleeford in Linkhornsheire	1	6

6

September 25th given to M^ris Margarett Talbott and M^ris Penelope Courtney and to 7 more wch lost 2300*li.* and upwards by certificate	2	6
Oct. 14th given to the Ringers for ringing on the kings birthday	10	0
Nov. 6th layd out by my partner at the George when 2 schollers made their declemations (4)	4	0
Jan. 18th pd to the parritor for a booke of prayer on the 30th Inst and on the sixt of ffebruary	1	0
Feb. 6th given to the ringers for ringing that day	6	8
ffebruary 9th given to 2 seamen wch lost 150*li.* wch came from Ireland and going to Lin	1	0
Feb. 21st payd to Mrs. Aynsworth for a bottle of wyne when Dr. Goodman pretcht	2	0
„ 25th pd to Nicholas Tyler for the comunion Rayles and for worke and Timber in the church and Church howses	12 10	0
March 21st pd to Allen How for a journey to Sr Samuell Husbands to knowe whether he would stand steward for the schoole ffeast	5	0
April 5th pd to Robert Bonns (?) for 2 hoggsheads of water and for help to use the Ingin		8

1686.

April 23 Given to the Ringers upon Coronation day	10	0
May 10 spent upon the Townsmen when they went to Mr. Hales to looke after the peece of meadow	2	6
June 3 pd to the paritor for syting us to Ware, the lord of London two letters, and the ffrench Breife	2	0
August 10 pd to the paritor for syting the Churchwardens and sidesmen to Stortford Court	2	0
pd to Mr. Betts for the ffees of the Court	4	8
ffebruary 6 pd to the Ringers for wringing that day	6	8
„ 18 pd to the parritor for the claudiunce Letter		6

1687.

July 2 payd for two Pessocks for the Pullpett and Deske		8
October 5 payd to Hanchett for the ffences he left about the Orchard	6	0

January 26th payd to the Parritor for the proclamation and order for Prayers and Thanksgiving for the Queen	1	0
April 16th payd to Robert Bonns for exercising the Ingen	6	0

1688.

May 22 Given to Mr. Wainkfords mayd when wee went a possessioning	2	0
,, 24th paid to the parritor for the Kings declaration (1)	1	0
,, 26th payd Mr. Rutland for Cloath to cover the clock	3	0
June 12th Given to the Ringers for ringing for the Prince (2)	5	0
,, 28th payd to the parritor for the Kings proclamation and for the forme of prayer and Thanksgiven to be kept for the prince	1	0
July 23rd payd to the parritor for the forme of prayer for the prince of Whales		6
November 2 payd to Robert Bonns for playing the Ingen	6	0
Jany. 4th payd to Mary Knight for going to Thorley to make affidavy for the souldier that dyed heere	1	0
Feb. 9th payd to the parritor for the books of prayers for the prince of Orringe and the day of Thanksgiving to be kept ffeb. 14th	1	0
,, 14th Given to the Ringers upon the Thanksgiving day	10	0
,, 21st and for ringing when King William and Queene Mary were proclaymed	10	0
,, 24th payd for a bottle of connary when Mr. Sanders preached	2	0

1692.

Rec^d. of the last Churchwardens	1	7	0
Of Mr. Edward Denny as arrears of Rent for the Bark Barne recovered by the Decree	10	00	00
Of Mr. Edward Denny for Costs given by the Decree	6	00	00
Of Mr. Edward Denny towards repairs of the said Barne by order of the Decree	1	17	0
Rec^d. of Mrs. Mary Barnard as arrears of Rent recovered by the Decree	6	0	0
Of Mrs. Mary Miller as arrears of rent and costs recovered by the Decree	1	0	4

Of Mr. Thomas Clayton as arrears of rent (for Sextons mead and other Churchland in Hockerhill field which hee held att an under rent) by agreement   5   0   0

The sume Totall of the Arrears and Costs Received as within £31 4s. 4d.

Memorand^m as to what is entred in the same account as Rec^d. more of Mrs. Mary Maplesden and Mrs. Judeth Rochell for Debt and Interest. It is to be noted that the principle being £27 15s. 0d. was paid over to Willm Bayford one of the Churchwardens, for which mony hee is to account with the Trustees next year. As to the Sixteen Pounds and four shillings, being Interest mony, it is of the same nature wth the most part of the £31 4s. 4d. above recited and according to the Decree may be disposed off att the descretion of the Trustees in defraying necessary Charges :—

Memorandum as to the Disbursements, etc.

June 8th, 1692. P^d by the hands of Dr. Yardley to Mr. James Altham as Attorney in part of his Bill as appears by his receipt upon ye ffiles   7   1   6

July 27, 1692. More paid by the hands of Dr. Yardley to Mr. John Hyde imploy'd as our Attorney as appears by Receipt upon the ffile .   1   0   0

Septem^r. 22, 1692. More paid by the hands of the said Dr. Yardley to Mr. John Hale Cleark to the Commissioners as appears by his Receipt upon the ffile . . .   6   11   0

April 20, 1693. Paid by the Churchwardens in person to Mr. James Altham aforesaid in part of his Bill as by acquittance upon the File   5   0   0

Aug. 7, 1693. Paid to Mrs. Stafford at the Rein-Deer in full for the Commissioners and Jurors Dinner at their sitting there on Feb. 22, 169$\frac{2}{3}$, upon a Tryall about Stortford Charities, as appears by her acquittance upon the File   9   0   0

Augst. 7, 1693. More paid to Mrs. Stafford for a dinner for the Trustees at their generall meeting to take these accounts on Augst 7th, 1693, as appears by her acquittance on the File   1   10   0

Augst. 7th, 1693. More paid by the said Churchwardens to Mr. James Altham aforesaid in full of his Bill for Attendance and service done by him as our attorney and disbursements made by him relating to the Decree, as appears by his acquittance at the end of his Bill upon the File   5   0   0

Repairs of the Church and Churchhouses, etc.

Augt. 24, Paid Robt Underwood for work done at the Lattin School . . .   2   0   11

And paid Robt Underwood also for work done at the Writeing School .   1   17   6

Novem^r 17 paid Nich. Ayley for Thatching ffour days and a halfe at the Church-houses .   6   9

„ 17 paid Nich. Ayley's Wife for yelmeing Two days and a halfe . . .   2   6

Jany. 31 paid Willm Theabalds for nailes used at the Church ffence in Water lane . .   6   8

April 10th paid Robt Bonns for wood burnt in the vestry when they examined the Writeings   6

1693.

July ye 18. P^d Mr. Saunders for a Register Book for the Feoffees in Trust . . .   10   6

1696.

Pd. Nick. Richardson for setting ye Yew Tree (1) .   6

pd for a rope for the Saints Bell . . .   2   8

1698.

Mr. Gill for horseman ditch for six yeares (1) .

Mr. Tooke for Susan Nicholls Roome under the librarie

Jan. 30 paid to Risby the baylie quit rent for the church tenements (2)   1   1

1703.

pd Henry Wallis for repairing Robt Bonests House and the old Schoole after the Great Storme (1)   3   2   0

1710.

May 8th, 1714. paid Mr. Smallwood by order of the Trustees for Beautifieng the Church .   22   10   10

June 11, 1714. paid Mr. Smallwood by order of the Trustees for puting up the Queens arms, etc.   12   10   10

Jany. 18, 1716. paid Mr. Hoy a solicitor in the Court of Chancery by order of the Trustees .   13   10   0

1712.
Receipts.

Of John Dorrington for ye old Scoole	5	0	0

Disbursements.

July 18th P^d Henry Barns a Plumers Bill	22	1	0
Oct. 26th P^d Jethro Newland for doing up ye Garden at ye Church Barn		3	0

1713.
Receipts.

Mr. Starford for a shopp		14	0
Wid^o Perry for ye Barley Hill		17	0
Jno Dorrington for ye old Schoole	5	0	0
Rec^d. by 12 bushells of Oats growing in Comon Downe		18	0
By straw and Chaff from ye same		2	0
Rec^d. of Mr. Sanders and Jeff. Newland for fruit growing in Bark barn Orchard		5	8½

Disbursements.

May 23rd P^d for Plowing Comon Downe Land 2 acres		12	0
pd for sowing ye same		2	0
pd for harrowing d^o		2	0
pd for 7 bush^{lls} of Oates at 22½d. p^r bushell		13	1½
pd for moweing ye same		2	0
pd for harrowing d^o		1	0
pd for carting in ye Corne		3	0
pd for Thrashing and dressing d^o		2	0
pd for ye use of ye Barne to lay ye Corne in		1	6
Sepr. 11 P^d Jno Waylett Bellfounder for new Casting ye bells as per his bill and receipt (1)	44	17	6
Novr. 18 pd Richd Osborne Tanner for hair		6	0

1714.
Receipts.

Wid^o Warman for a Shopp by ye Rain Deer	4	0	0
Mr. Gill for horsemans Ditch			1

1718.

Rec^d. the Gift of Dr. Stanley	2	2	0
By Cash to Matt Hanscomb Ceiling ye Ile	7	0	0
D^{tto} Jno Tyler for ye middle Ile	15	0	0
D^{tto} Matt Hanscomb Ceiling ye Ile	12	0	0
expended at Several meetings ab^t ye Ile		2	8

1720.

Of the Widd. Dorrington for the old grammar School	5	0	0
P^d John Poulter his Bill for work done to the old Grammar Schoole	1	2	2

1743.

March 16th. To Phill. Glascock	2	3	10
March 20. To Mr. Wankford for Straw (1)	1	10	0

1744.

June 27. To Charles Perry 1 y^{rs} Sallery	1	0	0
To Mr. Popeley 1 y^{rs} d^o	20	0	0

1785.

Money Rec^d. on the Trust account.

Rec^d. June 27th of Thos Jackson two years rent due Christmas 1784	14	0	0
Rec^d. July 9th of the Rev^d Mr. Gibson	10	10	0
Rec^d. July 9th of William Hughes one years rent due Michalmas 1784	3	5	0
Decr. 22nd paid Robert Perry half a years Salery for playing the Orgin and a stamp	10	0	2
July 20th paid Mr. Ramsey a bill for cleaning the Church Brasses	2	2	0

THE MINUTE BOOK NOW USED BY THE CHURCHWARDENS OF ST. MICHAEL'S COMMENCES IN 1712, AND THE FOLLOWING ARE A FEW EXTRACTS FROM IT.

1713.

At a Court Leet and Barron held at the Crown at Hockrell ye 15th day of Aprill 1713

Jonathan Carter Junr. } were elected Constables for the year
Robt Lumkin } ensueing.

1830.

NOTE.—This year for the first time the Head-Borough, Ale Tasters, Fish and Flesh Tasters, and Cattle Drivers, were appointed by the Vestry. These Officers of the Parish were originally appointed by the Court Leet. Their appointment being considered of no practical use in modern times, they ceased to exist in 1872.

1836.

This year at a Public meeting it was unanimously resolved to appoint a paid Surveyor.

It was proposed by Mr. Frederic Chaplin and sec^d by Mr. Jo^s Fairman that Mr. Weeks be nominated and appointed Surveyor of the Highways at a salary of £40 0s. 0d. per an.—car^d unan^y.

This year the Vicar (Rev^d. Charles Spencer) relinquished his right of appointing one of the Churchwardens.

1837.

Five Persons being nominated this year for the Office of Churchwarden, a poll was demanded. The polling occupied two days, from 9 until 4, and at the close the numbers were:

Mr. Joseph Heath, Junr.	0
Mr. Robert Cole	64
Fred^k Vandermeulen, Esq.	0
Mr. James Hillat Summers	65
Mr. Joseph Fairman	1

1846.

Three Persons being nominated this year, a poll was demanded by Mr. W. M. Ley. The polling occupied two days, from 9 to 4.

	Ratepayers.	Votes.
Mr. W. M. Ley	98	114
George F. Grounds	78	160
Robert Clayden	95	177

Mr. Clayden and Mr. Grounds were elected.

1847.

This year a public meeting was called to consider the state of the Charities.

NOTES TO THE CHURCHWARDENS' ACCOUNTS.

1489.

Peter Pence was an ancient levy or tax of a penny on each house (provided there were thirty pence belonging to it) throughout England, paid to the Pope. It was called Peter-pence, because collected on the day of St. Peter ad vincula. Edward III. first forbade the payment; but it soon returned, and continued till the time of King Henry VIII. It was abolished under that Prince, and restored under Philip and Mary, but finally prohibited under Queen Elizabeth. [Chambers's "Cyclopædia," 1741.]

1495.

[Page 22, line 15]. Sir H. Chauncy ["Hist. Herts"] has transcribed this item thus: "Lib. vocat. the Crowcher jacen. ante crucem (quære annon potius the Crowcher nam Crowch est Crosse)."

1496.

[Page 23, line 4]. "Estriche bordis" = wainscot.

1500.

(1) See note (1) 1505.

1502.

(1) Every church was anciently provided with one or more banners to bear in the processions on Rogations and other holy days. A processional banner had usually the patron saint of the particular church where it was used painted or wrought upon it. [Staunton's "Ecclesiastical Dictionary"]. See also the items in the accounts for 1520 and 1525.

1482.

(1) In 1476 one Elizabeth Spycere gave 13s. 4d. at Waites Cross to repair the church.

(2) It was at this time customary on Good Friday to erect in the chancel a small building to represent the Holy Sepulchre. In this was placed the Host, and a person was set to watch it both that night and the next, then very early on the following morning (Easter Sunday) the Host was taken out, thus representing the burial and resurrection of our Lord.

I find from this and subsequent items in these accounts that the sepulchre here mentioned was of wood, so framed that it could be easily erected in the church and taken down again. There are a few instances of permanent sepulchres being formed in the chancel wall; one of these may be seen in the church of Sandon, Herts.

(3) "in grete" = altogether, in one sum, signifying that the work was done for a previously agreed upon price.

(4) "Nares in his Glossary, p. 103, says this festival was held annually on the Thursday after Trinity Sunday, in memory, as was supposed, of the

miraculous confirmation of the doctrine of Transubstantiation under Pope Urban IV. Its origin, however, is involved in great obscurity." [Brand's "Pop. Antiq."]

This festival appears to have been thoroughly observed at St. Michael's; there was a religious procession and a pageant, and then the Mystery or Miracle Play. The principal feature of the procession was the Pyx containing the consecrated bread: this was carried through the church and the adjacent streets; other figures followed, representing favourite saints, e.g., St. George killing the dragon.

(For further information regarding Corpus Christi day, read Googe's translation of Naogeorgus, f. 53, "Then doth ensue," etc. Brand's "Pop. Antiq.," i. 295.)

1484.

(1) Previous to the Reformation most parishes possessed a "Church House," or "Parish House," as it is also sometimes called. The Church House may at times have been used for the transaction of the secular affairs of the parish, but its name is more intimately associated with the then popular periodical games and festivities. These festive gatherings were known by the name of "Ales;" there were "Church Ales," "Clerk's Ales," "Whitsun Ales," "Hocking Ales," etc. The following extract relating to the "Church House" is taken from some papers drawn up by John Aubrey, an English gentleman-scholar, who flourished in the latter half of the 17th century. "Before the Reformation there were no poor rates; the charitable doles given at Religious Houses and the Church Ale in every parish did the business. In every parish there was a Church House, to which belonged spits, pots, crocks, etc., for dressing provisions. Here the housekeepers met and were merry, and gave their charity. The young people came there too, and had dancing, bowling, and shooting at the butts. Mr. Antony Wood assures me there were few or no Alms houses before the time of King Henry VIII.; that at Oxford opposite Christ Church is one of the most ancient in England. In every church was a poor man's box, and the like at great inns." [This extract is quoted in Chambers's "Book of Days," ii. 440.]

(2) Hocktide began on the Monday following the second Sunday after Easter. Monday was the men's day and Tuesday the women's. (For an account of the festivities of Hocktide read Brand's "Pop. Antiq.," i. 184, Dyer's "British Pop. Customs," p. 188, and Chambers's "Book of Days," i. 498.)

(3) Baldwin or Bawdwyn Victor was the founder of the Chantry of St. John the Baptist here. It would appear from this and subsequent items relating to his obit that he was interred within the church.

(4) "Prikkyd songge" = manuscript music. "To prick" = to copy.

1491.

(1) Sir H. Chauncy in his "Antiquities of Hertfordshire" says: "Three Gylds and a Chantry were founded in this church; the Gyld of St. Mary, the Gyld of St. Michael, and the Gyld of St. John the Baptist. These saints had their Altars, and St. Michael his Tabernacle, on which much cost has been bestowed."

I find that St. John also had a tabernacle, and that in 1520 a new tabernacle was made, which might possibly have been for St. Mary.

(2) Jenyns or Jennings. The first mention of this name in these accounts is in 1431, when John Janyn (or Jenyn) was paid 3*d*. for nails for the great chest. From that date down to the present time (1881) members of the family have resided here.

(3) It was at this time customary to light in churches what were called

Paschall Tapers. These tapers or candles were generally very large; they were lighted on Easter Eve and continued burning until Ascension.

1503.

(1) This item is followed by items for materials and labour amounting to £4 8s. 2d.

1504.

Previous to this date the year over which these accounts extended was reckoned from Michaelmas to Michaelmas, but in 1504 and the subsequent years until 1611 the reckoning is from Palm Sunday to Palm Sunday.

(1) The orthography and writing of these two accounts (1503 and 1504) are so bad that I had very great difficulty in deciphering them: "brawyng playe" I take to be "Braughing Play." The Churchwardens of Stortford owned a "dragon" [see Inventory], and it would appear from this item that they occasionally let him out.

1505.

(1) I have been unable to ascertain the exact meaning of "Luntis Yeld," or "Luntys Gylde" as it is written in 1500. Toulmin Smith, in speaking of Sir H. Chauncy's extracts from the Accounts of the Churchwardens of Stortford, says: "The ale called 'Luntis yield,' which, though I cannot find any trace of in the archæological works treating of these matters, I take to be an 'Ale' held at the time of paying the 'Smoke farthing' or 'wax silver.' Lunt is an old word meaning 'match,' and often used for 'smoke,' and nothing was more consistent with ordinary practice than that as funds for other purposes were raised by means of other regular 'Ales,' so the Smoke-farthing and Wax-silver should in some parishes be gathered at an ale."

(2) It was the custom in the Romish Church to extinguish all the fires on Easter Eve. The "wood and coles" here mentioned were therefore provided on Easter Eve for renewing the fires on Easter Day; when, however, they were kindled again, it was done by pure elemental fire, produced by a flint and steel, and not from unhallowed embers. From this fire the Paschal taper was also lighted. [See also Naogeorgus's "Popish Kingdom," by Googe: "On Easter Eve the fire all is quencht in every place," etc.]

1506.

(1) Paschal silver I take to be either synonymous with Wex-silver, or Wax-silver, which was a contribution made towards the expense of the candles used in the Roman Catholic Ceremonial, or a collection made on Easter Eve especially for the Paschal taper.

(2) "Funeral tapers, however thought of by some, are of harmless import. Their meaning is to show that the departed soules are not quite put out, but having walked here as the children of light, are now gone to walk before God in the light of the living." ["Gregorii Opuscula," p. 112.]

To have a great many torches was a special mark of esteem in the person who made the funeral to the deceased. The Churchwardens provided the torches and let them out at funerals, charging, as in this item, for the waste of them.

(3) "Bowers" I take to mean booths or covered stalls used on the fair days. It was at this period the custom to hold these fairs on the day of the feast of dedication and in or near to the churchyard.

(4) It would appear from this and other items in these accounts that at this period it was usual to go to London by way of Hoddesdon.

(5) bellf.

1509.

(1) On these days the souls of the departed were had in special remembrance, and some office or obsequies said for them, as obits, dirges, etc.

1510.

(1) This watercourse was in South Street.
(2) See note (1) 1491.
(3) This was for three parishioners engaged to go round the bounds of the parish with the religious procession in Rogation week; they probably had to carry the cross or the banner staves.

1513.

(1) This cross is not mentioned by Sir H. Chauncy.
(2) See note (3) 1482.
(3) Probably a staff or handle for the cross that was carried in the processions.
(4) The flasks or cruets in which was kept the consecrated oil blessed on Holy Thursday.
(5) Candlemas Day. The Purification of the Virgin Mary. For information regarding the religious observances on this day read Brand's "Pop. Antiq.," i. 43, Chambers's "Book of Days," i. 212.

1514.

(1) I have been unable to ascertain what connection Sir Edward Hayward, Knt. had with the town or church of Stortford. His name is not mentioned by Sir H. Chauncy, Clutterbuck, Morant, or Wright in their County Histories.
(2) *i.e.* letting three dwelling-houses (see N. and Q., 5th S. xi. 194.)
(3) The amice (so called from *amicire*, to cover) was a piece of fine linen in the form of an oblong square. When the priest put on the amice, he rested it for a moment upon the crown of his head, and then spread it upon his shoulders.
(4) "Beting" candle was a candle made of rosin and pitch.

1515.

(1) Sir H. Chauncy ["Hist. of Herts"] has transcribed this "Mary Ale," but the original is plainly "May Ale."
"May Ale" I take to be another name for the games and revelries of May-day. The good folk of Stortford were probably amused on this day with the frolics of the Morris dancers. [For information regarding May-day read Brand's "Pop. Antiq.," i. 212, Dyer's "British Pop. Customs," and "The Book of Days."]
(2) These were the torches used at funerals, and month minds, and for the use or waste of which a payment was made to the Churchwardens.
(3) Robert Savill was the Chantry Priest.
(4) As an instance of the way in which surnames may become corrupted through ignorance or carelessness, I quote the name of Dugarde, which is at first spelt correctly; it then becomes "Dewgard," and finally "Dogood."
"Tawyer" was the mediæval name for "Tanner." The leather was used by the churchwardens for making baldricks for the bells.

1516.

(1) See note (1) 1502.
(2) "strykyng" = moulding or making.

1519.

(1) These bonfires were lighted on Midsummer Eve or on St. John the Baptist's day.

"Then doth the joyful feast of John the Baptist take his turne,
When bonfiers great with loftie flame in everie towne doe burne."
[Googe's translation of Naogeorgus.]

(2) "obligacon" = an agreement.
(3) Nothing is left to show where this cross formerly stood, but in all probability it was on the south side of the church, and near to the path leading to the south or principal entrance. From an item in the account for 1643 I am inclined to think it was taken down that year. Sir H. Chauncy (1700) does not mention it; there were, therefore, probably no remains of it in his time. Mr. J. E. Cussans, in his "Hist. of Herts," states that during the restoration of the church in 1868 a portion of a cross was found under the floor; this he imagines was a fragment of one of the old town crosses. I have never seen this fragment, but as it was found buried *in* the church, I think it might possibly be a portion of the old churchyard cross.
(4) See note (2) 1520.

1520.

(1) "begger" = collector (?).
(2) "Grate." Possibly this was another name for the cage or lock-up. In the accounts of the churchwardens of Reading I find the following item:
"1552. Of the Mayor and burges for the gaol called the grate p^r. a^m xij$d$."
In N. and Q. 5th S. xi. 194, Mr. John Parkin says: "The 'grate' was a sort of lattice that served instead of a window."
(3) See note (1) 1502.
(4) No mention is made of the dedication of this new tabernacle. See note (1) 1491.

1521.

(1) "Furbisher" was the mediæval term for a maker of swords and scabbards.
(2) "Fox tells us of one Gray, a smith of this town, accused for denying the Sacrament of the Altar to be Christ, was therefore sent for to London, but was there deliver'd by means of the Lord Cromwell." [Chauncy's "Antiq. of Herts," i. 326.]

1523.

(1) There is a similar item in the accounts of Great Dunmow: "Item to make up ye shott at Lynsell Maye xij$d$." Mr. Scott in his book says of this item, "This looks as if they had gone to Lindsell, but the inhabitants had not contributed enough to pay their public house score."

See also the item in 1541 relating to Stansted Play.

1525.

(1) Palm Cross. "This name was given to churchyard crosses because they were ornamented with wreaths of palm on Palm Sunday for processions," (Scott's "Dunmow").
(2) This inventory is lost; the earliest one is dated 1537, which is transcribed in full further on.

1529.

(1) At this period the organ was, I believe, very much akin to the present bagpipe, and we find the instrument is generally spoken of in the plural as "the orgons" or "a payre of orgons," but I think I am correct in saying that only one instrument was meant. The earliest mention of "the organs" in Stortford Church is in 1490, when the churchwardens paid a strange priest or clerk 8d. for playing on them.

1530.

(1) Sir William Say, Kt., was Lord of the Manor of Baas, in the parish of Broxbourne. He was interred in Broxbourne Church, and a handsome monument is erected to him there. (See also 1489.)

1531.

(1) The Leather Market was that portion of the present Market Square immediately in front of the Plume of Feathers Inn and the shop of Mr. Joscelyne. It would appear from this and other items that at this period tanning and the sale of leather formed an important branch of the trade of the town.

(2) In the churchwardens' accounts of St. Mary at Hill, London, I find this item: "1501 for paintynge the crosse staffe for lent iiij*d*."

1534.

(1) "Childern" = Choristers.

1535.

(1) The Fish Market, or Fishrow as it was sometimes also called, stood upon that portion of Market Square to the west of the present Corn Exchange.

1538.

"Grene wex." Estreats were delivered to the Sheriffs under the Exchequer seal of "Green Wax," levied in counties; sometimes the churchwardens assisted at the collection. (N. and Q. 5th S. xi. 194.)

1539.

(1) This item refers to the perambulation or beating of the bounds of the parish in Rogation week. [See Brand's "Pop. Antiq.," i. 202.]

1540.

(1) This Item probably relates to the dissolution of the Guild of the Virgin Mary.

(2) Rent Resolute was a rent anciently paid to the Crown from the lands of religious houses.

(3) Possibly this was a quit rent paid by the churchwardens to the bailiff of the Bishop of London.

1542.

(1) This Bible was probably purchased in order to comply with the King's proclamation of May, 1540. The dates relative to the use of the Bible in the English Church are as follows:

1536. Cromwell orders every parson to cause a Bible in Latin and English to be set up in the choir for the perusal of the people.
1538. Cromwell orders a Bible of the largest volume to be set up in every church in some place convenient for reading.
1540. A King's proclamation orders a Bible of the largest volume to be provided by the curate and parishioners under a penalty of 40*s*. per month.
1541. A brief published directing the same.
1543. The Bible was again suppressed (Strype's "Cranmer," i. 121).
1547. Edward's injunctions directed that the whole Bible in English of the largest volume should be set up in every church.
1559. Elizabeth issued the same injunction.

(2) The "care cloth" was a kind of pall or canopy held over the heads of the bride and bridegroom during the marriage ceremony (see Brand's "Pop. Antiq.," ii. 141).

(3) See note (2) 1520.

1545.

(1) Chapel—see note (1) 1561.

1546.

(1) 6s. 8d. was the fee paid to the churchwardens for an interment within the walls of the church. There is nothing in these accounts indicating that the fees varied according to the position of the grave within the church.

(2) *i.e.* The feast of the dedication of the church.

"This feast was at first regularly kept on that day in every week on which the church was dedicated; but it being observed and complained of that the number of holidays was excessively increased, to the detriment of civil government and secular affairs, and also that great irregularities and licentiousness, which had crept into these festivities by degrees, especially in the churches, chapels, and churchyards, were found highly injurious to piety, virtue, and good manners; there were therefore both statutes and canons made to regulate and restrain them; and by an act of Convocation passed by Henry VIII., 1536, their number was in some measure lessened. [Brand "Pop. Antiq."]

For a more detailed account of what took place at these wakes or feasts of dedication read Brand, ii. 1—15, and "Book of Days," ii. 404.

In the June number of the *Fortnightly Review*, 1880, there is a very interesting article on "The Cost of the Mediæval Church in England." Speaking of the festivals of the Church, the writer observes: "It was a chief characteristic of the Church system to abstract in festivals and holidays probably a fourth of the time of the lay people; and what is more, to levy onerous fines in money or goods on all who availed themselves of these spiritual dissipations. But the economic effect of all this expenditure was as nearly as possible waste. It produced no single commodity for sustaining human life; it yielded not one solitary article which could increase the exports, and therefore buy goods from the foreigner. Some alms doubtless were given to the indigent, and propagated 'sturdy rogues and valiant beggars.' In a few instances rudimentary learning was fostered among the few students who redeemed the swarming fraternities of idle and debauched monks from utter uselessness. But the general and prolonged effect on the nation was a hindrance and a calamity exactly analogous to reducing the quantity of daylight by one-half, or adding several months to the reign of winter."

I trust it will not be considered out of place to transcribe here the last paragraph from the article mentioned above, in which the writer sums up the utility of the Mediæval Church in the following words:

"No one has ever pretended that the institution of the Mediæval Church in this and other countries was wholly evil. Unless there had been mitigating circumstances of some kind, society would have broken down by the increasing pressure of a burden chiefly wasteful and pernicious. Among the greatest services rendered by the Church was the assistance it gave to the growth of a middle class. Generally the ecclesiastical landlords were indulgent to their tenants, and in effect shared the profits of their lands with the bailiffs and labourers, the more industrious and intelligent of whom became themselves owners. The plebeian origin of the majority of the monks and regular clergy disposed them to assist, when possible, their lay relatives, and many snug tenancies and profitable leases took their origin in such motives. It was the same circumstance of the plebeian complexion of the church which, during the earlier part of its career especially, did render it a refuge for the studious, the gentle, and the oppressed, and by constantly raising the child of the meanest villein to the dignity of a spiritual prince or peer, put a curb on the savage soldiery of feudalism. To some of the earlier monks also belongs the eminent merit of fostering and advancing those useful arts which lay at the very bottom of all national progress. The Cistercian Abbeys were for nearly two hundred years pioneers and patterns in the reclamation of forests and wildernesses, and for a longer period schools of agriculture and the industrial arts.

"The services rendered by the Mediæval Church in this country to the cause of enlightenment and learning was of a bad and false sort; and no real enlightenment could possibly come out of the arid discussions and distressing puerilities which constituted the only orthodox mental exercises permitted by the Church. The increasing demand for cathedrals, abbeys, hospitals and churches raised to rapid eminence an order of architects among the most original, daring, and successful that has ever flourished. These cultivators of one of the noblest, most difficult, and most useful of all the arts and sciences which advance and adorn a country, will always be counted among the greatest benefactors of Western Europe. By the simple and enduring force of beauty and fitness the principal edifices raised by the mediæval architects, whether clerics or laymen, have become models of their kind for all subsequent ages.

"These are the principal considerations which can be urged in favour of the Mediæval Church. I do not discuss its theology or its traditions. But the considerations of an opposite and evil nature—some of the most important of which have been indicated in the foregoing pages—far outweigh the good."

(3) It would appear that at this time the clock was fixed outside the tower or steeple. The amounts expended hardly warrant the supposition that a new clock and chimes were made this year. I therefore read "makyng" in the sense of "renovating."

1547—1st of Edward VI.

(1) This is the first mention of an alms-house in these accounts.

(2) These items relate to the sale of plate, etc. The amount given by the churchwardens when before the King's Commissioners is £38 16s. 9d.

(3) There were doubtless mural paintings in the church at this time. Mr. Cussans says (1870) that one was discovered a short time ago on the north wall; it represented a winged figure holding in one hand a Tau Cross, all within the monogram IHS, repeated four times and arranged in the form of a lozenge.

(4) The church book here mentioned was probably the first Parish Register, which unfortunately is not extant, and was never copied into the existing Register Book, which dates from 1561.

(5) This, I imagine, was the injunction issued by Edward VI. (1547), and which related amongst other things to the appointment of churchwardens by the parish, the distribution of the fortieth part of the revenues of the benefice among the poor, the devotion of surplus stock to the repairs of the highways, the sending of boys to school or college at the expense of the benefice, etc. [For further particulars of the injunction read "The Parish," by Toulmin Smith, pp. 80, 95, 106, 188, 307, 325, 603.]

(6) In 1547 it was enjoined that "the parson, vicar, or curate and parishioners of every parish within this realm, shall in their churches and chappels keep one book or register, wherein they shall write the day and year of every wedding, christening, and burial made within their parish for their time, and so every man succeeding them likewise; and therein shall write every person's name that shall be so wedded, christened or buried, and for the safe keeping of the same book, the parish shall be bound to provide of their common charges one sure coffer, with two locks and keys, whereof the one to remain with the parson, vicar, or curate, and the other with the wardens of every parish church or chappel, wherein the said book shall be laid up; which book they shall every Sunday take forth, and in the presence of the said wardens, or one of them, write and record in the same all the weddings, christenings, and burials made the whole week before, and that done to lay up the book in the said coffer as afore. And for every time that the same shall be

omitted, the party that shall be in fault thereof shall forfeit to the said church 3s. 4d., to be employed to the Poor men's box of that Parish."

(7) The Commissioners for Hertfordshire were Sir John Butler, K^t, Sir John Brockett, K^t, John Pen. Esqr., and Nicholas Bristow, Esqr. Mr. Cussans in his "Church Goods in Hertfordshire" transcribes their certificate in full. The following extracts relating to Stortford are taken from his work :—

"Thinge don by men dead.

"Item Sr Henry Parkar layt of Pellam Knight in the said county of Herts haithe clearlie desolved and puld down the chappell of Allswike in the said Shiar and haithe sold the Belle lead Tymbre and stone to Willyam hammonde and Henry Grave of Buntingford in the said Countye for the sum of xl*li*. and the said Sr Henrye Durynge his Lyff did hold the chappell yard of Alswike aforesaid as parcell of his inheritaunce Sainge he bought the said Chappell wyth thapptenne of the Kinge maiestie Allso the said S^r henry haith in his hande more of the Goodde of the said chappell and ij Challisses of Syllver the verrie contente therof we know not but estimate to the value of vj*li*. Allso then habitaunte of Stortforde say that thei wear commaunded bie Sr Henric parker aforesaid to Delyuer unto thuse of the said Sr Henrie To John Ellyot and Thomas Diar of Stortford in the said countie xxxij*li*. iij*s*. iiij*d*. Delyvered out of the churche box of the said Town and in lyk manner the said S^r henrie Receiued of the parrisshioners of Muche Haddam owt of the Church box ther xxxix*li*. which Sumes the said Sr Henrye did convert unto his own use The Sum therof in the hoall amountethe to cxvij*li*. iij*s*. iiij*d*. The said S^r henrie beinge dead and the Kinge Maiestie seased in part of his Gooddes and the rest so separated ande deuyded That we the said Commyssioners know not whear the said Sum may be aunswered nor levied."

"Goodd' sold and embesylled by not resiant in the Countie of Hertf.
Item. The inhabitants of Stortford say that lorde Morley haythe Resayued into his hande out of the Church Box of the Towne aforsaid iiij*li*. which was employed as thei say Towarde the setting ffurthe of a Demyelaunce.
Item. Mychaell Cammyswell layte of Saint Andrewe parryshe in Harf and now dwellinge besidde Coventrie haythe embessillede a Crose and ij Candellsticke of silluer ffrom the Church aforsaid the value therof we know not.

Goodde solde by common assente of the inhabitaunte of the parrishes in the countie aforsaid.
Stortfford. Item the Parysshiners of Stortfforde haue sold all their goodde which was Belonginge to the church of Stortford aforsaid except the Belles whiche as yt is reported was a Ryche Churche."

,, Hundred of Brawghin.

Startforde. Made the ffirst daie of Novembre, &c., and John Ellyot of Startforde, &c., belongy'g to the pyshe charche of Startforde, &c.
Imp'mis. A vestment on albe and ij ould copes and a lytle pello of sylke.
p'ecclia. Item v oulde Diaper aulter clothes and iiij^{or} other Diaper clothes of ye best.
Item vj playne Aulter clothes and iiij^{or} Diaper Towelle.
Item v playne Towells.
Item ij latten candlesteke ij^o hande belle & a saunce bell.
Item in the steple v Belle and a lytle cloke bell.
Item a lector of Brasse.
p'ecclia. Item a payse of Organes.

Item ij. paynted **Curtens.**
Item a care clothe "
(State Papers: Domestic, Edward VI. v. 5. Art. 19).
Certificate of the churchwardens of the parishes within the city of London and the several deaneries in Essex and Hertfordshire within the diocese of London, of the sale of all the church plate, ornaments, jewels, bells, vestments, &c., lately belonging to their respective churches, and of the appropriation of the proceeds.

(1548)

The Deanery of Braughing:

Storteforde John Bayforde) Churchewardens have solde of the Churchiss Edwarde Wylley (Plate there Thees parcells folowing viz.: A crosse wth a foote sylver and gylte a chalys wth a patent of sylver a paxe ij sensers of sylver and the Toppe gylt and two Cruetts of sylver for the some of xxxviijli. xvj$s$. ix$d$. of the wch Some there remayneth in thandes of S^r henry park' Knighte xxxvijli. ij$s$. ix$d$. and the resydue ys bestowd in repayring the same churche. ("Church Goods in Hertfordshire," J. E. Cussans, F.R. Hist. S.)

(8) This certificate is now in the P.R.O. [Chantry Certificates, Edward VI. an II.] and the following is a verbatim transcript of it.

The valuation of all the londs ten^{ts} and hereditaments, stokks off cattell and redie money wch were geven willed and assigned for and towards the maintenance of any lamps lyghts obbits and anniv'saries w^{t}in the said countie of Hertff.

Stortford.   v acres of Londe called the hospittales lyinge in Ugley and Stansted Mountfichet wch were geven and p'chased
(a)   by the Brotherne and Sisterne of the ffraternite of Stortf' to the fyndinge of an yerelie Obite. And byn letten by the yere for . . . . . . xs.

A rente goynge owt of iij acres of londe geven to the Sexten of the churche of Stortf' for the findinge of an
(b)   yerelie obite . . . . xij$d$.

A Rente geven for the findinge of an obite goyng owt of a crofte lyinge at Tenter hill cont^g j acre in thandes of the Vicar and his successors yerelie . . . xij$d$.

A rente goynge out of an acre of londe lyinge at muche halfeacres now in the hands of John Jardefilde geven for the kepinge of an obite yerelie . . . . xij$d$.

A Rente goinge owt of a ten^{te} in thands of Thoms. Massell geven for the said intent yerelie . . xij$d$.

A Rent goynge owt of a Ten^{te} in thands of Henry Johnson geven also for the said Intent yerelie . . xiiij$d$.

A Rente goynge owt of a Ten^{te} at Northgate geven for the kepinge of an obite now in thandes of Rich. Bedell by the yere . . . . . . xij$d$.

A Rente goynge owt of an acre of londe geven to the
(c)   Intent abovesaid lyinge in Aptonfilde now in the handes of Ales Pileston wydowe by the yere . . . xij$d$.

A Rente goyinge owt of a parcell of lande in prestley gyven by Trossher for an obite now in thandes of Robt Goodfray by the yere . . . . . xij$d$.

A Rente goyinge owt of a crofte lyinge at Mapilcros geven by John Nobill for the kepinge of an obite now in thandes of John Alberd yeerlie . . . . xij$d$.

A Rente goyinge yeerlie owt of a meade in thandes of

NOTES TO THE CHURCHWARDENS' ACCOUNTS.

John Jardefilde geven by   Strowde for the maynten'nce of a lampe before the Roode yerelie   .   .   ij$s.$
A Rente goyinge yerelie out of a ten^{te} in thandes of
John Goodinge gyven for the findinge of the lyghtes
before the Roode by the yere   .   .   .   .   ij$s.$
A Rente goynge owt of ij peces of lande now in thandes
of Richard Jardefilde wch was gyven by Willm ffraunces
towards the kepinge of the lyghtes in the said Rood lofte
yerelie   .   .   .   .   ij$s.$
A Rente goynge out of a Ten^{te} w^t a Garden in South-
streate in thandes of Thoms. Chaundeler the elder gyven
to the maynten'nce of lyghts yerelie   .   .   .   xvij$d.$
Total xxvj$s.$ viij$d.$

NOTE.—In the margin is written in a different hand at
   (a) Henry P'ker gent hath p'chased this p'cell.
   (b) John Cokkes esq^{re} hath p'chased all the p'cells following.
   (c) sold to Reve and Catton and was paten. dat. iij maii an° iij° Reg. Edward vj$^{th.}$

1548.

(1) See note 1561.
(2) The communion table.

1549.

NOTE.—Both the spelling and writing of this account are very bad, and consequently difficult to decipher.
   (1) Percy was the church clerk.
   (2) See note (7) 1547.
   (3) The King's Book here mentioned was probably the first **Book of Common Prayer**—the use of which was enjoined by Parliament in the first Act of Uniformity, Jan., 1549—or "A Necessary Doctrine and Erudition for any Christian Man, set forth by the King's Majesty of England, etc., 1543." This latter was addressed by the King to the people, and is therefore called the King's Book.

1553.

NOTE.—The main point of interest in this account is its evidence of the prompt return to the Roman Catholic form of worship immediately upon the accession of Queen Mary.
   (1) The Holy Water Stoup was a stone basin usually built in the wall at the entrance of the church. The remains of one may still be seen in the south porch of St. Michael's.
   (2) The Ship was a vessel in the shape of a boat in which the incense was stored; when in use the incense was taken out with a spoon and thrown on the censer.
   (3) See note (4) 1514.

1554.

(1) These veils or hangings were sometimes used to divide the chancel from the rest of the church.

1557.

(1) The custom of adorning the top of a steeple with a **cock** is one of great antiquity. The cock was supposed by some to remind the clergy of watchfulness (Du Cange, Gloss.); others think it had reference to the cock's crowing when St. Peter denied his Lord; and another reason for the adoption of this form of vane is this: "The manner of adorning the tops of steeples with a cross and a cock is derived from the Goths, who bore that as their warlike ensign." (Minute Book of the Soc. of Antiq., I. 105.)

1558.

(1) This is the only occurrence of an assessment in the churchwardens accounts.

1559.

(1) "obligacon" = an agreement.

1560.

(1) The rood loft was pulled down and sold this year. Other items follow this relating to the sale by the churchwardens of iron and old materials, all belonging to the rood loft.

(2) The Paraphrase of Erasmus was ordered to be set up in every parish church in order to assist the unlearned in the interpretation of Scripture.

NOTE.—At the foot of this account is written "Colect^r for y^e heyghwaye," but no name is added.

1561.

(1) The chapel mentioned here, and in 1545 and 1548, was probably either the Chantry Chapel or the chapel of St. Paul within the castle.

(2) Queen Elizabeth. Possibly on her way to little Hadham Hall.

1562.

(1) "Pytell" = a small enclosure.

1563.

(1) The Second Book of Homilies. The most important editions of the Homilies are:

First Book, first edition, 1547, last of July, I. Edward VI.
Second, divided as at present, 1549, August.
Second Book, 1st 1563. That on Wilful Rebellion was added 1571.
Last, by authority, 1623.

1564.

(1) This item is the first instance in these accounts of payment for tolling a bell at the death or burial of a parishioner. [For information regarding the passing bell, or "soul bell," read Brand's "Pop. Antiq.," ii. 202.]

(2) See note (1) 1560.

1565.

(1) Questmen = sidesmen.

1566.

(1) The following extracts are from the churchwardens' accounts of the parish of St. Peter, Cheapside, London:

1564. Item payde for foure prayer bookes against the turke . iiij$d$.
    Item pd for three bookes of thankesgevinge for the turkes ou'throw . . . . . vj$d$.
1565. Pd for ij prayer bookes ag^t the Turke . . . iiij$d$.
1571. Geven to the Ringers for the victorye over the Turk and at the thawght of the queenes ma^{ties} reigne . xvj$d$.

From the accounts of the churchwardens of St. Matthews, Friday Street, London:

156$\frac{5}{6}$. Item pd for to praier bocks against y^e turke . . iiij$d$.

1567.

(1) Edward Parker, Lord Morley, great-grandson and heir of Henry (Parker) Lord Morley, was one of the peers who pronounced judgement of death on Mary, Queen of Scots, at Foderinghay on January 16th, anno 29 Elizabeth, on Phillip, Earl of Arundel, anno 32 Elizabeth, and on Robert, Earl of Essex,

anno 43 Elizabeth. William Lord Morley, and Monteagle, his son, in the third of James I. (bearing then in his father's lifetime the title of Lord Monteagle only), discovered the plot by which the King and Parliament were intended to be assassinated on the 5th of November. Lord Morley resided at Hallingbury Place, at present the seat of John Archer Houblon, esq.

1570.

(1) See note (1) 1563.

(2) This word is probably intended for "monuments," as Foxe's "Monuments" was one of those books that were specially ordered to be chained in parish churches.

1573.

(1) Previous to the Reformation this church must have possessed some very fine stained glass. Sir H. Chauncy gives a description of some remnants existing in his time.

1574.

(1) I am told that there was formerly a well at the north east angle of the church yard.

1575.

(1) Query, is this the house which was afterwards known as the Cock-pit House, and which formerly stood on the south side of Taintor Hill, near the top?

(2) St. Hugh's Day, November 17th, was afterwards (1679) celebrated as Queen Elizabeth's Day [see "Book of Days," ii. 588.]

1576.

(1) See note (1) 1622.

1578.

(1) At this period Little Hadham Hall was a seat of the Capell family.

(2) In a previous year there is an item "for painting Jack vj*d*." I suppose this means a jack for the chimes; see also 1583.

1579 or 1580.

(1) The earthquake here referred to occurred on the evening of Easter Wednesday (April 6th), 1580. "The great Clock at Westminster struck at the shock and the bells, of the various churches were set jangling. The people rushed out of the Theatres."

This earthquake was felt pretty generally throughout the kingdom, and was the cause of much damage in Kent. So alarmed were all classes that Queen Elizabeth thought it advisable to cause a form of prayer to be used by all householders with their whole family every evening before going to bed.

(2) This, I imagine, is what is called, in a former account, the "school loft."

1581.

(1) The fashion of employing hour-glasses in churches was chiefly introduced after the Reformation, when long sermons became the order of the day. Previous to that period pulpit discourses appear to have been generally characterised by brevity. They lingered in country churches, but ceased to be in anything like general use after the Restoration.

(2) This item, I imagine, refers to the making of a book similar to that called "Ye Churchwardens' Booke, 1642." These books appear to have been made almost every year, and it is therefore somewhat strange that only one should now be found among the parish papers.

1582.

(1) This year the town was visited with the plague. The sickness com-

menced about the middle of June, 1582, and lasted until the following March. The following extract from the Parish Register will give an idea of the death-rate at this period :

In 1579 (reckoning O.S. from March to March) the number of burials registered was 14.

In 1580	,,	,,	,,	was 20
In 1581	,,	,,	,,	,, 19
In 1582	,,	,,	,,	,, 94

Out of the 94 who were buried in 1582, 66 died of the plague.

1583.
(1) See note (2) 1578, and items in 1590 and 1592.

1586.
(1) See note (6) 1547.
(2) The book of articles were the usual episcopal inquiries with which the churchwardens needed to provide themselves for the visitations.

1587.
(1) From the churchwardens' accounts of St. Matthew, Friday Street, London.

1588-9. Pd. for a proklemasson of wayghts with a bord to put it on. . x*d*. From the churchwardens' accounts of St. Peter Cheap, London :

1589. Item for a proclamacōn concerninge waights to be sette in the churche . . . . vj*d*.
See also the item in 1602.

1588.
(1) These items refer to the defeat of the Spanish Armada, which took place in July, 1588.

1589.
(1) I have examined the entries in the Burial Register for this year, and it does not appear that there was a visitation of sickness, the number of deaths being about the same as the previous and subsequent years. The "tyme of ye trouble" possibly refers to a time of scarcity.

1590.
(1) The King here referred to was Henry IV. (Henry of Navarre, who succeeded to the throne after the assassination of Henry III.), and the fact that in 1590 Queen Elizabeth sent him £22,000 and 4,000 men under Lord Willoughby to assist him in fighting against the "League," will, I think, sufficiently explain why his "good successe" was prayed for.

1598.
(1) This is the Parish Register which is still in the church ; and the baptisms, marriages and burials were now copied into it ; the earliest entry is in 1561.

1601.
(1) Tanning seems to have been carried on in Water Lane in 1482, and the tannery continued for several generations in the Jardfield family. This is the first time I find any allusion to malting in these accounts; the word after malt I have been unable to decipher satisfactorily, but it looks like " ck (or l) oss (or h) e."

(2) In 1601 was passed the second Compulsory Poor Law.
"Justices to assess all dwellings ; churchwardens and overseers to provide work, build poor-houses, and apprentice paupers." This Act extended to the time of William IV, 1834.

(3) Edward Stanhope, LL.D., was Prebend of Cantlers in St. Paul's Cathedral in 1591. He was Chancellor to the Bishop of London and Vicar-General to the Archbishop of Canterbury.

1602.
(1) See note 1587.

1603.
(1) James I. was crowned on July 25, St. James's Day. Queen Elizabeth died on March 24, 1603.
(2) This item probably refers to a brief for the relief of some distress in Geneva.
(3) It would appear from these items that assizes were at this period occasionally held at Stortford.

1611.
NOTE.—The reckoning this year is from Easter Monday to Easter Monday, and the account is this year signed by twenty-five parishioners.

1612.
(1) The Bible purchased this year would be the authorised version which was published in 1611.

1614.
(1) The 5th of August was at this time observed as a holiday in England to commemorate the escape of King James (then King of Scotland only) from the Gowrie Conspiracy.
(2) Skull-hole, probably another name for Bone-House.

1619.
(1) A letter of request was simply a license to solicit alms or relief; other terms are also used implying the same permission, as in the following extracts from the accounts of the churchwardens of Ryton, near Coventry:

1618. Item given to a minister wh his patente for fyre on the weke day about St. Andrew's tyde	5*d*.
1619. Item layd downe to a brieffe for a Darbyshyre man . .	iij*d*.
1619. Item to a poore woman with a passe about ye same tyme .	ij*d*.
1629. Item to a Scottish marchand with a license . .	iiij*d*.

These licenses, etc., were granted in accordance with an Act passed in 1530, 22 Henry VIII. c. 12, which enabled justices to grant licenses to impotent persons allowing them to beg within certain limits, and if found begging out of their limits they were to be set in the stocks. All persons able to labour who begged or were vagrant were to be whipped and sent to the place of their birth.
(2) Probably the house which covered the clock.

1622.
(1) The Bill of presentments was probably a report to the full vestry of the way in which the duties to be done by the parishioners, and which the respective officers had each under his particular charge, had been fulfilled during the past year. The churchwardens were also empowered to make a presentment as to the character of the minister and the mode in which he performed his duties.

1623.
(1) This, I imagine, means the degrees of affinity.
(2) This probably refers to the return of the Prince of Wales (Charles I.) from the continent, where he and Buckingham had this year been travelling under the names of John and Thomas Smith.

1625.

(1) Charles I. succeeded to the throne March 27th, 1625.

(2) The plague this year compelled Parliament to remove from Westminster to Oxford; 35,417 persons died in London. I have examined the entries in the Burial Register for this year, but it does not appear that the visitation extended to Stortford.

1629.

(1) The minister and churchwardens were bound by law to send a copy of the christenings, marriages and burials to the Bishop of the diocese, or his chancellor, within a month after the 25th of March. For further information regarding "Bishops Transcripts" read Burn's "History of Parish Registers."

1630.

(1) Probably Mr. Henry Glascock of Hertishobury or Hassobury, Farnham, County Essex. In 1625 this rent was paid by a Mr. Angell of London.

(2) John Dane, by deed dated 21st of July, 1630, in consideration of the parish having been at great charge in relieving Margaret his mother-in-law, the wife of Thomas Bowyer, after the death of her husband, etc., conveyed a parcel of ground taken out of a great yard belonging to John Dane, with a heremail there, or booth, and half part of a well lying in Hockerill Street, for the benefit of the chief inhabitants of this parish for ever.

1631.

(1) William Laud, afterwards Archbishop of Canterbury.

1633.

(1) These items probably refer to "Faculty Pews," of which I am told there were three in this church. A Mr. Butler was instituted vicar here in 1632.

(2) This was the "Book of Sports," which was this year again ordered to be read by the clergy in their churches.

1634..

(1) Sir H. Chauncy says that Maplecross was on the south of the town.

(2) I presume that the chancellor of the Bishop of London is meant here. His name was Thomas Turner, S.I.B.; he was collated to the office Oct. 29, 1629, and died Oct. 8, 1672, aged 81. He was domestic chaplain to Archbishop Laud, Chaplain to the King, and Dean of Canterbury.

1635.

(1) The Palsgrave here referred to was Charles Lodowick, the Prince Palatine, who came to England this year. For information as to the object of his visit read Aikin's "Charles I.," i. ch. xi. He probably passed through Stortford, and the bells were rung in his honour.

(2) As there is no item in the account for this year showing that the window itself was enlarged, the inference is that some of the old stained glass was removed and replaced by new plain glass.

1640.

(1) "On Saturday the 24th of November, 1640, a proclamation was put forth for a general fast to be held in this part the 17th of this instant, November, and elsewhere upon the 8th of December."

[Historical notices of the reign of Charles I. by Nehemiah Wallington.]

NOTE.—One of the sidesmen this year was "John Gladwin of Dane-at-Coyves."

1641.

(1) On the 3rd of May, 1641, the House finding that there have been and having cause to suspect that there still are, even during the sittings of Parliament, endeavours made to subvert the fundamental laws of England and

Ireland . . . . . . whereupon the subjects have been prosecuted and grieved, and that divers innovations have been brought into the church, multitudes driven out of his Majesty's dominions, jealousies created between the king and his people, and a Popish army levied in Ireland, and two armies brought into the bowels of the kingdom, and that endeavours have been and are used to bring the English army into misunderstanding of this Parliament, thereby to incline that army by force to bring to pass those wicked counsels, adopt the following form of protestation :

"I, A. B., do in the presence of Almighty God, promise, vow, and protest to maintain and to defend as I lawfully may, with my life, power, and estate, the true Reformed religion, expressed in the doctrine of the Church of England, against all Popery and Popish innovation within this realm, contrary to the said doctrine ; and, according to the duty of my allegiance, I will maintain and defend his Majesty's royal person, honour, and estate, also the power and privilege of Parliament, the lawful rights and liberties of the subjects, and every person that shall make this protestation, in whatsoever he shall do in the lawful performance of the same ; and to my power, as far as lawfully I may, I will oppose, and by all good ways and means endeavour to bring condign punishment on all such as shall by force, practices, counsels, plots, conspiracies, or otherwise, do anything to the contrary in this present protestation contained. And further that I shall in all just and honourable ways endeavour to preserve the union and peace between the three kingdoms of England, Scotland, and Ireland ; and neither for hope, fear, or any other respect shall relinquish this promise, vow, and protestation."

This protestation was immediately taken by all the members of the House then present, and the next day it was sent up to the House of Lords, where it was also taken by all who were present, with only two exceptions. It was afterwards taken very generally by the absentees of either House. On the 5th this protestation was sent down into all the counties, with an intimation that it would be agreeable to the House if it were also taken by all corporations, sheriffs, and justices of the peace. Directions were also given that it should be also submitted to the ministers and inhabitants of the different parishes, to whom it should be read "on the afternoon of some Lord's Day after sermon ;" and that "there be a register book provided in which every man taking it should subscribe his name, and that the names be taken of such as do refuse the same." Several of the Parish Registers of Essex contain this "protestation," together with the signatures of the minister and the parishioners appended to it.

[David's "Annals of Evangelical Nonconformity in Essex," p. 193.]

1642.

(1) I am not certain what this item means, but it may have some reference to the "protestation" or the Popish army levied in Ireland.

1643.

(1) I think there is very little doubt that the items marked A in 1641-42-43 relate to the destruction or removal of the stained glass and brasses with the so-called "Popish inscriptions or images." At this period very many of our fine old parish churches were thoroughly despoiled of everything in the shape of a cross, stained glass, or brasses with such inscriptions as "Orate pro anima," etc., by ignorant zealots, who went about the country doing this work only too well. The following extract from Burn's "History of Parish Registers," p. 101, will perhaps best illustrate the character of these men and their work :

"Dr. Berwick, in his 'Querela Cantabrigiensis,' notices one of these zealots.

" 'One who calls himself John' (it should be William) 'Dowsing, and by virtue of a pretended Commission, goes about ye country, like a Bedlam, breaking glasse windows, having battered and beaten downe all our painted glasse, not only in our chappels, but (contrary to order) in our Publique Schools, Colledge Halls, Libraries, and Chambers, mistaking, perhaps, y*e* liberall Artes for Saints (which they intend in time to pull down too), and having (against an order) defaced and digged up y*e* floors of our Chappels, many of which had lien so for two or three hundred years together, not regarding y*e* dust of our founders and predecessors, who likely were buried there; compelled us by armed souldiers to pay forty shillings a Colledge for not mending what he had spoyled and defaced, or forthwith to goe to prison.'"

In the churchwardens' accounts of Walberswich, Suffolk is:

1644. April 8. Paid to Master Dowson that came with the troopers to our church, about the taking down of Images and Brasses off Stones	. . . . .	0 6 0
1644. Paid that day to others for taking up the brasses of grave stones before the officer Dowson came	. . . .	0 1 0

This William Dowsing, it appears, kept a journal of his ecclesiastical exploits. With reference to the church of Toffe, he says:

"Will. Disborough, Churchwarden, Richard Basly, and John Newman, Cunstable, 27 Superstitious pictures in glass and ten other in stone, three brass inscriptions, Pray for y*e* Soules, and a Cross to be taken of the Steeple (6*s*. 8*d*.), and there was divers Orate pro Animabus in y*e* windows, and on a bell, Ora pro Anima Sanctæ Catharinæ.

"Trinity Parish, Cambridge, M. Frog, Churchwarden. December 25 we brake down 80 Popish pictures, and one of Christ and God y*e* Father above."

"At Clare we brake down 1,000 pictures superstitious."

"Cochie, there were divers pictures in the windows which we could not reach, neither would they help us to raise the ladders.

"1643. Jan. 1. Edward's parish, we digged up the steps, and brake down 40 pictures, and took off 10 superstitious inscriptions."

Mr. Cole, in his MSS., observes:

"From this last entry we may clearly see to whom we are obliged for the dismantling of almost all the grave stones that had brasses on them, both in town and country; a sacrilegious sanctified rascal, that was afraid, or too proud to call it St. Edward's Church, but not ashamed to rob the dead of their honours, and the church of its ornaments.—W. C."

"Lowestoft (1644). In the same year also, on the 12th of June, there came one Jessop, with a commission from the Earl of Manchester, to take away from gravestones all inscriptions on which he found Orate pro Anima—a wretched commissioner, not able to read or find out that which his commission enjoyned him to remove, he took up in one church so much brasse, as he sold to Mr. Josiah Wild for five shillings, which was afterwards (contrary to my knowledge) runn into the little bell that hangs in the Town House. There were taken up in the middle Ayl twelve pieces belonging to twelve generations of the Jettours."

It is not to be wondered at that Mr. Cole's wrath should be kindled against this individual, who left in Mr. Cole's native county so many marks of his devastating presence, and more especially, as monuments, etc., for the dead were excepted in the Act under which this Wm. Dowsing claimed to derive his authority. In that year (1643) one of the Bills proposed to King Charles at Oxford by the Lords and Commons enacts:

"That all altars and rails be taken away out of Churches and Chapels before April 18, 1643, and that the Communion-Table be fixed in some convenient part in the Body of the Church. That all Tapers, Candlesticks, Basons, Crucifixes, Crosses, Images, Pictures of Saints, and superstitious inscriptions in Churches or Churchyards be taken away or defaced. This is not to extend to any Image, Picture, or Monument for the Dead."—[Burn's "Parish Registers."]

The officer of the Earl of Manchester mentioned in this item, if not the notorious Dowsing himself, was another officer appointed to see carried out here a destruction similar to that which took place in the County of Suffolk.

1644.

NOTE.—At the foot of this account is written:

"Md. that the 9th day of ffebruary, 1647, Thomas Kinge hath pd. to Willm. Reade the elder, one of the Collectors for the poore, according to the order of Sir John Gore and Mr. Scroggs, the Remaynder of the Stocke he had in his hand to sett the poore on worke the sume of v*li.* iiij*s.* vij*d. ob.*, wch wth the sume above allowed him makes up the full sume of xij*li.* and v*s.* wch he had of the Stocke.

Wm. M Reade.

"Witnes hereto me, Tho. Barnard."

NOTE.—Since the year 1561 the names of the Parishioners elected to fill the Offices of Churchwardens, Sidesmen, and Surveyors of the Highways for the ensuing year, have been written at the foot of the accounts. This year's account contains, in addition to the above, the appointment of constables, collectors for the poor, collectors of the market house rents, and leather sealers. Four parishioners are also nominated to receive the town stock.

1647.

(1) It is little to be wondered at that there are so many errors of omission and commission in our old parish registers, when we find that a period of nineteen years is allowed to pass before the memoranda of the various christenings, marriages, and deaths are entered into the parchment book.

1648.

(1) The arithmetic of the churchwardens is a little faulty here.

(2) During the Civil War it was by no means an uncommon thing for soldiers to be quartered in churches. The soldiers here referred to were possibly a portion of Cromwell's army from Walden, on the march to London.

NOTE.—The houses in the churchyard appear at this time, and for some years past, to have been let out in rooms or chambers, generally to widows.

1649.

(1) See Note (1), 1647.

1654.

(1) From 1652 to 1656 a large number of poor and distressed persons were relieved by the churchwardens here; in 1655 the greater number of recipients were "women w^h came out of Ireland."

From a note at the foot of this year's account, it appears that the late churchwarden delivered up to his successor (?) "3 . . . of bucketts, 2 flaggons, a communion cup, and the grene cloth, and a dyaper coverlid."

1680.

(1) This is the house in the market square at present (1881) the residence of Mr. A. Rushall.

(2) See note (10).

(3) This house, I presume, stood upon the site now occupied by the Plume of Feathers Inn.

(4) Fockinghams stood in Basbow Lane. The house was pulled down a few years ago by the owner, Mr. G. E. Sworder.

(5) See note (4) 1515.

(6) Paradise was the name of a piece of ground on the south of Apton Field.

(7) Sextons Mead was the name of a field neartheend of Dane Street, or (as it was lately called) Dell Lane. This field was purchased by the railway company.

(8) Chalkcroft is a field between the "Cricket-field Lane" and the rifle butts.

(9) Comon Down is to the north of the road leading from Stortford to Farnham.

(10) This Mrs. Aynsworth was the notorious "Betty Aynsworth," landlady of the Reindeer Inn which stood at the corner of the High Street, on the site now occupied by the house of Mr. Robert Cole. Her character will be best illustrated by the following extract from the diary of Samuel Pepys:

"1667, Oct. 7. . . . So we to Enfield, and there bayted, it being but a foul, bad day, and there Lowther and Mr. Burford, an acquaintance of his, did overtake us, and there drank and eat together; and by-and-by we parted, we going before them, and very merry, my wife and girl talking, and telling tales, and singing, and before night come to Bishop Stafford, where Lowther and his friend did meet us again, and carried us to the Rayne-deere, where Mrs. Aynsworth, who lived heretofore at Cambridge, and whom I knew better than they think for, do live. It was the woman that among other things was great with my cozen Barnston of Cottenham, and did use to sing to him, and did teach me. 'Full forty times over,' a very lewd song; a woman they are well acquainted with, and is here what she was at Cambridge, and all the good fellows of the country come hither. Lowther and his friend staid and drank, and then went further this night; but here we stayed, and supped and lodged . . . . so that being done, and my mind at ease, we to supper, and so to bed, my wife and I in one bed and the girl in another, in the same room, and lay very well, but there was so much tearing company in the house that we could not see the landlady, so I had no opportunity of renewing my old acquaintance with her."

"1668, May 23rd. Up by four o'clock, and getting my things ready, and recommending the care of my house to W. Hewer, I with my boy Tom, whom I take with me to the Bull in Bishopsgate Street, and there, about six, took coach, he and I and a gentleman and his man, there being another coach also with as many more in it; and so away to Bishop's Stafford. Dined and changed horses and coach, at Mrs. Aynsworth's; but I took no knowledge of her. To dinner, and in comes Captain Forster, that do belong to my Lord Anglesey, who had been at the late horse-races at Newmarket, where the King now is, and says that they had fair weather there yesterday, though we here and at London had nothing but rain, insomuch that the ways are mighty full of water, so as hardly to be passed. I hear Mrs. Aynsworth is going to live at London; but, I believe, will be mistaken in it, for it will be found better for her to be chief where she is than to have little to do at London."

Lord Braybrooke in a note says:

"Elizabeth Aynsworth, here mentioned, was a noted Procuress at Cambridge, banished from that town by the University authorities for her evil courses. She subsequently kept the Rein Deer Inn at Bishop's Stortford, at which the Vice-Chancellor and some of the heads of Colleges had occasion to sleep, in their way to London, and were nobly entertained, their supper being served off plate. The next morning their hostess refused to make any charge, saying that she was still indebted to the Vice-Chancellor, who by driving her out of Cambridge had made her fortune. No tradition of this woman has been preserved at Bishop's Stortford; but it appears from the register of that parish that she was buried there 26th March, 1686. It is recorded in the History of Essex, iii. 130, 8vo., 1770, and in a pamphlet in the British Museum entitled 'Boteler's Case,' that she was implicated in the murder of Captain Wood, a Hertfordshire gentleman, at Mannden, in Essex, and for which offence a person named Boteler was executed at Chelmsford 10th Sept., 1667, and that Mrs. Aynsworth, tried at the same time as an accessory before the fact, was acquitted for want of evidence; though in her way to the jail she endeavoured to throw herself into the river, but was prevented."

["Diary and Correspondence of Samuel Pepys" by Richard Lord Braybrooke.]

1684.

(1) The house formerly known as the "Dog's Head in the Pot," is still standing in the Market Square in rear of the Corn Exchange. Modern signpainters have, however, robbed the dog of his pot.

(2) That is, for those of the parishioners who went "beating the bounds" of the parish.

(3) See the account for the destruction of vermin.

1685.

(1) It would appear from this item that in beating the bounds of the parish it was necessary for the procession, or "possessioning" party to pass through the house, garden, or premises of a Mr. Waynckford, and that on these occasions it was customary for the churchwardens to "tip" his maid. Mr. Thomas Slater informs me that he remembers as a boy going round the bounds of the parish, and that in so doing they passed through Wickham Hall, one of the rooms there being partly in Farnham and partly in Stortford parish. Possibly Mr. Waynckford occupied Wickham Hall in 1685.

(2) The "chimney men"=the men who collected the hearth tax.

(3) The Duke of Monmouth, who headed the rebellion in the south of England.

(4) The scholars mentioned here were probably scholars of the Stortford school.

1688.

(1) This no doubt refers to the second "Declaration of Indulgence," which was ordered by James II. to be read in all churches on the two Sundays, May 20 and 27.

(2) The prince mentioned here is James Francis Edward, the son of James II. He was born on June 10, 1688, but as news travelled slowly in these times, it is not to be wondered at that the bells of Stortford were not rung until the 12th.

1696.

(1) Most probably this was the yew-tree, which is now standing on the south side of the church. It is supposed that yew-trees were originally planted in churchyards to secure the trees from the cattle, and thus preserve them for the encouragement of archery.

1698.

(1) Horseman Ditch was a piece of ground lying next the vicarage yard, containing one rood.

(2) The Bishop of London appointed a bailiff for his manor here.

1703.

(1) The great storm of 1703 was a violent hurricane of a week's duration; it reached its height on the morning of Saturday, November 27. For an account of its ravages, see Chambers's "Book of Days," ii. 622.

1713.

(1) See the decree of the Court of Chancery.

1718.

(1) From these items it would appear that the open timbered roof was this year ceiled. At this period in the history of architecture, this kind of work was know as "beautyfying." See the item in 1710.

1743.

(1) See note, 1685.

THE VICARS AND CHURCHWARDENS OF ST. MICHAEL'S.

THE VICARS.

Names.   Date of Institution.

John De Strathern, Aug. 31, 1332.
Richard ac Brugg, Nov. 5, 1361.
Nicholas Germain, Oct. 24, 1409, upon the death of Richard ac Brugg.
John Wryght.
Henry Alderby, July 6, 1426, upon resig. of John Wright.
William Wodehall, Oct. 13, 1443, upon resig. of Henry Alderby.
John Snoring.
John Palmer, Nov. 17, 1447, upon dec. of John Snoring.
John Elwyne, Nov. 10, 1454, upon resig. of John Palmer.
John Isaac, May 8, 1472, upon dec. of John Elwyne.
Walter Nywton, June 18, 1476, upon resig. of John Isaac.
William London, B.D., May 16, 1482, upon resig. of Walter Nywton.
Thomas Saunte, D.D., Sep. 8, 1494, upon resig. William London.
Nicholas Townley, March 7, 1513, upon dec. of Thomas Saunte.
Richard Betynson.
Richard Fletcher, Clk., June 19, 1551, upon resig. of Richard Betynson.
John Bartlett, Clk., Feb. 23, 1555, upon the preferment of Richard Fletcher.
Thomas Sympson, Clk., March 5, 1560, upon removal of John Bartlett.
John Gravett, M.A., Jan. 12, 1571, upon resig. of Thomas Sympson.
Jonas Jerdfeld, June 23, 1575, upon resig. of John Gravett.
John Cory, Clk., Aug. 10, 1580, upon resig. of Jonas Jerdfeld.
John Lane, Clk., March 1, 1581, upon resig. of John Cory.
John Bishop, M.A., June 6, 1583, upon dec. of John Lane.
David Sandye, 1586, upon resig. of John Bishop.
Francis Burlye, Clk., June 13, 1590, upon dec. of David Sandye.
William Bendish, S.T.B., Dec. 8, 1604, upon resig. of Francis Burlye.

Thomas Bendish, M.A., Nov. 1, 1616, upon cession of William Bendish.
Richard Butler, M.A., Jan. 24, 1632, upon dec. of Thomas Bendish.
———— Fish.
Jonathan Paine.
Nathaniel Crowcher, Clk., Sept. 13, 1662, by the removal of the last Vicar.
Thomas Leigh, S.T.B., Oct. 9, 1680, upon dec. of Nathaniel Crowcher.
Christopher Cooper, M.A., March 11, 1686, upon dec. of Thomas Leigh.
William Polhill, M.A., June 13, 1698, upon dec. of Christopher Cooper.
Robert Styleman, Clk., LL.B., June 5, 1722, upon dec. of William Polhill.
William Jackson, Clk., M.A., Jan. 9, 1749, upon dec. of Robert Styleman.
Richard Hind, D.D., May 17, 1754, by cession of William Jackson.
Edmund Gibson, Clk., May 27, 1766, upon resig. of Rich. Hind.
Plaxton Dickenson, Clk., March 20, 1798., upon dec. of Edmund Gibson.
Raymond-Edward-Lorance-Rogers, B.A., Jan. 20, 1799, upon dec. of P. Dickenson.
Charles Spencer, M.A., Jan. 31, 1817, upon dec. of R. E. L. Rogers.
Francis William Rhodes, M.A., June 15, 1849, upon dec. of C. Spencer.
George Smith Bayne, M.A., Nov. 17, 1876, upon dec. of F. W. Rhodes.

————

THE CHURCHWARDENS.

1430. Thomas Pygeon.
John Clapton.
1431 John Wolverston.
to 1440. John Busch.
1482. J. Jardewill the young^r.
John Grace.
1483. John Grace.
Wm. Schepperd.
1491. John Setcok.
John Marian.
1494. John Jenyns.
John Sadde.
1496. John Jenyns.
John Sadde.

1499. Jo. Wood.
Jo. Davy.
1500. Richard Jardevyll.
John Bussh.
1502. Robert Bardney.
John Marchant.
1503. Robt. Bardney.
Jo. Marchant.
1504. Richard Pelham.
William Crowe.
1505. Thomas Jocelyn.
Thomas Crabbe.
1507. Rob. Bardney.
Ric. Newman.

CHURCHWARDENS.

1498. Thos. Josselyn.
Jo. Davy.
1510. Ric. Jardefeld.
And. Clifton.
1513. Jo. Payne.
Nic. Redwood.
1514. Jo. Payne.
Wm. Bardney.
1515. Wm. Bardney.
Tho. Papys.
1516. Thomas Papis.
Thomas Jegon.
1517. Thomas Jegon.
William Abbot.
1518. John Josselyn.
Wm. Abbott.
1519. Jo. Josselyn.
Jo. Hawkyn.
1520. Jo. Hawkyn.
Rob. Barnard.
1521. Robt. Barnard.
Thos. Chaundeler.
1522. Thos. Chaundeler.
John Newman.
1523. J. Newman.
Nic. Redwood.
1524. J. Newman.
Nic. Redwood.
1525. Nic Redwood.
John Wylley.
1526. John Wylley.
Ric. Glascok.
1527. Ric. Glascok.
Ric. Jardefeld.
1528. Ric. Jardefeld.
Jo. Jacob.
1529. Jo. Jacob.
Jo. Alys.
1530. Jo. Jacob.
Jo. Alys.
1531. Jo. Jacob.
Jo. Alys.
1532. John Jacobbe.
John Hawkyn.
1533. John Hawkyn.
John Maryon.

1509. Thos. Whepill.
Thos. Josselyn.
1536. Thomas Chandeler.
John Smyth.
1537. John Smyth.
Ric. Jardefeld.
1538. Ric. Jardefeld.
John Dowsehed.
1539. Ric. Jardevyle.
Ric. Glascok.
1540. Ric. Glascok.
Matt. Calyday.
1543. John Wylley.
Mat. Calyday.
1546. T. Chandeler.
J. Bayford.
1547. Jo. Bayford.
Edw. Wylley.
1548. Thos. Chaundeler.
1549. Edw. Wylley.
1553. Jo. Smyth.
Tho. Chandler.
1554. John Cheny.
Thomas Snowe.
1556. Thomas Snowe.
Thomas Crabbe.
1557. Thomas Crabbe.
Robt. Goodaye.
1558. Robt. Goodaye.
Thomas Crabbe.
1559. Richard Bedwell.
George Jacob.
1560. George Jacob.
William Miller.
1561. George Jacob.
William Miller.
1562. George Jacob.
Thomas Chandler.
1563. Thomas Chaundler.
Henry Parsley.
1564. Henry Parsley.
George Hawkyn.
1565. George Hawkyn.
Ralfe Clarke.
1566. Thomas Parsons, Esq.
George Hawkyn.

CHURCHWARDENS.

1567. Thomas Parsons, Esq.
Jo. Parsmith, alias Cheny.
1568. Jo. Passmith, alias Cheny.
Wm. Barnard.
1569. Thomas Crabbe.
Willm. Barnard.
1570. Thos. Crabb.
Jo. Myller.
1571. John Miller.
William Pylston.
1572. William Pylston.
Thomas Wilsemer.
1573. Edward Hake.
Thomas Wylsemer.
1574. Thomas Chaundeler.
Edward Gybson.
1575. Edward Gybson.
William Brett.
1576. William Bret.
John Jardfeld.
1577. John Jardfeld.
John Gate.
1578. John Gate.
William Barnard.
1579. William Snow.
William Barnard.
1581. Henry Parsley.
William Snow.
1582. John Gybbe, gent.
Henry Parsley.
1583. John Gybbe, gent.
Thomas Jernegan.
1584. Thomas Jernegan.
John Skyngell.
1585. John Skyngell.
William Barnard.
1586. William Barnard.
Phillip Mountjoy.
1587. Phillip Mountjoy.
John Gace.
1588. Phillip Mountjoy.
John Gace.
1589. John Gace.
John Gates.
1590. John Gates.
William Barnard.

1591. William Barnard.
John Myller.
1592. John Myller.
George Hawkyn.
1595. George Jacobbe.
John Gates.
1596. John Gate.
Thomas Myller.
1598. Tobias Chaundeler.
Thomas Jennynge.
1600. John Melles.
John Bull.
1601. John Bull.
Robert Colt.
1602. Robert Colte.
Thomas Tendering.
1603. Thomas Tendering.
Abraham Warde.
1604. John Smyth.
Abraham Warde.
1606 (?). Frauncis Abell.
William Dennyson.
1608. George Abbott.
Thomas Barnard.
1609. Thomas Barnard.
Thomas Jennyngs.
1610. Thomas Jennyngs.
Thomas Miller.
1611. Thomas Miller.
John Miller.
1612. Robt. Colte.
Robt. Bowycre.
1614. Robt. Colte.
Edward Chandeler.
1616. William Dixon.
Thomas Jennyngs.
1617. Thomas Jennyngs.
Thomas Tydie.
1618. Thomas Tydie.
John Mathewe.
1619. John Mathewe.
John Gibbs.
1620. John Gibbs.
John Parseley.
1621. Thomas Crabb.
John Parseley.

8

1622. Thomas Crabbe.
       Thomas Jennyngs.
1623. Thomas Jennyngs.
       John Miller, junr.
1624. John Miller.
       George Jacob.
1625. George Jacob.
       George Hawkin.
1626. George Hawkin.
       William Ellis.
1627. William Ellis.
       John Ramsey.
1628. John Ramsey.
       Thomas Mowton.
1629. Thomas Mowton.
       Thomas Barnard.
1630. Thomas Barnard.
       John Bull, the elder.
1631. John Bull.
       Robert Colt.
1632. Leonard Knight.
       George Denyson.
1633. George Denyson.
       Robert Bowyere.
1634. George Denyson.
       Robert Bowyere.
1635. George Denyson.
       Robert Ffreemam.
1636. Robert Ffreeman.
       John Miller.
1637. John Miller.
       John Chandler.
1638. John Chandler.
       Thomas Jennyngs.
1639. Thomas Jennyngs.
       Mr. Aylmer.
1640. Mr. Aylmer.
       William Barnard.
1641. William Barnard.
       Ralfe Bull.
1642. William Barnard.
       Ralfe Bull.
1643. Ralph Bull.
       Thomas Kinge.
1644. Thomas King.
       William Holgate.

1645. William Holgate.
       William Reade the elder.
1647. Thomas Barnard.
       Thomas Stevens.
1648. Thomas Stevens.
       George Denyson.
1649. George Denyson.
       John Scott.
1650. John Scott.
       John Bull.
1651. John Bull.
       Edward Hawkins.
1652. Edward Hawkins.
       John Jacklin.
1653. John Jacklin.
       John Ashbie.
1654. John Ashbie.
       William Palmer.
1655. William Palmer.
       Leonard Knight.
1656. Leonard Knight.
       William Read, junr.
1657. William Read, junr.
       Ralph Manester.
1658. Ralph Manistey.
       Ralph Bull.
1661. Ralph Bull.
       Humphrey Dixon.
1680 to 1682. Edward Maplesden.
       Robert Lay.
1683. Robert Lay.
       Thomas Barnard.
1684 and 1685. Thomas Barnard.
       Simon Rutland.
1686 and 1687. Simon Rutland.
       Edward Bayford.
1688. Edward Bayford.
       William Sanders.
1692. Samuell Jocelyn.
       William Bayford.
1696. Thomas Clayton, senr.
       Samuel Bayford.

CHURCHWARDENS.

1698. Geo. Chandler.
      Ed. Ashby.
1699. Edward Ashby.
      John Jennens.
1700. John Jennens.
1701. John Taverner.
      Matthew Game.
1703. Wm. Saunders.
      Thomas Barnard.
1704. Thomas Barnard.
1706. John Carter.
1709. Thomas Wheatly.
1710. Samuel Bayford.
      Nicholas Tyler.
1712. John Green.
      Thomas Clayton.
1713. Thomas Clayton.
      Thomas Scott.
1714 and 1715. Thomas Scott.
              Christopher Webb.
1716 and 1717. Christopher Webb.
              John Wood.
1718. John Wood.
      John Rose.
1719. John Rose.
      Henry Barns.
1720. Henry Barnes.
      Richard Osborne.
1721. Jeffery Archer.
1722. Jeff. Archer.
      Tho. Fowle.
1723. Jonathan Carter.
1724. Jonathan Carter.
      John Rous.
1725. Sheffield Warren, Baker.
1726. Sheff. Warren.
      Jno. Reynolds.
1727 and Roger Boltwood.
        Jno. Reynolds.
1728. Wm. Speeringe (in the place of Jno. Reynolds, dec^d.

1729 and 1730. Thomas Mott.
              Wm. Speeringe.
1731. Tho. Mott.
      Jno. Boultwood.
1732. Samuel Taylor, Malster.
      John Boultwood.
1733. Saml. Taylor.
      Arthur Wankford.
1734 and 1735. Samuel Taylor.
              Henry Robinson.
1736. Samuel Bayford.
1737. John Cole.
      Samuel Bayford.
1738. Edward Juby.
      John Cole.
1739. Edward Juby.
      Wm. Fairchild.
1740. Wm. Fairchild.
      Fitch Lea Wood.
1741. Wm. Hitchin, senr.
      Wm. Fairchild.
1742. Wm. Hitchin.
      Fitch Lea Wood.
1743. Fitch Lea Wood.
      John Bush, Glover.
1744. John Bush, of Collins Cross.
      William Hitchin.
1745. John Bush, Glover.
      John Bush.
1746. John Bush.
      John Robinson, Salesman.
1747 and 1748. John Robinson.
              William Palmer, Victualler.
1749. John Robinson.
      Thomas Rankin, Grocer.
1750. Thomas Rankin.
      Samuel Scott.
1751 and Saml. Scott.
        John Chapman for Thos.
1752. Hayden.

S—2

CHURCHWARDENS.

1753.	Saml. Scott. Jonas Reynolds.	1797 and 1798.	Arthur Mountford. Wm. Machin.
1754.	Jonas Reynolds. John Dellow.	1799 and 1800.	William Francis. John Jones.
1755.	John Dellow. Francis Jones.	1801.	William Francis. John Perry.
1756.	Francis Jones. John Boultwood of Windhill.	1802.	William Francis. Affable Yardley.
1757.	John Boultwood. Samuel Warner.	1803.	James Jones. Affable Yardley.
1758.	Samuel Warner. Thomas Scott.	1804.	James Jones. Peter Norris.
1759.	Thomas Scott. John Jones.	1805.	James Jones. James Summers.
1760.	John Jones. Affable Yardley.	1806.	James Summers. William Stacey.
1761.	Affable Yardley. Thos. Adderley.	1807.	William Stacey. George Perry.
1762 to 1764.	Thos. Adderley. Hannibal Hill.	1808.	George Perry. John Rolfe.
1765 to 1777.	Hannibal Hill. Nathl. Smith.	1809.	John Rolfe. Thomas Clough.
1778 to 1782.	Hannibal Hill. Trimer Robinson.	1810.	Thomas Clough. Nathaniel Smith Machin.
1783 and 1784.	George Juby. Trimer Robinson.	1811.	Nathaniel Smith Machin. Thomas Scott.
1785 to 1788.	Trimer Robinson. Thos. Scott, senr.	1812.	Nathaniel Smith Machin. Robert Hawke.
1789 and 1790.	Thos. Scott, senr. John Boultwood.	1813. and 1814.	Robert Cole. Samuel Francis.
1791 to 1793.	John Boultwood. Affable Yardley.	1815.	Robert Cole. John Baynes.
1794.	John Boultwood. Arthur Mountford.	1816.	Joseph Fairman. John Baynes.
1795.	John Boultwood. Thos. Scott.	1817 to 1819.	Joseph Fairman. William Francis.
1796.	John Boultwood. Thomas Clough.	1820 and 1821.	Robert Hawke. John Scott.
		1822.	William Stacey. Joseph Taylor.

CHURCHWARDENS.

1823. William Stacey.
Thomas Clifford.
1824 and 1825. Joseph Glasscock.
Samuel Francis.
1826. Joseph Glasscock.
James Summers.
1827. Joshua Cheffins.
James Summers.
1828. Joshua Cheffins.
John Baynes.
1829. Joshua Cheffins.
Samuel Emson.
1830. William Tyler.
William Stacey.
1831. Isaac Denning.
John Baynes.
1832. Isaac Denning.
George Perry, senr.
1833. James H. Summers.
George Seymour, senr.
1834. James H. Summers.
R. T. Patmore.
1835. George Perry, senr.
Joseph Taylor, senr.
1836. John Cater Canning.
William Palmer.
1837. Robert Cole.
James Hillat Summers.
1838. Thomas Wilby, esq.
George Perry, junr.
1839. Thomas Coote.
Michael Greata.

1840. James Odams.
John Baynes.
1841 and 1842. Joseph Fairman.
William Walford.
1843. Frederick Pindar.
John Barnard Glasscock.
1844. George Seymour, junr.
George Edward Sworder.
1845. Robert Clayden.
Edwin Phillips.
1846. Robert Clayden.
George Field Grounds.
1847. William Merriman Ley.
Frederick Pinder.
1848 and 1849. William M. Ley.
Henry William Young.
1850. Joseph Fairman.
William M. Ley.
1851 to 1859. Joseph Fairman.
Robert Clayden.
1860 to 1872. George Augustus Starling, M.D.
Robert Clayden.
1873 and 1874. Robert Clayden.
George Speechly.
1875. Henry Baker.
George Speechly.
The present churchwardens, 1881.

THE CHANTRY AND GUILD OF ST. JOHN THE BAPTIST.

Among the Church papers are two very much dilapidated, which have been endorsed on the back by some one, "Relating to the Chantry."

No. 1 appears to me to be the account of the Collectors of the Guild or Fraternity of St. John the Baptist in this town for eight years.

No. 2 is the account of the expenses relating to the establishment and endowment of the Chantry of St. John the Baptist by Baldwin Victor, in the second year of King Richard III.

The parts filled out with dots indicate the portions of the pages that are torn off.

No. 1.

Storteford.
Thes ben the parcells resseyved by John ffullere ....
Jone Baptyste the ij day July the first yere of the ....
ffirste Resseyvyd by the seid Collectors of William Depon in party of....................
Twyfford mylle late of the Gyfte of Richard Wylde xiijs. iiijd. Item............................
Gyfte of John Algore xxvjs. viijd. Item Resseyvyd in yere sylvyr of......................
xijs. iiijd. Item resseyvyd of John Jardevill for the fferme of the Crofts at Sowthmylle iijs. viijd..............
        Summa iiijli. ...... iiijd.
Thes ben the parcells Resseyvyd by John Boukker (?) and John halle Colle...................................
gelde the viij day July the ij yere of the reigne Kyng Richard the..................................
ffirst resseyvyd of William Depom for the messuage afore seid in party of............
Sume xiijs. iiijd. Item resseyvyd in yere sylvur the seid yere........
Jardevill for ferme of v acre land ijs. ijd. Item of John ffullere......
Crofts at Sowthmylle the same yere iijs. viijd. Item rᵈ of William...
        Summa lijs.

THE CHANTRY AND GUILD OF ST. JOHN THE BAPTIST. 119

Thes ben the pcells Resseyvyd by William Seynden (?) and
  John G................................
fore seyd Brethrede the vj day of July the iij yere of the reigne ...
ffirst rec. of William Depom by the seyd Collectors in party of
  paym.................................
of Amere (?) xiijs. iiijd. Item rec. in yere sylvur ....
xjs. xd. Item rec. of John Jardevill for the yere fferme of v acre
  lond.......................................
John ffullere for ferme of ij crofts at Sowthmylle iijs. viijd. Item
  rec. of...............
John Marchaunt the older iijs. iiijd. Item rec. of Roberd Russele
  to...... ....
same gelde xijd.
                    Summa xxxvs. iiijd.

Thes ben the parcells resseyvyd by John Sturdy and John Grace
  Col......................................
Brethered the xxvj day of Junii the ffirste yere of Kyng Herry ...
ffirst resseyvyd of Wyllyam Depom by the seyd Collectors for......
...messuage at................
of payment of amere (?) Sm xiijs. iiijd. Item red of the Brethe......
sylvyr xijs. vijd. Item red of John Jardevill for fferme of v acr......
rec. of John ffullere for ferme of the crofts...............ylle iijs......
yere fferme of Salyng (?) xxxs...

Thes ben the parcells resseyvyd by herry Redyngt ....
Brethered the xx day of Juun the ij yere of the R......................
ffirst recd of William Depom in party of payment of...................
Item recd in yere silvyr the same yere xijs. iiijd. Item rec..........
Sowthmylle towards the purchase of the Chauntrie lands............
v acre land towards the same purchase vjli. viijs. iiijd...............

Thes ben the parcells resseyvyd by John Jardevill jun..............
seid Bretherede there the xxvj day of Juun the iijde of..............
ffirst resseyvyd of the execors of William Depom in f..............
xiijs. iiijd. Item recd in yere sylvyr of the Bret.................
recd of the Gyfte of margerie Crowe............................
iijs. iiijd. Item recd of the Gyfte of..................
Item recd of the Gyfte of........................
Spicer xiijs. iiijd. Item recd of the......... ...
the Gyfte of mergit Garole vjs. viijd.
                    Summa ....

Thes ben the parcells resseyvyd by John Thurgood and John......
  rion Coll...............
Bretherede there the xxvj day of Juun the iiijth yere of Kyng
  her....................

ffirst resseyvyd by the seyd collectors in yere sylvyr of the
  Breth... ....
rec. of Sr John marchaunt of the Gyfte of Alis pern... vjs. viijd....
of John Clarvyce iijs. iiijd. Item recd of the Gyfte of John
  Marcha... ....
rec. of the Gyfte of John Papworth xxd.
Summa xxiijs.
Summa totalis xxvijli. x..................

Item resseyvyd of the Bretherin and Susteres by particular
  parcell..................
by Writyng lxvjli. xixs. iiijd. Item resseyvyd of margerie............
Item resseyvyd of Sr John Marchaunt of the Gyfte of Alis per
  nell (?)
Summa lxxvli. ....

No. 2.

Theisse been the parcells that mayster William..................
Jardevill jun and John Grace of the same towne to............
victor wyllyd by his last wylle to make a chauntrie............
Jone Baptiste in the cherche of Storteford.
ffyrst payd to Kyng Rychard Resseyvor to..............
Bawdwyn Victor wyllid to the same..................
prevye Signet lxs. Item pd for..................
Clerke of the wex xijd. Item pd for by..................
for Rollyng in the Chaunceri xiijs. iiijd. Item............
Chaunceri xxs. Item pd to mr Whittnow for d............
Item pd to mr Chatirton for his labor and for..........fful......
wrytyng ouure supplication in parchemyne wt..................
the cheffe lords of the ffee of Gestyngthorpp Bel..................
Summa.........

Item pd to Thomas Host for makyng of the yeveden............
Gestyngthorpp vs. Item pd for the fyne of the la..................
Astate xxiiijs. viijd. Item payd at the Jerge in Storte............
and mr John Barlee wt the Bretherin ijs. ijd. Item pd............
ije yere of kyng Richard the iije xxd. Item..................
a bowre to mr Richard Barlee iiijd. Item pd in Expen............
the lands of v persones vs. Item pd in Expencs of Rob............
the yevedens to Stebyng Bermeston Henham and to hatfe........
of the lands in Berdefeld Salyng and Gestyngthorpp of............
london next takyng ouwre estate of the lands shewyng............
mete and manys mete xijs. vjd. Item pd in Expenc............
takyng of Kyng Richards Broode seale upon his graunte............
for the borweyng of xvli.   ijd. Item pd in Expe............
to make the fyne for the lands in Berdefeld wt............
Expencs of v p'sones to ffulbo'ne to bye of (?) mr Ormysby.........

for rede wex to seale the yevedens of Berdefeld....................
Item pd in expens takyng the estate of m^r Or......................
to m^r Philpot for drawyng the ffunda...................................
Item pd to Thomas host for............the same p..................
for the same ffundacion and for the...................
Shepperd to sette the stent of the lands in Gesty...... ....
in expens of m^r Philpot m^r Josselyn and m^r Marks w^t h.......... ..
Item pd in expens of m^r Vicar John Jardevill and ....
to m^r Philpot and to m^r Browne of the tempill vj*s*...................
the stent of the lands in Storteford Gestyngthorpp..................
vj*li*. viij*s*. vj*d*. (in margin)
Item pd to my lord Schropis Clerke for makyng of..............
Item pd in expens on Shroffe munday the ffirst yere of............
At Westmester ij*s*...
m^r Philpot m^r Josselyn ....xvj*d*.....................
at Chelmysford to bring theiss ....to gedir.....................
Expens John Jardevill John Grace and William Shepperd to......
Barlee by the permittement of m^r Philpot xiiij*d*.....................
and William Shepperd the xxvj day of Janeur' to bring m^r Ph......
london viij*s*. iiij*d*. Item pd the weke next after C..................
of m Richard Barlee m^r Philpot and m^r Josselyn John Grace......
Item pd to m^r Philpot for his labo^r the same tyme for ouurę......
xxiij*s*. Item pd into the hampir for o' confurmacion and for......
ij writs into the chaunsseri iij*s*. pd in Expens of.....................
At Shorffetyde the ij^de yere ....ing the wri............
there being m^r Philpot m^r...
of herry vijth in horsse mete and m ....
Clerke in money xvj*d*. Item pd in expens of John Sturdy.........
Storteford xij*d*. Item pd in expens of John Grace and ij............
the purchasse of his lands in Storteford ij*s*. j*d*. Item pd to.........
At the Jerge in Storteford xiij*s*. iiij*d*. Item pd to Richard..........
for a bote to ffullham for m^r Philpot to speke w^t my lord of lon...
Shepperd to speke w^t m^r Barlee and m^r Josselyn for to have made......................
iij*s*. viij*d*. Item pd to Sr. Roberd from the ij^de weke of len.........
pd for writyng the stent of the land in Gestyngthorpp Stort.........
Chauntrie lands in Storteford xiij*li*. vj*s*. viij*d*. Item ....
Item pd in expens of Roberd Bloss......for diverse..................
his men at Blossmes v*s*.

The following certificate of Baldwins Chantry I copied from the original in the Public Record Office [Chantry Certificates, anno ii. Edward VI.]

Stortforde.

The Chauntrie founded w^tin the parisshe Churche of Stortford by Baldwin Victor to have a contynnaunce for ever.

Valued in

{
The fferme of one messuage w^t a ten^te called the Chauntre howse together w^t all howses Buildings medds pastures and ffedyngs w^t all other the appertennces to the said chauntre belongynge w^tin the parisshes of Stortforde Thorle muche halingburie and ffarnham letten to fferme by Indenture date the x day of September an° xxv^to Hy. VIII. to John Jacob for terme of xxx yeres then next ensuinge yeldinge and payinge therefore yerelie — lxxv*s*. viij*d*.

The fferme of one messuage called Mennants (A) w^t all howses Barnes stables londs medds ffedings and pastures w^t all and singler ther appertennces lyinge w^tin the parisshe of Gestingthorpe or ells wher in the Countie of Essex letten to fferme to Willm Clerke by Indenture as it is said, and payeth therefore yerelie at iiij termes of the yere — xj*s*. iij*d*.
}

iv*li*. vj*s*. vj*d*.

Whereof.

Rent Resolute

Stortforde {
Manor de Erles Bury per an^m vij*s*.
To the Bisshop of London vj*s*. ij*d*.
To the Churchwardens of Stortford ij*s*. vj*d*.
} xv*s*. viij*d*.

Gestingthorpe {
The Sheref of Essex at the shirifes turne . . vj*d*.
Bailiff of the hundred of mistowe . . . ij*d*.
Erle of Oxford . . viij*d*.
To diverse persones viz. to the manor of mery haule vij*s*. iiij*d*. the manor of butters viij*d*. Goldingham hall viij*d*. The manor of lytyll mapested haule vij*d*. and to the manor of upper halle ij*d*. In the holle
} xj*s*. iij*d*.

ix*s*. vj*d*.

xxvj*s*. xj*d*.

And so Rent viij*li*.

(A) Gestingthorp C° Essex.

Plate belonginge to the same Chauntrie, parcell gilte poz. viij onz. Goods and ornaments appertenynge to the said Chauntrie lviijs. ijd. M^d the seid Chauntrie is fformed w^tin the parish Church of Stortforde whereof Thom^s Symson is Incumbent. A man of honest behaviour and indeferently lerned, and is of the age of xxxiiij yeres havinge none other lyvynge but the Revenues of the said Chauntrie. Also ther is non other prest to mynistre to the holle parisshe of Stortforde Beynge a market Towne and a thorowghfare but the vicar there, havinge in Cure about DCC hostlinge people whois Benefice is aboute the yerelie valew of xii*li.*

Quite distinct from Baldwin's Chantry *within* the parish church of Stortford, was the Chantry which existed within the Chapel of St. Paul in Stortford Castle.

In the "Rotulorum Patentium," Edward III., anno 26, I find: " Pro præpositio et capellanis S. Pauli infra Castrum de Stortford." This I find was a license from the King to Ralph de Stratford, Bishop of London, to found and endow a college or large chantry of secular priests to be governed by a provost within the chapel of Saint Paul in his castle here. They were to pray for the souls of Queen Philippa and the Bishop; a place of habitation was assigned for them *in the castle*, to have and to hold, and they were to have temporalities to the amount of £20 per annum.

" Here were certain messuages and Tenements in the Parish called Menants or Monants belonging to a Chantry in B^p Stortford, in Hertfordshire, of the foundation of Baldwin Victor, which in 3 Edw. VI. were granted to Henry Parker and Peter Gray, which Messuages and Tenements in the 4th Edw. VI. were by virtue of the King's license alienated by the said Henry Parker to John Welborne or Melborne, who by like license alienated the same 4th and 5th of Phil. and Mary to Thomas Brown of Little Easton, who 1 Eliz. held the same." [Newcourt's " Repert."]

THE INVENTORIES OF THE CHURCH GOODS.

Among the MSS. in the church there are nine papers of inventories and memoranda relating to the sale of the church goods. The earliest (1537) is written upon parchment and the others upon paper. They are now placed in the MS Book. No. 1. But before giving a transcript of them it may be as well to say a few words as to why they were taken.

At the commencement of the Reformation in England, and after the seizure of the revenues of the monasteries and religious houses by King Henry VIII., the people, following the example of their King, began to help themselves to the goods, furniture, and plate belonging to the various parish churches. When Edward VI. succeeded to the throne this abuse had reached such a pitch that it was found necessary to put an end to it. Cromwell, the Vicar-General, hit upon the happy expedient of stopping robbery by individuals by taking the whole of the treasures of the Church into the King's coffers. He, therefore, in the second of Edward VI., issued a commission to inquire into the quantity and value of church goods in England, and it was in obedience to this commission that these inventories of church goods at Stortford were drawn up.

(The previous inventory, 1537, was probably drawn up by the order of the churchwardens, who were responsible to the parishioners for the safe custody of their goods.)

In the sixth year of Edward VI. another commission was appointed for the same business, but during the time which elapsed between the first and second commissions, the inhabitants of Stortford disposed of their goods. The account that the churchwardens of Stortford rendered to this second commission is given in the extract from Mr. Cussan's book, which I have printed at page 97. If the reader will go carefully through these inventories and compare the items with the amounts of the receipts in the accounts for the years 1547—48, and then compare these again with the amounts mentioned in the depositions of the churchwardens when before the King's commissioners, he will then ascertain how much of the money actually reached the King's coffers, how much was laid out upon the repairs of the church, and how much was not.

On parchment, date 1537.

Stortford.

This is the Inventorye of the goods and ornaments beying in the kepyng of Thomas Scharpe parisshe Clerke ther at the ffest of Palm sonday in the yere of oure lord god mccccexxxvij as hereafter folowith :

ffyrst a cros of silver and gilte with a foote of the same.

Item iiij hoole chalyes and a broken chalyses.[1]

Item ij sensers and a schip of silver.[2]

Item ij cruetts and a pax of silver.[3]

Item a pix of silver and gilte w^t a cros upon it for Corpus x$\overline{pi}$ day closed abowte w^t birrall.[4]

Item a litill box of silver and birrall and two of silver and gylt w^t relykes therein.

Item a cros of silver brokyn w^t a brode round holow bottm.

Item a sewte of vestments with a cope all of guld and rede damaske.

Item a sewte of vestments with a cope all of Crymsyn velvett.

Item a sute of vestments with a cope all of white fustian.[5]

Item a sute of vestments w^t a cope all broyderd with guld and wrought w^t birds and fowlis.

Item a sute of vestments with a cope of grene silke and rede.

Item a sute of blew vestments w^t iij copis to the same wrought with guld.

Item a cope of blew damaske.

Item a cope of grene sylke.

Item a cope of white silke wrought with guld and perle.

[1] *Chalice.* The cup in which the consecrated wine is administered in the celebration of Holy Communion.

[2] *Ship.* A vessel, in the shape of a boat, to store the incense, from which sufficient was taken out with a spoon and thrown into the censer, when required for use.

[3] *Cruetts.* The flasks containing the wine and water used at the altar.

Pax. A small tablet on which was a representation of our Lord's Passion. It was kissed by the priest in the Mass at the words "Pax Domini sit semper vobiscum," and afterwards passed round to be kissed by the congregation.

[4] *Pyx.* The vessel in which the Holy Eucharist was preserved. It was usually in the form of a cup of gold or silver or some less precious metal.

Birral = Beryl, and a species of crystal.

[5] *Cope.* The mantle or outer garment of the priest. It had no sleeves, was open in front, and fastened round the neck by a brooch.

Fustian. Was originally wove at Fustal, on the Nile, with a warp of linen thread and a woof of thick cotton, which was so twilled and cut that it showed on one side a thick but low pile, and the web so managed took its name of fustian from that Egyptian city.

Item ij old copis of sylke.
Item a vestment of grene wusted w^t an obe.
Item a rayed vestment with an obe.[6]
Item vij old vestments and v obis.
Item a rede vestment for good fryday w^t owte an obe.
Item ij vestments and ij obis whereof on is for requiem and the other is for eny day.
Item j old vestement a myter and a peece of Crymsyn velvett for the bysship and (?) Crosyer.
Item vestments of saten of bredgis w^t obis.[7]
Item a herse cloth of velvett.[8]
Item xj corporosis with vj clothis whereof vj be good and vij be old.[9]
Item a whyte veyle.[10]
Item v old diaper awter clothis.
Item iiij diaper awter clothis of the best.
Item v playne awter clothis.
Item iiij diaper towells whereof on conteyneth vij yard and di.
Item ij playne towells myled and ij litill playn towells.
Item a fyne scheet w^t ij cut hoolis.
Item a blew velvet purse w^t perle to beer in the sakerment.
Item a diaper auter cloth and iij playn awter clothis.
Item a Canapy cloth.
Item an awter cloth and ij curteyns.
Item a peyntid awter cloth ou' (over ?) the Auter w^t a frenge.
Item ij awter clothis of grene silke.
Item a pany (?) awter cloth of sylke.
Item ij pillowes of silke.
Item a cros cloth of silke and another of pewke.[11]
Item a litill playne towell and ij playne awter clothis.

[6] *Raye.* Silk of its natural colour that has never been coloured or dyed.
Alb, from Alba, white; an ample tunic of white linen reaching to the feet.
[7] Satin made at Bruges in Flanders.
[8] *Herse.* The herse was an open framework of iron or wood set up over the coffins of deceased persons, and covered with tapers, to support the pall when the service for the dead was being used.
Herse Cloth. The pall or bier cloth.
[9] *Corporas, Corporal.* A cloth of fine white linen on which the sacred elements were consecrated; so called from the body (*corpus*) of Christ which rested thereon. The corporal cloths, when not in use, were carefully preserved in a case somewhat resembling a portfolio, usually made of silk and enriched with embroidery. The corporal cloth itself was always of white linen, and seldom more than a foot square; but it was frequently inserted in the middle of a large piece of coloured silk or other material.
[10] *Veil.* The curtain which during Lent was drawn across dividing the chancel from the rest of the church.
[11] *Puke* or *Puce.* A colour between black and russet.

Item a fine scheet.
Item half a black herse cloth with a white cros.[8]
Item a wretyn masbooke and iiij antiphenals.[12]
Item a legend iiij graylis and ij manuellis.[13]
Item an Imnall pryntedj and iiij precessionals of parchement.[14]
Item v processionals in paper and ij parchement masbooks.
Item iij pryntid masbooke and a venyte booke.[15]
Item j lecturn clothis a care cloth and ij cusshyns.[16]
Item the vykers surples and an old surples for a preest.
Item ix surplesis for men and vij for chyldern.
Item an Ewer and ij basons.[17]
Item ij joyned stoolis.
Item a peyntid cloth for the roods cote.
Item a cote of sylke for the rood.
Item a cote of sylke for o^r lady.
Item iiij forefrunts for the awter w^t frenges.[18]
Item a lenyn old cloth that was for the rode loft.
Item ij peyntid awter clothis.
Item ij peyntid clothis that servyd for the trynyte.

[8] See note [8] p. 126.

[12] *Antiphonal.* The book of antiphons, containing the music for the anthems, hymns, and psalms noted in plain chant.

[13] *Legend.* The books containing lessons to be read in the public service taken out of the Holy Scriptures, the lives of saints, the writings of the ancient fathers, and other doctors of the Church. [Burn's " Ecclesiastical Law."]

Gradual, Gradale or *Greyle.* In the Romish Church properly, a sentence in the Communion Office sung after the Epistle. But the term, in its usual signification, not only includes the sentence called the Gradual, but also all the other parts of the office of the Holy Eucharist which were sung, viz., Asperges, Introit, Kyrie Eleison, Gloria in Excelsis, Hallelujah, Tract, Sequence, Creed, Offertory, Sanctus, Agnus Dei, etc. The name indicates that some of these anthems were chanted from the steps of the chancel or ambon. [Staunton's "Ecclesiastical Dictionary."]

Manual. So called from *manu,* as being required to be constantly at hand. It seems to be the same as the ritual, and contains all things belonging to the ministration of sacraments and sacramentals; also the blessing of fonts, and other things by the use of the Church requiring benediction; also the whole service used at processions. [Burn's " Ecclesiastical Law."]

[14] *Processionale.* A book containing services to be said or sung in processions.

[15] *Venyte book,* possibly a book containing the 95th Psalm, commencing "Venite exultemus," etc.

[16] *Care cloth.* A cloth about six or eight feet long by three feet wide, held over the heads of the bride and bridegroom during the marriage ceremony.

[17] *Ewer, Bason.* A basin and ewer for the font, for the priest to wash his hands.

[18] *Altar Front, Awlter Cloth, Front Cloth, Frontletts,* etc. The altar frontal was a movable front of metal, wood, silk, or other material put close to the fore part of the altar, reaching from the slab to the top of the ground. The frontals were usually of the same colours as the vestments, and were changed at the same times, according to the festivals. Sometimes the silken frontals veiled the two sides as well as the front of the altar. ["Church Goods in Berkshire," by Walter Money, F.S.A.]

Item ij endis of torchis.
Item a stondyng ffawcon of bras for a lecturn.
Item a sepulker of bourde.
M^d delyv'd to old Chaundeler ij canstiks.
Item to Th. Snow ij canstyks.
Item of Iren xlvij peecs.
Item ij canstyks on the awter.
Item ij standards of latyn.[19]
Item liij ends of Canstykes of latyn.
Item a brokyn peyer of orgyns.
Item a . . . . . . deske.
Item a lytill . . . . . . cofer in the queer.
Item a sakeryng bell.[20]

Inventory, date Edward VI. an° II.
Stortford.

{ Edward Wylley cherchewarden Syr Th Symson.
Thomas Patmer gent.
George Thompson gent.
John Elyatt gent.
Wyll^m Pygott. }

This is the certificat of Edward Wylley cherchewarden ther and of Thomas P. gent. G. T. gent. John Elyat and Willm Pygott inhabytants of the same parisshe and of Syr Thomas Symson Curate the xix day of marche in a° ij° E. sexti unto the ryght Wursehipfull Sr Henry Parker K^t and Wyll^m Barlee Esquyer Commyssioners of oure sofereign lord the kyng consernyng the bells leds vestments chalecs and other goods belongyng to the seyd cherch accordyng to ther precepte.

Stortford an Inventorye of the cherche goods ther.
ffyrst ij chalyces of sylver and gylte w^t patents.
Item a pix of silver and gylte w^t a cros upon it and the middis thereof is of burall.
Item a lytill box of sylver and burall.
Item a sute of vestments with obis w^t a cope to them of guld and rede damaske.
Item a sute of vestments and obis w^t a cope to them of crymsyn velvett.
Item a sute of vestments and obis w^t a cope to them of white ffustyan.
Item a sute of vestments and obis w^t a cope abbroyderid w^t guld and fowlis w^t birdes.

---

[19] *Latten, Laten.* A kind of bronze alloy. The name was also applied to brass.
[20] *Sacring Bell.* In the Romish Church a small bell used to call attention to the more solemn parts of the service of the Mass.

Item a sute of vestments and obis w⁺ a cope of grene sylke and rede sylke.
Item a sute of blew vestments and obis w⁺ iij copis to them wrought w⁺ guld.
Item a cope of blew damaske.
Item a cope of grene sylke.
Item a cope of white sylke wrought w⁺ gulde and perlis.
Item ij old copis of sylke.
Item a vestment of grene wusted w⁺ an obe to it.
Item a rayed vestment w⁺ an obe.
Item vij old vestments w⁺ v obis.
Item a rede vestment for good fryday w⁺ owte an obe.
Item a vestment and an obe for buryall.
Item a vestment w⁺ an obe for euery day.
Item a vestment of saten of bredges w⁺ an obe.
Item xj corporossis w⁺ vj corporys clothis.
Item v old diaper awter clothis.
Item iiij diaper awter clothis of the best.
Item vj playne awter clothis.
Item iiij diaper towells.
Item ij playne towells milid.
Item iij litill playne towells.
Item a fyne scheet w⁺ ij cut holis.
Item a canapy clothe.[21]
Item an awter cloth w⁺ ij curtens of peyntid lenyn cloth.
Item a peyntid awter cloth ouer the awter w⁺ a frenge.
Item a panyd awter cloth of sylke.
Item ij litill pyllowes of sylke.
Item a cros cloth of sylke and another of pewke.
Item halfe a blak herse cloth of cloth.[8]
Item a wretyn massebooke and iiij antiphenals.
Item a legend iiij graylis and ij manuellis wretyn.
Item an Imnall pryntid and iij old processionals in parchement.
Item iiij precessioners in paper of the new ynglysshe.
Item ij pryntid masse books.
Item ij masse boks in parchement and a venyte boke.
Item a lecturne clothe a care cloth and ij cusshyns.
Item the vycars surples iiij surpleces for men and ij for ladds.
Item an Ewer and ij basons and a pix of latyn.
Item ij joyned stoolis.
Item a peyntid cote of silke for the roods cote.
Item another cote of sylke that was for the roode.
Item a cote of sylke that was before the images of old.

[21] *Canopy.* A hood suspended over the altar.
ᵇ See note 8, p. 125.

Item iij forefrunts to hang on the awter w^t frenges for them.
Item an old leenyn cloth that was for the rood loft.
Item ij old peyntid awter clothis.
Item ij peyntid clothis that dide hang before the trynyte and an old lynyng of an awter cloth beyng of blew bukkeram.[22]
Item ij ends of torchis and ij litill curtens in the queer.
Item a stondyng fawcon of bras for a lecturn to lay on the bybyll.
Item a sepulker of bourde.
Item ij canstyks on the awter of laten beyng gilte.
Item ij standerds of laten and ij cruetts.
Item a brokyn peyer of orgyns.
Item a tymber lecturn for the queer.
Item a litill coffer in the queer to put in books and surpleces.
Item fyve hutchis in the vestre wherof on is a grete chest bendyd with Iren.
Item of old laten and bras cccxx*li*.
Item of old Iren ccc*li*. and di. sold for xxxviij*s*. vj*d*.
Item a peyer of orgons.
Item v bells in the steepill w^t the chyme hammers as they hang w^t roopis to them.
Item a litill clok bell hangyng w^t owte the stepill.
Item a saunsebell and a sakeryng bell.[23 and 20]
Item the poremens chest.
Item wex weyng cv li. sold by Chaundler.
Item ij hand bells and a sakeryng bell.
Item of stremers of sylke ij.
Item of steyned clothe.
Item ij standard clothis whereoff on is of silke and the other of cloth.
Item ij canstyks left standyng on the awter.
Item of baner clothis of silke iiij and of peyntid cloth v and ij curtens before sold all vij for v*s*. iiij*d*.
Item of cros clothis of sylke ij.
Item iiij canstikes delyvered to old Chaundeler and Thomas Snowe.
Item ij baner clothis sold to Edward Wylley for v*s*.

On the other side of the same sheet.

Left owte of this Inventory at the makyng of yt that is caryed

---

[22] *Buckram.* A cotton textile. All along the Middle Ages buckram was much esteemed for being costly and very fine, and consequently fit for use in Church vestments, and for secular personal wear. The coarse thick fabric which now goes by the name was anything but the olden production known as "bokeram." [Introduction to Rock's "Textile Fabrics."]

[23] *Sanctus Bell* or *Saunce Bell.* A bell fixed outside the church and rung at the elevation of the Host at the Mass.

away bysydis the thyngs that they left forth of ther inventory at Ware that they have caried away in lyke maner w^t owte the assent of the parisshoners ther.

ffyrst the frame belongyng to the sepulker.
Item the hole portall at the chaunsell dore w^t the Iren werke to the same.
Item the Schryvyng howse.
Item a grete stone morter.
Item an old seetyl hutche to syt on in the belfree.
Item a frame to set in Torchis.
Item an old chest owte of the stepyll.
Item ij chests owte of the rode loft w^t mary and John and other pictors.
Item a Dragon made of hoopis and couered w^t canvas.
Item of lede forth of the stepill that servyd for the chyme and clok.
Item for Iren that served for to tye the wyer to for to drawe on the clothe before the roode loft.
Item ij Torchis and iiij lynks.
Item the box for oyle w^t the sendell therto.
Item a grete yerne pyn that was ouer the vestry doore.
Item the weyneschot of the rode loft that was taken downe and had to Wylleys.
  The baner stavis and cros stavis.
Item Canstykes delyvered to Chaundeler and Snowe beyng sold.
Item for the Cypers cloth w^t a brode wrought bend and frenge of guld that was abowte the pix w^t a long sylkyn gyrdell w^t Tasselles to pull yt up and downe w^t all.[24]
Item the laten hoopis and frenges that was abowte the same pixe.
Item the tabills ouer the awters w^t v Images.
Item on litill Tabernakyll for Images.
Item a Tabill of the Doome.
Item a frame w^t lynes to pull up the pix w^t all.
Item the iiij heryn (?) awter clothis.
Item Irens for the auters curtens and for the queer curtens to runne on.
Item a trendyll for a towell ayenst the awter end.
Item Alabaster tabylls and picturfur (?) old tymber peeces.
Item the stondard for the pascall.
Item banar stavis ix of crostavis ij.
Item Canapie stavys iiij a grete . . . . ke.

---

[24] The Pix was suspended over the altar, decorated by a corona, and enclosed in a *sacrament cloth* of semi-transparent muslin. [Peacock, "English Church Furniture."]

On another Sheet.

Stortford in aº ijº R. Edwardi Sexti.

M^d that Edward Wylley and John Bayford weer then ther Cherchewardens and they sold theis parcells of plate and ornaments belongyng to the Cherche ther heer after wretyn.

ffyrst a crosse of Sylver and gylte w^t a fote to the same.

Item a Chaleys of Sylver and gylte w^t a paten to yt.

Item a pax of sylver and gylte.

Item ij sensers of sylver w^t the toppis of them beyng gylte and j schyp of sylver and ij cruetts of sylver.

Alle the seid parcellis dide wey seven score unces and xiij and was sold for vs. jd. an unce sume xxxviij*li*. xvij*s*. ix*d*.

Item they sold j brokyn chaleys and other brokyn sylver weyyng together xxxiiij unces and an halfe and halfe a quarter of an unce and was sold for vs. an unce sume viij*li*. xiij*s*. *ob*.

The hole sume by them receyved for the seid plate ys xlvij*li*. xs. ix*d*. *ob*.

Whereof they delyvered to my lord morley iiij*li*.

Item they delyvered to Syr harry Parker xxxij*li*. iiijs. v*d*.

    Sume pd so by them ys xxxvj*li*. iiijs. v*d*.

Item ther remayned in the hands of the seid Edward Wylley upon the foote of the seid cherchwardens account v*li*. xij*s*. x*d*.

M^d that all the rest of the seyd mony that they receyved for the seid plate they dide ley forth for reparacons and other necessaryes belongyng to the seid cherche as yt apperyth by ther seyd account.

On another sheet.

  Aº iijº Regis Edwardi Sexti.

Stortford. This is the copye of the Inventory of the cherch goods that was takyn at Ware for the kyngs magestye by Syr harry Parker knyght and Wyll^m Barlee Esquyer.

weyyng lvij unces and iij quarters and sold by m^r bayley and other for ix*s*. vj*d*. the unce sume of all ys xxvij*li*. viij*s*. vij*d*. *ob*.	{ ffyrst ij chalyces of sylver and gylte w^t patents Item on pix of sylver and gylte w^t a cros upon it and the middis therof ys burrall. Item a lytyll box of sylver and burrall.
sold to Gooday by the cherchewardens for the sume of ix*li*.	{ Item a sewte of vestments of clothe of gulde the ground therof ys tawny sylke Chamlet w^t obys to them and a cope of the same.[25]

[25] *Chamlett, Camlet.* A material originally made of camel's hair; a cloth made of silk and wool.

sold by the cherchewardens to Mr. Thomas Parsons for v*li*.	Item a sewte of vestments w' obys to them and a cope alle of Reede Velvett.
sold to m' patmer for the sume of xxxj*s.* viij*d.*	Item a sewte of vestments w' obys to them of whyte fustyen and a coope of the same.
sold to m' patm' for iij*li.* (?) xvj*d.*	Item a sewte of vestements w' obys to them and a coope of blewe sylke wrought w' byrds and ffowlys.
sold to Rafe Smyth for xl*s.*	Item a sewte of vestments w' obys to them of grene sylke and rede sylke and a cope of the same.
sold to mast' patmer for iij*li.*	Item a sewte of vestments w' obys to them of blewe sylke wrought w' gulde and iij coopis of the same.
in the hands of Edward Wylley for x*s.*	Item j cope of blewe damaske.
In the hands of E. Wylley.	Item a cope of grene sylke.
sold to Edward Wylley for xiij*s.* iiij*d.*	Item a cope of whyte sylke wrought w' guld and small peerl - - (? pearls).
remayning in the cherch.	Item ij old coopis of sylke.
sold to herry parcely for viij*s.*	Item j vestment of grene wusted w' an obe to yt.

Item vij old vestments w' v obys to them wherof remayneth on vestment and j obe in the cherche and other ij vestments and ij obis of them were sold to E. Wylley for xj*s.* iiij*d.* and j vestment and j obe sold to Th. Snowe for v*s.* and to John Smyth ij vest' and ij obis viij*s.*

sold to Rafe Smyth for x*s.*	Item a rede vestment for good fryday w' owte an obe.
sold to Roger Trenham for v*s.* iiij*d.*	Item a vestment of saten of bredges w an obe for every day.
Wherof sold x to Edward Wylley and Th. Snowe for vj*s.*	Item xj corperosys w' vj corperos clothis in them.[9]

[9] See note 9.

remayneth in the cherch ther.	Item v old **dyaper** awter clothis. Item iiij dyaper awter clothis of the best. Item vj playne awter clothis. Item iiij dyaper towells. Item ij playne towells mylyd w^t blewe. Item iij lytyll playne towells.
sold to Cheyne for vj$s$.	Item a fyne scheete with ij hoolys in yt.
In E. Wylleys hands.	Item a Canapye cloth.
sold to Ric. Jardefeld for xx$d$.	Item I awter clothe of leenyn w^t ij peyntid curtens.
In the hands of mast^r patmer.	Item j peyntid awter clothe of sylke ouer the awter w^t frenges.
	Item ij lytyll pelowes of sylke wherof on remayneth in the cherche and the other not delyvered m^r patmer bought for xij$d$.
sold to m^r hubberd for ij$s$.	Item I cros clothe of sylke and another of Pewke.[26]

Goods belongyng to Stortford cherche and to the parissheners ther and beyng sold to dyverse persons the xij day of June in the vth yere of the Reyn of Kyng Edward the sixte for the necessary reparacons of the seid cherche by Thomas Chaundeler and John Smyth cherchewardens, and by Thomas Patmer gent. mast^r parson beyng bayly, Rafe Smyth, John Cheyne, Thomas Snowe, Roberd Gooday, Ric. Jardefeld, Edward Wylley and others.

ffyrst to Roberd Gooday a sute of vestments w^t obis and a cope to them belongyng for the sume of   ixli.   xx$d$.
Item to herry parcely a vestment and an obe of grene wusted for the sume of . . . . viij$s$.
Item to John Smyth iiij vestments and ij obis for   viij$s$.
Item to Roger Trenham a vestment and an obe for .   vs.   iiij$d$.
Item to Ric. Jardefeld a vestment with an obe .   viij$s$.
Item to Edward Wylley iiij Corporocis w^t clothis for   vs.
Item to Th. Snowe vj Corporocis w^t ij clothis for .   xij$d$.
Item to John Cheyne a fyne scheet for . . vs.
Item to m^r hubberd iij fore frunts w^t frenges to hang on an awter for . . . . . vij$s$.   iiij$d$.

[26] *Cross Cloth*. A hanging before the rood, that could be raised, lowered, or drawn aside by a cord.

Item to the same mr hubberd iij stremer clothis iiij banner clothis and ij cros clothis for . xiijs.
Item to Rychard Jardefeld v banner clothis and ij curtens . . . . . . vs. iiijd.
Item ij standard clothis sold to Edward Wylley for . vs.
Sume rec. ys xij*li*. xiiijs. viijd.

Theis parcellis heer under wretyn be sold and the money as yet on receyved.
ffyrst to mr bayly a sute of vestments wt obys and a cope for . . . . v*li*.
Item to mr patmer three sutes of vestments wt obis to them and v copis for . . . vij*li*. xiijs.
Item to Rafe Smyth a sute of vestments wt obis and a cope for . . . . . xls.
Item to hym a rede vestment for . . . xs.
Item to Edward Wylley a blew cope for . . xs.
Item to the same Edward Wylley a whyte cope for . xiijs. iiijd.
Item to the same Edward a vestment and an obe for vjs. iiijd.
Item to the same Edward a vestment and an obe for vjs.
Item to Th. Snowe a vestment for . . . vs.
Item of Edward Wylley for ccc li. and di of Iren by hym sold for . . . . . xxxviijs. vjd.

Theis parcellis heer under wretyn ar yet to be sold and no money receyved for them.
ffyrst ij chalyces of sylver and gylte wt patents weyyng
Item a pix of sylver and gylte wherof the myddis is of berall weyyng .
Item a lytill box of sylver and berall.
Item of old laten and bras weyyng cccxx li.
Item ij hand bells and a sakeryng bell.
Item an Ewer ij basons and a pix of latyn.
Item ij crewetts.

The weyght of the plate lvij onces and iij (? quarters) at ixs. vjd. the once xxvij*li*. viijs. vijd. ob.

Theis thyngs heer under wretyn do remayn in the cherche wardens kepyng to the cherche.
ffyrst v bells wt ropis and the chym hammers.
Item the clok bell.
Item the saunse bell.
Item the fawcon for the bybill.
Item a deske of tree in the chaunsell.
Item ij stoolis in the queer and ij cusshens.

Item the Comunyon Tabyll.
Item the pore mans chest.
Item a vestment w^t an obe.
Item ij coopis of sylke.
Item ix dyaper awter clothis of good and bad.
Item vj awter clothis of playne clothe.
Item iiij dyaper towells.
Item v towells of playne cloth wherof ij be milid w^t blewe.
Item a long Seetill for boyes to syt on wher as oure lady awter dyde stond.
Item ij peyntid Curtens in the queer w^t irens for them to rune on.
Item a peyer of orgons.
Item a Care clothe.
Item the bybill and other bokes.
Item the vycares surples and other surpleces.
Item a lytill pyllowe of sylke.

On another sheet.

Theis parcells heer wretyn were sold at master Patmers and pd for to the Cherche wardens.

ffyrst to Wyll^m lytill an old chest for . . .		xij$d$.
Item to Th. Snowe xv peeces of old payntid clothis . iiij$s$.		ij$d$.
Item to Th. Chaundeler a peyntid awter clothe for .		xvj$d$.
Item to m^r bayly ij banner stavys for . .		xij$d$.
Item to Edward Wylley iij banner stavys for . .		xvj$d$.
Item to Richard Jardefeld for ij banner stavys .		iiij$d$.
Item to John Cheyne a schyp chest for . . xs.		
Item to herry parcely the Torch chest for . . vs.		
Item to Edward Wylley the roode chest for . .		viij$d$.
Item the sepulker sold to Th. Westwood for . . vs.		
Item to Rafe Smyth ij round Irens for curtens for .		viij$d$.

The foreseid parcellis heer above wretyn were rec. by the cherchwardens.

Theis parcells be sold ther and not payed for.

ffyrst to m^r patmer ij coots for the roode and a lytill pyllowe for	vj$s$.	viij$d$.
Item to the seyd mast^r patmer ij litill old chests for .		xx$d$.
Item to the seid m^r patmer ij banner stavys . .		xij$d$.

There doth remayne ther as yet theis parcellis folowyng and to account fore.

Item the tymber and bourds of the schreevyng howse of the old orgons and of the sepulker price .	vj$s$.	vj$d$.
Item ij old peeces of torchis and iiij lynks price .	ij$s$.	

Item the old Orgon pypes price
Item the long Setill at Dewgards price . . viijs.
Item a chest sold to m^r patmers mayde for . . xijd.
Item a trendyll price . . . . . iiijd.
Item an awter clothe peyntid and a blewe cloth of
    bokeram sold to John Newman for . . ijs.
Item ij curtens of damaske werke price . . ijs.
Item old stolys sold to Barnard for . . . iijd.
Item for bookys sold to Roberd water and lyster for xijs.
Item iiij Canape stavys price . . . viijd.
Item iij peeces of old tymber price . . . iijd.
Item the pascall tre price . . . . ijd.
Item a deske price . . . . . ijd.
Item a stone morter price . . . . xxd.
Item v awter casys w^t a ffrunte price . . vs.
Item a long chest bound with Iren price . . xxxs.
Item an old chest crossid w^t iren price . . iijs. iiijd.
Item a portall price . . . . . vjs. viijd.
Item a Tabyll of Dome price . . . vjd.
Item a wyndles for the pix price[24] . . . iiijd.

The hole sume beyng chargyd upon mast^r Patmer in
    this boke ys . . . . . iijli. iiijs.
Wherof he pd to m^r John Elyat for the poverte . xiijs. iiijd.
and the rest of the seid sume he pd for the amendyng of the
kyngs hye wey agenst barells downe.

Theis parcells as yet do lak and be in the kyngs inventory.
ffyrst an old cope of sylke.
Item the Canapy clothe.
Item ij canstyks that dide stond on the awter.
Item the weynescot and the quarters that was in the rode loft.
Item the yernys that the curtens dide run on in the rode loft sold
    to marvell.
Item the gulden frenge and Cypres abowte the pix.
Item j Ewer ij basons and a pix of latyn and ij cruetts.

On a small piece of paper, no date.

receyts rec. by Th. Chaundeler for goods sold at m^r
    patmers the sume of . . . . xlijs. vjd.
Item for goods sold at Wylleys . . xxvli. vijs. viijd.
Item for wex . . . . . . xxixs. ijd.
Item for plate . . . . xxvijli. viijs. vijd. ob.
        Sume lvjli. vijs. xid. ob.

[24] See note 24

ffyrst alowed to Gooday		xx*d*.
Item to Roger Waren	x*li*.	
Item to Ric. Roberds	v*li*.	
Item to John Jacob	viij*li*.	
Item to Rafe Smyth	xvj*li*. xix*s*.	iiij*d*.
Item to Waren the smyth	x*li*.	
Item to the Glasyer	iiij*li*. iij*s*.	iiij*d*.
Item to the kawsyes	xxxj*s*.	iij*d*.
Item for reparacons of the cherche and cherche yarde	xxiij*s*.	viij*d*.
Item for the costs at the rydyng to the comyssyoners at dyverse tymes	xx*s*.	viij*d*.
Item Rado Smyth	xv*s*.	

CHURCH RENTALS.

There are twelve of these Rentals among the church papers, and the items throughout are similar to those in the receipts of the churchwardens for corresponding years, and from which extracts have been given.

I have transcribed the two following Rentals verbatim. There is no date on the first, but it is apparently *circa* Edward IV. or Richard III. The second is a portion only, dated 21st of Henry VIII.

(No. 1.)

Of . . . . . for his Ten^{te} in Sowthstrete late Gylbert Coks and Rentyth by yere . . . x*d*.
of the same Richard for a ten^{te} late T. Mallowes rentyth by yere . . . . . ij*d*.
of T. Blaunchflower by the right of his Wyff for a mesuage in Sowthstrete sometyme Nycholas Everads rentyth per an^m . . . . viij*d*. ij capons di. li. of comen.
of John harrington for a mesuage in Sowthstret sometyme T. Daynes rentyth by yere . viij*d*. di. li. of commyn.
of John Grace for a mesuage sometyme harman Skynners lying in Sowthstrete re. . . ix*d*.
of the same John Grace for a mesuage somtyme Raff Rosys lieng by arkebelds re. by yere . . xij*d*.
of Thomas Wheple for his mesuage somtyme John Sadds liing in Sowthstret re. by yere . . ix*d*.
of John marryon for hys mesuage in hockerell somtyme John myles and Rents by yere . . . viij*d*.
of herry Redyngton for hys mesuage somtyme Nycholas Tanner and now Wyll^m Redontone and rentyth by yere . . . . . . vj*d*.
of Thomas Sterdy (?) for his Ten^{te} somtyme steven Turk rent by yere . . . . ij*d*.
of John page for his ten^{te} in Northstrete somtyme John Smythes rent by yere . . . xij*d*.
of the same John Page for his mesuag w^t a garden

liing in Waterlane somtyme perce hychcoks rent
by yere, and now Ric. Jarfelds . . . xiiij*d*.
of John Norfolk for his mesuage in Waterlane somtyme
John hogans rent by yere . . . ij*d*.
of Wyll^m Sturdy holdyth by the right of his Wiff in
Waterlane somtyme John Sadds rent by yere . ij*d*.
of Sr Robt Savell for lynchWellmeddowe somtym John
Ormysby rent by yere . . . ij*d*.
of John Wylley for a meddowe caulled linchWell-
medowe somtyme Wyll^m harts rent by yere (1) . xij*d*.
of Julian Eton for a pece of land in Shepo late Wyll^m
langhames and somtyme Cicelle (?) Pelhams (?)
rent by yere . . . . . iiij*d*.
and for a stall liing betwen the stall of my lord of
london and the Church Stall of Stortf in the
spycery Rowe rent by yere . . . ij*s*. viij*d*.
of . . . hospytall of seynt Barthellmewes in london
for a pece of land liing in Dunton hyll sometyme
Cicelle (?) Pelham (?) rent by yere . . iij*d*.
of Wyll^m Prior of hallingbury for a pece of land liing
in Reding somtyme John lynne Rent by yere . iiij*d*.
of John Crawthorn for his mesuage lying in the northstret agaynst the ffleshstalls somtyme Ric. Pelhams Rent by yere . . . . xiiij*d*.
of John Tompson for a pece of lande in Bramble ffeld
somtyme Thomas Andrews rent by yere . ij*d*.
Summa xiiij*s*. ix*d*.
ij capons 1 li. of Comyn.

(No. 2.)

The parts filled out with dots indicate the portions torn off.

A Rentall. temp Hen. VIII. 21st.

Fyrste of the collecturs of ou^r ladyes gelde..............
Item of John Nobill for his mesuage in So............
Item of John Dane Pulter for a Wattercours att......
.........Southstrete............
Item of Clyfton for a mesuage in Southstrete late
Shorts.................................
Item of the same Clyfton for a mesuage in Southstrete
late John Jardefelds . . . .
Item of Jenyns wyfe for hir mesuage in Southstrete . ...

---

[1] Lynchwell meadow is the name of a field on the east of Rye Street in rear of The Fox.

CHURCH RENTALS.

Item of Willm Thurgood for his mesuage in Southstrete late John Smythers . . . .
Item of Johm Clerke of hatfeld for his mesuage in Southstrete . . . .
Item of Wyll^m Crowe for his mesuage in Southstrete . ...
Item of Richard Wood for a Wattercourse in Southstrete . . . . . . j*d*.
Item of Thomas Whepill for his mesuage in Southstrete late John Sadds . . . . iiij*d*.
Item of the same Thomas for his howse in Southstrete late Danes . . . . x*d*.
Item of John Wood for a pece of land lyenge in Shippoo late Algores . . . . . vj*d*.
Item of the same John for a pece of land in Aptonfeld late Algores . . . . vj*d*.
Item of Nicholas Redwood for his mesuage late John marchaunts . . . . . j*d*.
Item of the same Nicholas for his mesuage late Anne Rushe . . . . . . j*d*.
Item of John John for a pece of lond callyd Spetylacre ij*d*.
Item of the same John John for his mesuage in hokerell late Robert Chepe (?) . . . .
Item of Wyll^m Rynger for his place by the mille .
Item of Wyll^m Sybthorp for a gate Way in Watter layne late Thomas Rutters . . . viij*d*.
Item of Julian Eton for a pece of lond in Wyndelfeld late Nicholas bolyngtons . . . iij*d*.
Item of John Jacobbe for a gardyn late the seid Nicholas bolyngton . . . . . vij*d*.
Item of the sa. (? same) for his mesuage in Northstrete late the seid Nicholes . . . v*d*.
Item of the sa. for a mesuage ther late the seid Nicholes iij*d*.
Item of Julian Eton for a mesuage there sometyme Jakeleyn . . . . . . vj*d*.
Item of Richard Wood for his Barne in Wyndell . xij*d*.
Item of Thomas mede for his bakehowse att his mesuage late Skeppers . . . . j*d*.
Glascok
Item of Roberd Bardeney for his mesuage late Richard masons . . . . . . vj*d*.
Item of Richard Jardfeld for his mesuage in northstrete . . . . . . vj*d*.
Danyell
Item of John lytell of Stansted for his mesuage in Wyndell late Throsshers . . . vj*d*.

Item of old . . . . . . for a mesuage in highestrete .	j*d.*
Item of Thomas Papis for his mesuage in baysbowlayne late Isabell Hall	j*d.*
Item of the sayme Thomas for his mesuage att the Cornehill late herry Spencers' . . .	xiiij*d.*
Item of the same Thomas for a gardyn in basebolayne late John Bolyngtons	ix*d.*
Item of John Pylleston for his mesuage late hannyngs	vj*d.*
Item of Joone Ingrame Wydowe for a crofte callyd grove crofte	iiij*d.*
Item of the same Joone for a pece of lond in hokerelfeld agenst Tyegrene . . .	iiij*d.*
Item of the same Joone for a pece of lond in hokerelfeld late Thomas acastre . . .	vj*d.*
Item of the same Joone for a mede callyd lowmede (?)	iiij*d.*
Item of Thomas Clerke for his mesuage in hokerell .	iij*d.*
Item of John Clerke for his Ten^{te} in hokerell .	ij*s.*
Item of Wyll^m Bolyngton (?) for his Ten^{te} in hokerell late John Josselynes	vij*d.*
Item of the executors of John Joslyn for a pece of lond in Aptonfeld	
Item of the sa' executors for a mesuage in basebolayne callid fookynghams	iij*d.*
Item of Wyll^m Renyngton for his mesuage in hokerell late herry Renyngton	iij*d.*
Item of Sr Edward Pye chauntrie prest for a pece of lond in moche halfe acres callyd Shortlond .	iiij*d.*
Item of the sayme Sr Edward for an acre of lond in Kithalcroft	xviij*d.*
Item of the sayme Sr Edward for an acre of lond in Goodwynstile	viij*d.*
Item of margytt Sturdy wydowe for a Gardyn in Watterlayne late Wryghts . . .	vj*d.*
Item of Joone host wydoo for her mesuage in Watterlayne	j*d.*
Item of Robert Bretton for his mesuage in Southstrete	j*d.*
Item of Robert Hothe for his mesuage that he dwellith in late John hoth his ffather . . .	vj*d.*
Item of John Busshe of haseley for lond in the comondowne	iij*d.*
Item of Nicholas grene for his Ten^{te} in the highstret late marchall	ij*d.*
Item of Thomas Chamberlayne for his mesuage oue (? over) the Cornhill	viij*d.*
Item of Bats Wyfe for hir Ten^{te} in Watterlane late John Marchunts	iij*d.*

Item of Thomas Jegon for his mesuage in basebolane late Reynold Jegons	iij*d*.
Item of Thomas Crabbe for a parcell of a mesuage late John Davys in basebolane . . .	iij*d*.
Item of John maryon for a pece of lond in hokerelfeld	j*d*.
Item of the same John for a Gatewaye att his Ten^te in hockerell	viij*d*.
Item of Richard Gybbe for his mesuage in Northestret late Roberd Dykers . . .	iij*d*.
Item of John hopkyn for his Ten^te in Wyndell late John Johns	v j*d*.
Item of Richard Teybole for his Ten^te late cristmassis	j*d*.
Item of Andrew Clyfton for his stall . . .	j*d*.

ffarme lond.

ffyrst of Richard wood for farme of his Gardyn called Thorley Wyke	iij*d*.
Item of John Gybbe for farme of his Gardyn att Southstretend	vj*d*.
Item of John John for farme of halfe an acre of lond in hokerelfeld	vj*d*.
Item of Roberd ffuller for farme of his mesuage att Tent' hill	ij*s*.
Item of Wyll^m Butler for farme of his forge att potterscrose	ij*s*.
Item of Thomas helgay for farme of his mesuage att southstrete	ij*s*.
Item of Thomas Jegon for farme of a stall by his pents	vij*d*.
Item of Wyll^m best for farme of his schope in highestrete	
Item of John Peyn bocher for his stall in the bochery	
Item of the Ten^ts in the cherche yarde . .	
Item of Richard Jardefeld for farme of his mesuage in Watterlayne	

Extracts from the Rentals.

1644.

Willm Taylors land at Maplecrosse . . .	1	8
for Low-meade Mr. Woolly		4
Tho. Curtis for the Castle		6
for the Dogs head and pott		1
for the Raine Deare		6

for the boares head		2
Tho. Balam for the Bell		6
for the White Horse		6
for Bulls house late Glascocks		1
Mr. Glascocks piece in Comon downe late Billams		10

Lease Rents.

Mr. Robert Woolly for his ditch . . . 1
of Mr. Denny for the Tan house and Backside . 2 0 0

1782.

From Mr. John Jones Tanner one year will be due at Christmas next 1782 . . . . 3 0 0

From the Widow Chapman one year was due at old Michaelmas 1782 for what of the Rev^d Mr. Stanley's Lands remains untaken in by the Navigation 2 15 0

Rev^d Mr. Gibson always accounts for and pays in the Dividends of £350 Stock vested in the three Per cent South Sea Annuities of the year 1751 one year will be due at Midsummer 1783 . . 10 10 0

Poors Rental.

From John Carter for the late Coach and Horses on Windhill (Mr. Calverts) one year was due at old Lady day last 6 8

THE CHURCHWARDENS' BOOK, 1642.

From Items in the accounts of the Churchwardens it appears that from the time of Queen Elizabeth a book of this kind was made almost every year; it is therefore rather singular that only one should now be found among the parish papers.

This little book consists of 18 leaves stitched together. It is headed:

Stortford.

This is the Churchwardens booke there for the yeare 1642 Aº R. Caroli xviijº.

Willm Barnard and Ralfe Bull } Churchwardens.

The book commences with a list of the amounts collected for the church clerk's wages and for communion silver. This list probably contains the names of all the householders in the parish. I have therefore transcribed it *verbatim*.

Northstreate.

Of Elias Burling for church clarks wages for one yeare	iiijd.
Of him for comunion silver for himselfe	vd.
Of	
6d. Of Mr. Anthony Denny	iiijd.
of him Comunion silver for comunicants	
6d. Of Tho. Gladwin	iiijd.
Comunicants 2	ijd.
Of John Gray	iiijd.
Com. 2	ijd.
6d. of John Hutt	iiijd.
Com.	
Of	
6d. of Rich' Sawyere	iiijd.
Com. 2	ijd.
6d. Of william Bush	
6d. of Tho. Bowyere	iiijd.
Com. 2	ijd.
Of Nic. Morley	iiijd.
Com. 2	ijd.
Of John Stanes	iiijd.
Com. 2	ijd.
6 Richard Gladwyn	iiijd.
Com. 2	ijd.
W. Massum	iiijd.
Com. 2	ijd.
Edward Mathew	iiijd.
Com	
ffoulk ffrench	jd.
Will'm Bush	iiijd.
Com.	ijd.
6d. Edward Darling	iiijd.
Com. 2	ijd.

1*d*. Tho. Nayler	j*d*.	Henry Crab	iiij*d*.
8*d*. Mr. Rowe	iiij*d*.	Com.	
Com. 3	iij*d*.	ffr' Mathewe	iiij*d*.
7*d*. James Colte	iiij*d*.	Com.	
		Widow Jones	iiij*d*.
W. Heritage	iiij*d*.	Arr	iiij*d*.
Com. '.		Markall	iiij*d*.
7*d*. Tho. Hitcherson	iiij*d*.	Com.	
Com. 3	iij*d*.	ffr' Pasfeild	iiij*d*.
6*d*. M^{eis} Tendring	iiij*d*.	Com. 2	ij*d*.
Com.		Arr	
6*d*. Doth^e Sparke	iiij*d*.	Widow Palmer	iiij*d*.
Com. 2	ij*d*.	Com. 1	j*d*.
6*d*. Tho. Baynes	iiij*d*.	Arr	
Com.		James Hastler	iiij*d*.
7*d*. Widow Miller	iiij*d*.	Com. 3	iij*d*.
Com.		Bennett	iiij*d*.
6*d*. Ralfe Curtis	iiij*d*.	Com. 2	ij*d*.
Com. 2	ij*d*.		
6*d*. Ezechiell Ayrie	iiij*d*.	Water Lane.	
Com. 2	ij*d*.	Mr. Hyde	iiij*d*.
Ed. Hamond	iiij*d*.	Com. 3	iij*d*.
Com. 3	iij*d*.	Geo. Denyson	iiij*d*.
Allen Haynes	iiij*d*.	Com.	3
James Arch	iiij*d*.	Thomas Atwood	
Com. 4	iiij*d*.	Widow Chandlers	iiij*d*
Widow Ellis	iiij*d*.	Com. 1	j*d*.
Com		Robt Chandler	iiij*d*.
W. Sanders	iiij*d*.	Com. 2	ij*d*.
Com.		Will'm Skynner	iiij*d*.
Tho. Ashlocke	iiij*d*.	Com. 3	iij*d*.
Com. 2	ij*d*.	William Oates (?)	
Robert Campe	iiij*d*.		
Com.		Highe Streate.	
Henry Noone	iiij*d*.		
Com.		Nr. Newcomen	iiij*d*.
John Barnes	iiij*d*.	Com. 5	v*d*.
Com. 3	iij*d*.	John Wyberd	iiij*d*.
Henry Ive	iiij*d*.	Com. 2	ij*d*.
Com.		John Miller	iiij*d*.
Tho. Rannum (?)		Com.	
Will'm Almon	iiij*d*.	Rich' Wood	iiij*d*.
Com. 3	iij*d*.	Com.	2
John Phillipps	iiij*d*.	Roger Bancks	iiij*d*.
Com.		Com.	2

Tho. Stevens	. .	iiij*d*.
Com 4.	. .	iiij*d*.
Tho. Ramsey	. .	iiij*d*.
Com. 2	. .	ij*d*.
Tho. ffeast	. .	iiij*d*.
Com. 2	. .	ij*d*.
John Raynolds	. .	iiij*d*.
Com. . .	.	
Nath' Gary	. .	j*d*.
Justinian Aylmer	. .	iiij*d*.
Com. . .	.	
Edward Chandler	.	iiij*d*.
Com. . .	.	
Richard Holgate	.	iiij*d*.
Com. . .	.	
Tho. Ashbie	. .	iiij*d*.
Com. . .	.	
Mr. Hawkins	. .	iiij*d*.
Com. . .	.	
James Scrubie	. .	iiij*d*.
Com. . .	.	
Tho. Kinge jun'	.	iiij*d*.
Com. . .	.	
Tho. Barnard	. .	iiij*d*.
Com. 3	. .	iij*d*.
Will'm Dixon	. .	iiij*d*.
Com. 4	. .	iiij*d*.
Christ' Smith	. .	iiij*d*.
Com. . .	.	
Jo. Burch bookbynd'	.	j*d*.
Jo. Wilsem'	. .	4*d*.
Com. 2	. .	2*d*.
Gyles Rowell	. .	4*d*.
Com. 2	. .	2*d*.
John Trig	. .	4*d*.
Com. 2	. .	2*d*.
Rich' Chrichlowe	.	4*d*.
Com. . .	.	
ffr. Cramphorne	.	4*d*.
Com. . .	.	
Gurnard	. .	4*d*.
Com. 2	. .	2*d*.
Arr. .	. .	
W*y* Mathew	. .	4*d*.
Com. . .	.	

W*y* Wall	. .	4*d*.
Com. . .	.	
Samuell Duning	.	
Tho. Arch'	. .	4*d*.
Com. 2	. .	2*d*.
Tho. Roce	. .	4*d*.
Com. 2	. .	2*d*.
John Pond	. .	4*d*.
Com. 2	. .	2*d*.

Wyndhill.

John Nicolls	. .	4*d*.
Com. 2	. .	2*d*.
Arr. 6 yeres	.	

(A blank space here sufficient for four names.)

Geo. Oswald	. .	4*d*.
Com. 2	. .	2*d*.
Rob' Moncke	. .	4*d*.
Com. 2	. .	2*d*.
Wido Gary	. .	4*d*.
Com. 1	. .	1*d*.
Everist		4*d*.
Com. 2	. .	2*d*.
Henry Moncke	. .	4*d*.
Com. 2	. .	2*d*.
Roger Best	. .	4*d*.
Com. . .	.	
W*y* Westwood	. .	4*d*.
Com. 2	. .	2*d*.
Nic' Cooke	. .	4*d*.
Com. 2	. .	2*d*.
Arr. 6 yeres	.	
Geo. Miller	. .	4*d*.
Com. 2	. .	2*d*.
M*ris* Bendishe	. .	4*d*.
Com. . .	.	
Mr. Powell	. .	
W*y* Barnard	. .	4*d*.
Com. 4	. .	4*d*.
George Read	. .	4*d*.
Com. 2	. .	2*d*.
Arr. . .	. .	6*d*.

Mr. Leigh	4d.	James Derrington		4d.
Com. 4	4d.	Com. 2		2d.
Will'm Angell	4d.	Lawr' Osborne		4d.
Com. 2	2d.	Com. 2		2d.
Brooke	4d.	Will'm Gladwyn		4d.
Com. 2	2d.	Com. 5		5d.
Tho. Bond	4d.	W'y Reade		4d.
Com. 2	2d.	Com. 5		5d.
Geo. Bayford	4d.	Ralfe Earle		4d.
Com. 2	2d.	Com. 4		4d.
Arr.		ffr' Sabyn		4d.
John Bushe	4d.	Com. 2		2d.
Com. 2	2d.	Arr. 4 yere		
Arr.		Widow Griggs		
Will'm Bell	4d.	Jo. Bennett		4d.
Com. 2	2d.	Com. 2		2d.
Laur' Machin	4d.	Arr.		
Com. 2	2d.	Geo. ffreshwat'		4d.
Ed. Machin	4d.	Com. 2		2d.
Com.				
Wido Boltwood	4d.	ffishrow and Potter's Crosse.		
Com.		Andrew Brand		iiijd.
W'y ffletch'	4d.	Com.		
Com. 2	2d.	John Cooke		iiijd.
H. Chamberlein	4d.	Com.		
Com. 2	2d.	Richard Hoath		4d.
Jo. Jacklyn	4d.	Com.		
Com. 3	3d.	Widow Tolson		4d.
Symon ffabyan	4d.	Com.		
Com. 2	2d.	Robart Thurgood		
Mr. Garnett	4d.	Will'm Palmer		4d.
Com. 3	3d.	Com. 3		3d.
Wido Bowyere	4d.	Tho. Hodgkin		4d.
Com. 1	1d.	Com.		
Walter Stringer	4d.	Wido Chandler		4d.
Com. 2	2d.	Com. 1		1d.
		Russell		4d.
Basbowe lane.		Com. 2		2d.
Richard Bretten	4d.	Geo. Osborne		4d.
Com.		Com. 3		3d.
Wido Mathew	4d.	Thomas West		4d.
Com. 1	1d.	Com.		
Mr. Meade	4d.	Ezechias Leiffe, junr.		4d.
Com.		Com.		

Will'm Gray		4d.
Com. 2		2d.
Edward Ashbie		4d.
Com.		3d.
John Smith		4d.
Com.		
Wm Bennett		4d.
Com.		2d.

Southstreate.

Peter Pickering		4d.
Com. 2		2d.
Ben. Bull		iiijd.
Com. 2		ijd.
Wido Coller		iiijd.
Com.		
Wido Tydie		4d.
Com.		
John Pegrome		4d.
Com. 2		2d.
Ralfe Bull		4d.
Com.		
Will'm Bayford		4d.
Com.		
John Jones		4d.
Com.		2d.
John Bull		4d.
Com.		
Edward Marshall		4d.
Com.		
Robt Emerson		4d.
Com.		
Mr. Slater		4d.
Com.		
Edw. Bancks		4d.
Tho. Jennyngs		4d.
Com.		
Robert ffreeman		iiijd.
Com.		
Henry Gryce		iiijd.
Com.		
Lawr' ffreshwater		4d.
Com.		
John Crowch		4d.
Co. 2		2d.

Rich. Kirbye		4d.
Com.		
Mr. Keats		4d.
Com.		
Ezech' Leiffe, senr.		4d.
Com.		
Arr. 2 yere		
Widow Best		4d.
Com.		
Tho. Marden		4d.
Com. 2		2d.
Michell Mannyng		4d.
Com. 2		
John Mannyng		4d.
Com. 2		2d.
Henry Crab		4d.
Com. 2		2d.
Ben. Wall		4d.
Com.		
Thos Olyver		4d.
Com. 2		2d.
Arr.		4d.
James Marden		4d.
Com.		
W^y Andrewes		6d.
Tho. Angell		4d.
Com. 2		2d.
Arr. 2 yere		
Sam. Townsend		4d.
Com. 2		
Ar. 3 yeres		
Tho. Devenishe		4d.
Com. 2		2d.
W. Luckis		
John Chandler, senr.		4d.
Com.		
Mathew Bush		4d.
Com.		
Tho. Kinge, senr.		4d.
Com.		
Tho. Bush		4d.
Com.		
W^y peerson		4d.
Com.		

Jo. Brooks	. . .	4*d*.
Com. 2	. . .	2*d*.
Wy Waters	. . .	4*d*.
Com. 2	. . .	2*d*.
Mr. ffitch	. . .	4*d*.
Com.	. . .	
Toby Best	. . .	4*d*.
Com.	. . .	
Arr.	. . .	4*d*.
Ed. Bawcocke	. . .	iiij*d*.
Com. 2	. . .	ij*d*.
Tho. Pigott	. . .	iiij*d*.
Com. 2	. . .	ij*d*.
Widow Smith	. . .	4*d*.
Com. 1	. . .	1*d*.
Isaac Palmer	. . .	iiij*d*.
Com. 2	. . .	ij*d*.
Arr. 2	. . .	
Jo. Devenish	. . .	4*d*.
Com. 2	. . .	2*d*.
Arr.	. . .	6*d*.
Isaac Silvers	. . .	4*d*.
Com.	. . .	
Wy Stanes	. . .	
Edward Rowell	. . .	
Wy Justs wife	. . .	4*d*.
Com. 1	. . .	1*d*.
Arr.	. . .	2*d*.
Wy ffreshwater	. . .	4*d*.
Com. 2	. . .	2*d*.
Arr. 3	. . .	
Tho. Web	. . .	4*d*.
Com.	. . .	
Tho. Thurgood	. . .	4*d*.
Com. 2	. . .	2*d*.
Arr.	. . .	6*d*.
Tho. Mills	. . .	1*d*.
Wy Wright	. . .	4*d*.
Com. 1	. . .	1*d*.
Mris Perry	. . .	4*d*.
Com.	. . .	
Nic. Humfrey	. . .	iiij*d*.
Com. 1	. . .	j*d*.
Lapwood	. . .	j*d*.

Walsingham	. . .	4*d*.
Com. 2	. . .	2*d*.
John Rowell	. . .	4*d*.
Com. 3	. . .	3*d*.
Widowe Stokes	. . .	iiij*d*.
Com. 3	. . .	iij*d*.
Tho. Wyberd	. . .	4*d*.
Com. 3	. . .	3*d*.
Wy Smith	. . .	4*d*.
Com. 2	. . .	2*d*.
Arr.	. . .	
Ric. Payne	. . .	4*d*.
Com.	. . .	
Tho. Wall	. . .	4*d*.
Com.	. . .	
Richard Just	. . .	4*d*.
Com. 2	. . .	2*d*.
Tho. Tidie	. . .	4*d*.
Com. 2	. . .	2*d*.
Wy Tayler	. . .	4*d*.
Com. 2	. . .	2*d*.
Sam. Townsend, junr.	. . .	j*d*.
Wido Isaac	. . .	
Widow Bawcocke	. . .	
Widow Warman	. . .	
Gabr' Angell	. . .	4*d*.
Com.	. . .	
Arr.	. . .	6*d*.
John Jacob	. . .	1*d*.
John Eve, senr.	. . .	iiij*d*.
Com.	. . .	
Arr.	. . .	10*d*.
John Eve, junr.	. . .	iiij*d*.
Com. 2	. . .	ij*d*.
Wy Miller	. . .	iiij*d*.
Com. 2	. . .	ij*d*.
John Warman	. . .	4*d*.
Com. 2	. . .	2*d*.
Arr. 4 yeres	. . .	

Hockerell.

ffrancs Bingham	. . .	iiij*d*.
Com. 2	. . .	2*d*.
George Wood	. . .	iiij*d*.
Com. 2	. . .	

John Milton .	.	.		Nic. Raynold	.	4d.
Katherin Chandler		.		Com. 2	.	2d.
Widow White	.	.		Wido Knight	.	4d.
Widow Pinton	.	.		Com. 2	.	2d.
Wido Milton	.	.		Leonard Knight .	.	4d.
Mr. Wingate	.	.	iiijd.	Com.	.	
Com. .	.	.		ffoxe .	.	4d.
Wy Warner .	.	.	iiijd.	Com. .	.	
Com. .	.	.		Tho. Clarke .	.	4d.
Wy Cowell .	.	.	4d.	Com. 2	.	2d.
Com. 2	.	.	2d.	Arr. 5 yere	.	
Arr. 5 yeres .	.	.		John Tyler .	.	
Edward Savell	.	.	4d.	Geo. Noone .	.	4d.
Com. .	.	.		Com. .	.	
Wido Sanders	.	.	4d.	ffr' White	.	4d.
Com. .	.	.		Com. 2	.	2d.
Widow Lewis	.	.	jd.	John Howe .	.	4d.
John ffoster .	.	.	4d.	Com. 2	.	2d.
Com. 2	.	.	½. 2d.	John Wilson	.	4d.
Will'm Trapps	.	.	4d.	Com. 2	.	2d.
Com. 2 .	.	.	2d.	Arr.	.	4d.
Math' Ramsey	.	.	4d.	Tho. Cripps .	.	4d.
Com. .	.	.		Com. .	.	
Tho Prio'	.	.	4d.	Burges venter	.	4d.
Com. .	.	.		Com. 2	.	2d.
Phillip Stocke	.	.	4d.	Tho. Auncell	.	4d.
Com. .	.	.		Com. 2	.	2d.
Widow Ramsey .		.	4d.			
John Ramsey, senr.		.	4d.	Upland.		
Com. .	.	.				
Henry Payne	.	.	4d.	John Aylett .	.	iiijd.
Com. .	.	.		Com. 2	.	2d.
Tho. Baduley	.	.	4d.	John Stacie .	.	4d.
Com. .	.	.		Com. 3	.	3d.
Edward Gray	.	.	4d.	Robt Davie .	.	4d.
Com. .	.	.		Com. .	.	
John Glascocke	.	.	4d.	Arr.	.	6d.
Com. .	.	.		Lady Denny	.	6d.
John Bird	.	.	4d.	Com. .	.	
Com. .	.	.		John Gardiner	.	4d.
Tho. Browne	.	.		Arr.	.	5d.
Robert Gardiner .		.	4d.	Richard Harlowe .	.	4d.
Com. .	.	.		Com. .	.	
Tho. Mowton	.	.	jd.	Edward Plum	.	4d.
Arr.	.	.		Com. .	.	

152   THE CHURCHWARDENS' BOOK.

Ed. Goldsmith		4d.	Clanford		4d.
Com.			Com.		
John Ryce		4d.	Arthure Pitts		4d.
Com.			Com.		5d.
Mathew Harlow		4d.	Arr.		10d.
Com.			Danyell Bush		4d.
W^y Mills		4d.	Com. 2		2d.
Com.			M^{ris} Miller		4d.
W. Holgate		4d.	Com. 2		2d.
Com.			Alex. Osborne		4d.
Ed. Cooke, miller		4d.	Com.		
Com.			W^y Rawlyn		4d.
Geo. Baynes		4d.	Com. 2		2d.
Com.			John Scott		4d.
Robt Mills		4d.	Com.		
Com.			Edward Warner		4d.
John Wallis			Com.		
Ed. Palmer			Arr. last yere		8d.
John Hodge		4d.	Tho. Thorne		4d.
Com.			Com. 2		2d.
Arr.		6d.	ffr' Prior		4d.
Widow Coltie			Com.		
Thomas Walker		4d	John Speller		4d.
Com.			Com.		
Geo. Tingie		4d.	South miller		
John Killett		4d.	Geo. Pettitt		4d.
Com. 2		2d.	Com. 2		2d.
Tho. Strong		4d.			
Com.					

Then follows on leaf 13 a list of the Church rents, lease rents, receipts, and payments.

Church rents due the xxv of March, 1642.

Of Robt ffremans house	iiijd.
Of W^y Tayler for land at Maplecrosse	xxd.
Of him for his peece in Aptonfeild late Colts	vd.
Of Geo. Denysons house and yard	vjd.
Of John Chandlers house and yard	iiijd.
Of Ben. Walls late Caltons	iiijd.
Of Tho. Kings sen^r his house late a Barke Barne	jd.
Of W. Wrights house	iijd.
Of John Bulls late Collers (?)	iiijd.
Of Mr. Slaters house in South streat of old one Sadds	iiijd.

Of his oth' Ten te there called the fforge	xd.
Of him for his Chantry land in Kithall Crofte	xviijd.
Of Mr. ffitch arr. the last yere	xviijd.
Of a peece in much halfacres called Shortland sometime belonging to the chantry 4	
And an acre of land at Goodwin stile 8d. p an'm arr. of both for 32 yeres	
Of Tho. Jennyngs water lane where yonge Bancks house now is	jd.
Of the Ten'te late Burges where nic' humfrey dwel'	ixd.
Of wido Sanders gateway	viijd.
Of Hawkins late Hoaths	ob.
Of Spittle Acre	ijd.
Of Glascocks house	ob.
Of Tho. ffeasts	jd.
Of H. Godfreys peece in hockrellfeild	ijd.
Of John Millers house	ijd.
Of Rafe Curtis do.	viijd.
Of Wido Lyndsells do.	jd.
Of Wy Gaces house	jd.
Of West for Low mead	iijd.
Of Mr. Jacobs house where Mr Howe did late dwell	xvd.
Of Chr. Smithes house	vjd.
Of Ric. Gladwins do.	iijd.
Of Ed. Mathews do.	vjd.
Of Robt Chandlers house in Water lane	iijd.
Of Mris Bendishes house	vjd.
Of Wy Barnards barne	xijd.
Of him for grove crofte	iiijd.
Of John Barnes for parte of his close in Windlefeild	vjd.
Of Mr mead for ffockinghams	iijd.
Of Jo. Eve for Langhams land	iijd.
Of old ffletchers house	ijd.
Of Chamberlens do.	vjd.
Of John Triggs do.	viijd.
Of Wy Read late Covills	jd.
of Wy Dixons house	xiiijd.
Of Wy Gladwins	ixd.
Of Camps house	vjd.
Of Wy Mathewes peece at Claypond	vjd.
Of Knight for hallcroft	iiijd.
Of Ramseys house late pilstones	iijd.
Of Knights house	xd.
Of Baduleys	ijs.
Of a peece of land of Mr. Glascocks late in the tenure	

of Mr. Henry Denny lieng in Comon downe some time Mr. Billams	iijd.
Of Wy Walls house	ijd.
Of Tho. Hodgkins do.	iijd.
Of Henry Crabs ten't in Basbow lane	iijd.
Of the Whitehorse house	vjd.
Of Chandlers shop late Crabbs	jd.
Of John Cooks house	jd.
Of Ric. Hoaths house	vjd.
Of his oth' house where yonge Tidie dwelth	jd.
Of Isaac Palmers house	vjd.
Of Math' Bushes Tenement	xijd.

Lease Rents.

Of Henry Grices Tenement for halfe a yere ended at Mich^as 1642	viijs.	
and at o' Lady day after	viijs.	
Of Roger Bests pightle at paradice for half a yere at Mich^as 1642	xvd.	
And at o' Lady day after	xvd.	
Of Toby Best for the peece at Sowth Streat end in parte builded on for a yere ended at Mich^as 1642	vjd.	
Of George osbornes house for a yere ended on palme sonday last 1642	iijs.	
his lease is expired		
Of Edward Machin for the house at Sowthstreat end for halfe a yere at Mich^as 1642	xiijs.	iiijd.
and at o' Lady day after	xiijs.	iiijd.
Of wido Ramsey for the peece in Hockerellfeild for halfe a yere at Mich^as 1642	ijs.	
and at o' Lady day after	ijs.	
Of Mr. Hawkins stall for a yere at Mich^as 1642	viijd.	
Of Michell Mannyng for the house late Mr. parsons for a yeare then also	iijs.	
Of Willm Gladwyn for the peece in comondowne for halfe a yere at mich^as 1642	vs.	
and at o' Lady day after	vs.	
Of Robt Chandlers widow for Sextens mead and land in hockerelfeild for halfe a yere at mich^as 1642	xvs.	
and at o' Lady day after	xvs.	
Of Mr. Halton for the ditch for a yeare at mich^as	jd.	
Of Ralfe Bull for Marshalls house a yere then also	ijs.	
Of Strong for Chalncroft for halfe a yere at mich^as 1642	vjs.	
and at o' Lady day after	vjs.	

Of Tho. Barnard for the halfe acre peece in Apton
feild for halfe a yere at mich^as 1642 . . ijs.
and at o' Lady day after . . . . ijs.
Of Richard Sawyeres house at mich^as 1642 . . vs.
and at o' Lady day after . . . . vs.
Of Ralfe Earles shop at mich^as 1642 . . . xs.
and at o' Lady day . . . . . xs.
Of the houses in Water lane in Robt Chandlers tenure
for halfe a yere at mich^as 1642 . . . xs.
and at o' Lady day after . . . . xs.
Of Tho. Ashbie jun^r for the Butchers stalls for halfe a
yere at mich^as 1642 . . . . vjs.
and at o' Lady day . . . . . vjs.
of him arr. last yere . . . . . 6s.
Of Eliz. Russell for her lofte for a yere at midsomer
1642 . . . . . . viijs.
Of John Beamonds house at mich^as 1642 . . ijs. vjd.
and at o' Lady day aft. . . . . ijs. vjd.
Of Mother Wall for the rome wido Greene held in like
mann^er . . . . vs.
Of old Warman for the roume he holdeth by lease at
mich^as 1642 . . . . . ijs. vjd.
and at o' Lady day aft. . . . . ijs. vjd.
of him for his shop also . . . . vs.
Of the house where his sonne Tho. dwelth in like
mann^er .   .   .   .   .   .
Of Wido Thurgood for her house for a yere at Christmas 1642 . . . . . iiijs.
Of Ann Groome for her roume for a yere then also . iijs.
Of Geo. Denyson for the Stalls in the Barly Hill for a
yere at o' Lady day 1643 . . . xjs.
Of the Schoolelofte . . . . .

Now follow lists of receipts and payments, but as the items are for the most part a repetition of the items occurring in the accounts for the years 1641-42-43, I do not think it necessary to recopy them here.

THE DESTRUCTION OF VERMIN.

The Accounte and Reconynge of me Edward Wylley of Stortford, Collectore of all man' of veyrmane of ij yeres past both of Charge and Dyscharge as here aft' folloth frome the xij daye of App'lle in a° 1569 to this yere of a° 1571.

On the first page is what he terms his "charge," which is an account of moneys received by him from various persons "at v tymes;" he received altogether "lij*s.* viij½*d.*" Then follows his "Dyscharge," which consists of various payments made by him to the destroyers of vermin:

He paid for—

Hedge hoggs heads	2*d*. each
Crose eggs	2*d*. per doz.
pyse eggs	2*d*. „
vj yonge crose	1*d*.
vj crose hedds	1*d*.
vj hawkys hedes	1*d*.
xij Ratts hedes	4*d*.
1 mowlle	½*d*.
xij myse heddes	1*d*.
xij starlyngs hedes	1*d*.
a weysells hede	1*d*.
v hedds of the kyngs fyschers	5*d*.
a powlle Catts hedd	2*d*.
a boulle fynches hed	1*d*.

During the two years over which this account extends I find that vermin was destroyed within the parish of Stortford to the following extent, viz.:

141 hedgehogs, 53 moles, 6 weasels, 202 crows' eggs, 128 pies' eggs, 18 young crows, 80 rats, 18 crows, 2 bullfinches, 5 hawks, 24 starlings, 5 kingfishers, 1 polecat, 1,426 mice; and besides these there were 118 heads of crows, hawks, and "cadows" (jackdaws).

NOTE.—"There used to be a standing committee in every parish for the destruction of 'noyfull fowles and vermyn.' The practice still exists in some rural parishes. But many readers may be surprised to learn that this object was formerly felt to be so important that the practical use of it already then existing in many parishes received the express sanction of general suggestion by statute. A committee, consisting of the churchwardens together with six other parishioners, is named with power to tax and assess every person holding lands or tythes in any parish yearly at Easter, and whenever else it may be needful, in order to raise a sum of money to be put in the hands of two other persons, who are to distribute it. And these distributers are to pay this money in rewards for the different sorts of vermin brought in. The record is curious and interesting enough on its own account to be rescued from forgetfulness, if only for its bearing on the natural history of the country." [Toulmin Smith, "The Parish," p. 232.]

ACCOUNTS OF THE COLLECTORS FOR THE POOR.

The office of collector is a very ancient one, in fact, few are of older date.

The duty of these collectors, or distributors, as they were sometimes also called, appears to have been to collect the money once a quarter from the townsfolk for the use of the poor, and to assist the vicar and churchwardens in distributing alms. Collectors for the poor continued to be appointed in Stortford until 1653. Overseers of the poor, though created by a statute of the 39th of Elizabeth, were not appointed here until 1650.

Among the parish papers I find only nine accounts, or portions of the accounts, of these collectors. I have transcribed the account for 1566 in full, as a specimen, and have made the following extracts from the other years.

1564.

To the Prisoners[1] . . . . . xs. iiij*d*.

1565.

From the Receipts.

Mathew the Brasyer . . . . . j*d*.

From the Payments.

The Sowrgyns woymant[2] . . . . iij*s*.

1582.

The account for this year is unfortunately not complete; the portion extant contains the disbursements made to the sick from the 18th to the 25th of November, during a visitation of the plague (see notes to Churchwardens' Accounts, 1582).

The items for the 18th and 19th of November I have transcribed verbatim.

[1] This item may possibly refer to some prisoners confined in the castle dungeon, which at this period was used as a prison by the Bishops of London.
[2] Probably a woman employed by the surgeon to attend upon the sick.

18 die.

R^d the mony that came from Sabridgworth	xv$s$. ij$d$. ob.
R^d the mony came from Stansted Abbott	xj$s$. jd.
R^d the mony came from Gelston	iij$s$. jd.
R^d in mony 22 Days of the goodman Crabbe	xv$s$.
R^d in rent for warren dewe at michellmas last 1582	xiij$s$. iiij$d$.
Layd out for a pynt of mamsy for Barnes wiffe at twysse and suger and spice	vd.
Laide out as it apperith by the last accompt more then warren hath receyved	xv$s$. xj$d$.
Laide out to Mr. Gybbe at his last accompt wch he had layed out	xij$d$. ob.
Laied out for sack delivered to monshoe	iij$d$. and jd.
p^d to mother Lockier for wages	xviij$d$.
pd to mother williams	viij$d$.
pd for halfe a bushel of malt for monsho	ix$d$.
pd for grynding of a bushel and halfe	jd.

19 daye.

pd to mother lockier for monshoes howse for mylke	vj$d$.
pd to her for spice and hony for the same howse	iij$d$.
pd to Sawyers wiffe for barnes howse for milke spice and other nessiraeres	vj$d$.
pd for ij li. chesse and for drinck and mylke for morleyes howse and kyngs	viij$d$.
pd for a pecke of malt for Harrison	iiij$d$. ob.
pd for a peck of malt for kyngs wyffe	iiij$d$. ob.
pd for parte of a poynt of beeffe for morley and kyng	viij$d$.
pd for ij leggs and a rack of mutton	xvij$d$.
pd to Lambert for carrieing of wood to monsho	iij$d$.
pd for salt for morley and kyng	jd.
pd for a li. of Candell for barnes howse	iij$d$.
pd for morley and kyngs wiffe for a li. of candell and ottmell	iiij$d$.

The following are extracts from the disbursements from the 20th to the 25th November.

paid for butter frankencense and pitche	iiij$d$.
Laied out for a bushell and halfe of wheat and baking	iiij$s$.
pd for a loyne of mutton and a sheppes hed for barnarde	ix$d$.
pd for a showder of motton for Gostlyn	vd.
pd for a lege of motten for morley	vd.
pd for a spring of porke and a rack of motten for barnards howse	viij$d$.

pd for watching candell for barnes howse . . j*d. ob.*
pd for flower and eggs for morley to make poddings . iij*d.*
pd for a Mary bone and a spring of porke for Barnes
    Howse . . . . v*d.*

1593.

Stortford. The accompt of John Jennyngs and Benjamin Webbe Collectors for the Poore of the same Towne for and upon xx*s.* by them Receyved as the legacye of Thomas Pery late of Shinglehall deceased, and distributed to the poore ther the xxiij daye of Marche 1593 in manner and forme following, viz. :

To frengle (?) . . viij*d.*	to Graye . . . vj*d.*
to Little . . . viij*d.*	to Prenties . . . viij*d.*
to widow . . . . . . vj*d.*	to Oswald . . . vj*d.*
to Agnes Helgay . . vj*d.*	to Bond . . . vj*d.*
to Morgayne . . vj*d.*	to Rayment . . . vj*d.*
to mother francis . . xij*d.*	to Gornard . . . vj*d.*
to old Dane . . iiij*d.*	to Steven West . . vj*d.*
to James Stanes . . viij*d.*	to John Browne . . vj*d.*
to Skyngell . . . vj*d.*	to John Bowyere . . vj*d.*
to Graunt . . . vj*d.*	to widow Wood . . vj*d.*
to Gylsby . . . viij*d.*	to Low (?) . . .
to Pasfeild . . . vj*d.*	to Russell . . . vj*d.*
to mother bore . . iiij*d.*	to George pylston . vj*d.*
to Robson . . . xij*d.*	to widow Crab . . vj*d.*
to Lamberde . . iiij*d.*	to widow Hills . . vj*d.*
to Peerson . . . vj*d.*	to michell Sawyere . vj*d.*
to Morley . . . vj*d.*	to widow Cooke . . iiij*d.*
to Pamflyn . . . vj*d.*	pd for a quitaunce in dis-
to Tayler . . . vj*d.*	charging the Executors iiij*d.*
to Townesend . . vj*d.*	So xx*s.*

The Collection of y*e* Towneship of Stortford beginning at midsomer whiche is in y*e* yere of oure lord god mdlxvj for one yeare gathered of us William Miller and Richard Calidaye, Collectors.

Mr. Parsons . . xxvj*s.*	John Bowyer . iiij*s.* iiij*d.*
Mr. Elyot . . viij*s.* viij*d.*	Thomas Bowyer . iiij*s.* j*d.*
George Hawkyn . viij*s.* vj*d.*	John Sowthe . iiij*s.* iiij*d.*
William Pilesdon . viij*s.* ij*d.*	William Abbott . iiij*s.* iiij*d.*
Thomas Crabbe . viij*s.* iiij*d.*	Thomas Wilsemar . iiij*s.* ij*d.*
John Peresmyth . iiij*s.* iiij*d.*	Richard Hogate . iiij*s.* iiij*d.*
William Miller . iiij*s.* iiij*d.*	Robard Goodday . iiij*s.* iiij*d.*
Thomas Chamber . iiij*s.* iiij*d.*	Edward Gibson . iiij*s.* iiij*d.*
Henry Perselay . iiij*s.* iiij*d.*	John Marrion . iiij*s.* j*d.*

Richard Calyday .	iiijs.	iiijd.	Nicolas Marden .	ijs.	ijd.
Andrew Cawton .	iiijs.	iiijd.	John Crabbe .	ijs. jd. ob.	
Thomas Jurniman .	iiijs.	iiijd.	John Wifild .	ijs.	jd.
Richard Feaste .	ijs.	jd.	John Denison .		xiiijd.
Mathew Barnese .		vjd.	William Gare .	ijs.	ijd.
Thomas Nobse .	ijs.	ijd.	William Barre .	ijs.	ijd.
Mathew Ramsay .	iiijs.	iiijd.	Robard Bevis .	ijs.	ijd.
Richard Grave .	ijs.	ijd.	Robard Chambar .	ijs.	ijd.
Ffather Ayle .	ijs.	ijd.	Edward Growte .	ijs.	ijd.
John Crappes .	ijs.	ijd.	George Mathew .	ijs.	ijd.
Tyler .	ijs.		William Barnard .	ijs.	ijd.
Bushe .	ijs.	ijd.	Mr. Willaye .	iiijs.	iiijd.
		xvijd.	Thomas Mathew .	ijs.	
John Bayforde .	iiijs.	iiijd.	Giles Brett .		xviijd.
Maistris Glascoke .	iiijs.	iiijd.	John Hemyng .		vjd.
Goodwife Clarke .	ijs.	viijd.	John Strase .		xijd.
John Harlowe .	iiijs.	iiijd.	Ffather Solese .		xiiijd.
George Jacobe .	iijs.	xjd.	Mr. Grathorne .	xijd.—ijd.	
John Jardvilde .	iiijs.	iiijd.	Mr. Newman .	xijd.—ijd.	
Ffather Noke .	iiijs.	iiijd.	Mr. Plomer .		vjd.
John Miller .	iiijs.	iiijd.	Mr. Gibbe .		xd.
William Bret .	iiijs.	iiijd.	Mr. Edward Eliot (?)		ijd.
John Momford .	iiijs.	iiijd.	Mr. Carowe .		iiijd.
Peter Mede .	iiijs.	jd.	Strangers .	iiijs.	iiijd.
William Snowe .	ijs.	xjd.	John Hillse Tanner	nihill.	
Jemes Bull .	ijs.	jd.	Burges .		jd.

Summa xj*li.* xviijs. vjd. ob.

Payd oute of yᵉ Collection to these as folowyth.

Mother Roberdes for yᵉ Childe	xliijs.	iiijd.
Perse	xvijs.	iiijd.
Ffather Saunder	xvs.	iiijd.
Mother Alese	xvs.	vijd.
John Foster and his wife and his boyese hose	xxs.	xd.
Annes Gilson	xjs.	
Ffather Bett .	vijs.	xd.
Mother Corear	vs.	vjd.
Mother Etrige	vs.	ijd.
Mother Horwood	vs.	iiijd.
Mother Curtes	xs.	vd.
To Whetele for keping of foster fortenite	vs.	ijd.
To Grene yᵉ sawyer for howse Rome and keping of Foster		xijd.
Widdow Bowyer		iiijd.
Halese yᵉ Carpenter .	vijs.	jd.

Playle	ijs.
Alese Cater	ijs. iiij.ᵈ
Goodwife Little	ijs.
Staneses wife	ijs. ijd.
Ffather Monchow	vs.
An Papes	xvjd.
Marget Crabbe	vs. ijd.
Jean Gilson	xd.
Everedes Wife	ixd.
Thomas White	viijd.
Mother Tedsewell	xvd.
Swetinge	vs.
Etrige	xvjd.
	xxjd. ob.
Mother Write	iijs. vjd.
Balam	iiijd.
layde oute with Tabita Frier	xs.
for a peticote Clothe for yᵉ sayd Tabita and makyng a Cassake	vs. iiijd.
for a payer of shose and halfe a pound of wolle and carege of her to Burlse	xxijd.
for makyng of writyngs to Barnard	xiiijd.
layde oute to ij laser men yᵉ one of knits Bredge	xvjd.
To a poreman of mileende	viijd.
To a pore man yᵗ was burnde in yᵉ Countie of Kent	xijd.
To a poreman yᵗ came out of Essex beyng nombe	iiijd.
To a poreman of hamersmyth	viijd.
To yᵉ gatherers of yᵉ Kyngs Benche	viijd.
To a pore man of Colchester	viijd.
To John Mannsewell of London fishemonger and sitisin	viijd.
To yᵉ gatherer of Waltam spittel	viijd.

Summa xjli. xjs. xjd. ob.
Remayning in our hands of this Accounte vjs. vijd.
ther is to gather xiijs. xjd.

Richard Caliday and Wᵐ Myller discharged and William Brett and James Bull chosen in ther stede to be collectors aᵒ domⁱ 1567 22 die Junii.

EXTRACTS FROM THE OVERSEERS' BOOK.

1656. A booke of the Accomte of the Churchwardens, Overseers and the Officers of the pishe of Stortford.

1656. William Miller } Constables.
George Shepeorde }

There receipts for a rate made for a Robbery and ye town charge.

		£	s.	d.
1666. disbursed for the Plague[1]	. . .	46	10	0
1668. Disbursed by the fortnights collection	.	44	15	0
for Nurse Children	. . .	38	12	0

1669. April 12th George Holgate then gave accompt of all the moneyes Received of Mr. Browne and Mr. Duke and Mr. White John Bull and Robert Freeman of Stortford which was £82 7s. 3d.

---

[1] The plague appears to have raged in Stortford from about July to November, 1666; cases of death, however, occurred in 1667. In the parish register the entries of the burials of persons known to have died of the plague are marked Pl. And from this source I find that the following number of people died of the plague here, viz.:

	Deaths.
From July 13th to July 31st	24
in August	71
,, September	54
,, October	52
,, November	18
,, December	6
,, January	2
To May 6th	4
Total	231

Estimating the population of Stortford at this time to have been about 1200 or 1500, we find that nearly one-sixth of the people were carried off by this dreadful disease. It must be borne in mind that these 231 burials were actually registered, and that it is possible that some may have died of the plague here whose burials were not registered at the parish church.

which was Received in the time of the Sicknesse for ye Reliefe of the Poore.

Which was all disbursed to the intent aforesaid as appeare by his bill only 1*li*. 5*s*. 11*d*. which is now paid to Thomas Balam and James Brand Overseers of the Poore for ye yeare 1668.

The Constables had at the end of 1668 a balance in hand of £6 7*s*. 9*d*.

Whereof the same day (July 27, 1669) they Payed 17*s*. 9*d*. to Bennitt Thredcoab and Goodman Pryor towards their losse in going to Whitehall with the King's Carriages.

1670. Mr. Matthew Wooley, Mr. George Denison and Mr. Geo. Holgate are chosen by ye towne for surveyors for the Highways according to the new act of Parliament and that John Osborne and Thomas Clayton bee continued on to assist them in the sayd worke.[1]

1671. April 24th, Mr. Stevens Mr. Holgate Mr. Manistyes and Mr. Matthew Woolley's Accompt for a new Bell.

	£	s.	d.
Paid for the Bell Clappers brasses and wheles	60	10	0
Received of the Towne	39	16	6
due to Mr. Wolley	20	13	6

ordered that he receive the money of Tho. Scott untill satisfied.

NOTE.—The above-mentioned Thomas Scott collected the Market House Rents for the Town.

1671. William Mills } Overseers.
      Simon Rutland }

The above said William Mills being Constable of ye Hamlett was released from being Overseer for this present yeare. And according to an order of Sr Humphrey Gold (?) John Hutt was chosen overseer for ye poore for this year to come upon Tuesday ye 17th of May, 1671.

1672. Decr. 27th, it is ordered that John Grave be allowed 20*s*. out of the charge that he was at for his stall.

1675. This year two "tyled Stalls in the Fish market," one belonging to the church and the other to the poor, were pulled down and the ground let on lease to one Henry Wallis.

1677. Disbursements of Mr. Scott out of the Market House Rents:

	£	s.	d.
P^d to Wm Read for a Bell to ye Bellman	00	05	0

[1] 1670. The earliest recorded appointment of surveyors of the highways at Stortford is in 1616.

1679. This year £27 15s. 0d. was voted towards the chimes.

1681. Jan. 6th. Whereas Wm Speciall serving this yeare as a Surveyor of the Highways the parishioners doe promise that he shall be excused from any other office two or three years.

Oct. 31st, the day and year abovesaid Wee the inhabitants of Bpp Stortford whose names are hereunder written doe hereby consent and agree to meete at this parishe Church att the tolling of the Bell upon the first Fryday in every moneth for the settling the affaires and concernes of the parish upon the penalty of forfeiting sixpence for every default (unless some sufficient cause be showne to the contrary) to be payd to the overseers of the poore successively whom wee authorise to collect the same.

	£	s.	d.
1683. From Mr. Scott's disbursements.			
ffor Venison and carriage	02	12	00

1684. From Mr. Matthew Wolley's disbursements out of the Market House Rents.

	£	s.	d.
Layd out for a Gratuitye to Mr. Johnson and for a treat for him and his Lady att the Bull for beeing benefactors to the poore of Stortford .	1	18	0
1686. pd for a dark lanthorn for ye Bellman .	00	2	4
pd to make up ye Money for ye Engine	00	15	0
pd for water and helps to play ye Engine	00	2	0
1689. Sep. 10. P^d for mending the bellman's Bell	00	2	6
1690. Making cleane the gutter at the Market Hill carrying away the dirt .	00	00	06
1693. Nov. 4. The Ringers had ye King's birthday .	00	03	0

1695. Nov. 22. It is agreed upon and consented by all the Parishioners of the Parish of B^{pp} Stortford on the day above said, That no officer henceforth shall have allowed him by the said parish but four shillings unto Hertford or Ware for Justice, Two shillings unto Gilston, one shilling and sixpence to Sabridgeworth or Hadham and no more.

	£	s.	d.
1696. pd for a present to Mr. Johnson[1]	00	09	06
1697. a p'sent to Mr. Johnson	00	10	00
1698. ,, ,, ,,	00	08	06
1699. ,, ,, ,,	00	07	08

---

[1] 1699. With regard to the items of presents to Mr. Johnson I find he well deserved them, for he gave away between Michaelmas, 1695, and Christmas, 1702, £51 0s. 0d., in amounts of £3 0s. 0d., as "a gift of charity" to the poor. An account of these gifts is given at the end of the minute-book.

Sepr 15th. Att a publique Vestrey itt was then agreed that the present Churchwardens Mr. Edward Ashby and Mr. John Jennens shall allow unto John Baker the present Church Clerke as much Black cloth as shall make him a Gound to be used in the Church.

1706. Sep. 6. At a vestry then held it was ordered that the Constables do repair the Engine forthwith.

	£	s.	d.
Received by subscriptions for railing in the Causeway	08	15	0

1709. April 12th. At a vestry then held in the Parish Church of Bishop Stortford in the county of Hertford it is agreed and consented to by us the vicar Churchwardens and inhabitants of Bishop Stortford that the Revd Thomas Took Clerk master of the Grammar School in Bishop Stortford aforesayd may erect and build one gallery for the use of the schollars of the said Grammar School in time of divine service and sermons in the north Isle of the Parish Church aforesaid opposite to the pulpit from the second pillar Eastward to the fourth pillar westward to contain in depth fifteen feet and in front thirty three feet witness our hands this day and year first above written.

(The above is signed by the Vicar, Churchwardens, and 23 Parishioners.)

1712. John Reeve was this year elected Clerk of the Vestry and he was instructed to take out of the Church books an account of all Officers of the Parish that have not made up their account.

1713. April 12th. It is agreed that whereas Edwd Elkin and Eliz. his wife are committed to Hertford Goale for feloniously taking from Thos Stafford several Goods, the Overseers and Constables of this Parish shall become sureties to the keeper of the said Goale for their personal appearance at the next general Goale delivery of the County of Hertford to answer what shall then be objected against them by the s^d Thomas Stafford.

1718. Att a vestry held May 2nd 1718 Itt was agreed on for ye p'sent Survey^r for the high ways to enter and digg for Gravel for the use of ye high ways in ye p's of ground commonly called ye Luser Crofte (?) n^r ye Gravill pitt in Dels late in ye poseshion of John Warner and this vestery do hereby promise to stand by ye s^d surveyors to beare y^m harmless from all cost or charges that may arise thereby.

(From the disbursements of the Overseers.)

	£	s.	d.
The Pest House	16	6	6

1725. Disburst by Jn⁰ Ramsey for the Small Pox . 8 12 7
1728. By yᵉ small pox for Gase . . . 1 18 10½

1731. This year several sums of money were layd out upon "yᵉ workhouse."

1732. Easter Monday Aprill yᵉ 10 Wee the churchwardens and overseers of the Poor and other the Parishioners of the Parish of Bishop Stortford met at a Vestrey there held the day and year first above written doe agree with Mr. Samuel Ely, Apothecary, to find all medicines that the Poor of the said Parish shall have occasion to be administered to them upon all occasions except the Small Pox, and we doe promise to pay to him yᵉ said Samˡ Ely the sume of five pounds five shillings at the years end and if in case this agreement be too hard upon him wee doe promise to pay him half a guinea more.

1733. An agreement for the supply of Parish medicine for £5 5s. 0d. was made this year with Mr. Bishop.

1734. This year the Parish Apothecary had an advance of 5s. per anᵐ.

1735. From the disbursements of the overseers it appears that the workhouse was hired by them at an annual rental of £10 0s. 0d. per anᵐ.

The town was visited with small pox this year.

1736. This year a contract was made with "John Reynolds surgeon to find all medicines, both internal and external, both in Physick and Surgery, except the small pox, for Nine Guineas per anᵐ."

1741. Mem. Nath. Sweeting came to the vestrey to ask relief, and upon enquiry of himself he did acknowledge that he did rent Ten Pound five shillings in the Parish of King's Hatfield that is to say a field £6 15s. 0d., the House £3 10s. 0d., for several years the field of George Dorrington, the House of Esqʳ. Barrington.

1756. In February this year a vestry meeting was postponed one day on account of a Public Fast.

THE NAMES OF THE COLLECTORS AND OVERSEERS OF THE POOR.

Collectors for the Poor.

1563. John Parsmythe alias Cheny.
John Jardfeld.
1565. Thomas Crabbe.
Henry Parsley.
1566. William Miller.
Richard Calidaye.
1567. William Brett.
James Bull.
1569. John Harloo.
George Jacob.
1570. George Mathew.
William Snowe.
1593. John Jennyngs.
Benjamin Webbe.
1636. Thomas Emerson.
W^m. Tayler.
1637. Justinian Aylmer.
Nicholas Westwood.
1639. William Mathew.
William Palmer.
1640. Mr. Thomas Meade.
Thomas Kinge.
1641. Robert Freeman.
Thomas Stevens.
1642. John Bull.
Edward Plum.
1643. John Scott.
William Skinner.
1644. Edward Hawkins.
George Denyson.
1645. Richard Holgate.
William Bayford.
1648. Francis Mathewe.
Ralfe Curtis.
1649. William Holgate.
Thomas Plum.

Overseers for the Poor.

1650. William Reade the y^r.
Robert Chandler.

Collectors for the Poor.

1652. Edmund Goldsmith.
John Rowell.
1653. John Barnes.
Michell Mannyng.

Overseers.

1654. George Holgate.
Humfrey Dixon.
1655. Repentance Smith.
Richard Harryson.
1656. Edward Bayford.
George Baynes, Pikemaker.
1657. Henry Sanders.
John Josselyn.
1658. James Marden.
George Chandler.
1659. Thomas Scott.
Daniel Bull.
1662. Wiiliam Rochell.
William Chandler.
1663. Mathew Wooley.
Luke Cooke.
1664. Roger Banks.
Jeremiah Gardener.

COLLECTORS AND OVERSEERS OF THE POOR.

1665. John Barrons.
Richard Feast.
1666. William Bayford.
Nathaniel Jones.
1667. Henry Barnes.
Robert Allen.
1668. James Brand.
Thomas Balam.
1669. William Reade, junr.
Ralph Manesty.
1670. Mr. Edward Denny.
John Clarke.
1671. John Hutt.
William Mills.
Simon Rutland.
1672. Henry Perryn.
Robert Lay.
1673. Thomas Ingham.
John Reade.
1674. William Stock.
John Payne.
1675. Thomas Scott.
William Jones.
1676. Thos. Clayton.
John Osborne.
1677. Mr. Edward Maplesden.
W^m. Barnes.
1678. Thomas Clark.
William Bayford, junr.
1679. Ralph Manister.
Humphrey Dixon.
1680. Baldwin Skingle.
Jonathan Paine.
1681. William Parnell.
John Reynolds.
1682. Peter Sandford.
Richard Osborne.
1683. William Mills.
Thomas Wheatly.
1684. Joseph Scott.
John Grave.
1685. William Bayford, Currier.
Henry Wallis, Baker.
1686. John Taverner.
Samuel Bayford.

1687. John Reeves.
Zachary Blower.
1688. Samuel Jocelin.
John Perrin.
1689. Thomas Barnard.
Thomas Hide.
1690. George Jelliman.
Edward Ashby.
1691. William Speciall.
Thomas Cooke.
1692. John Boultwood.
William Furgeson.
1693. William Ely.
John Jennings.
1694. Nicholas Tyler.
Edward Jubey.
1695. John Cullick.
John Thorn.
1696. Saml. Scott.
W^m. Barnes, Pikemaker.
1697. Mr. Thomas Barnard.
David Joyce.
1698. John Schooling, senr.
Francis Fann.
1699. John Cornhill.
Thomas Appleby.
1700. William Helme.
Jonathan Carter.
1701. Henry Weeks.
Edward Bangham.
1702. Thomas Grove, senr.
John Green.
1703. Moses Patmore.
George Bass.
1704. Tobias Staines.
Affable Yardley.
1705. Mr. Thomas Clayton.
Samuel Bigamore.
1706. John Rouse.
James Ginn.
1707. Samuel Taylor.
John Wood.
1708. Joseph Scott.
Joseph Wilkinson.
1709. W^m. Spashall (? Speciall.)
Ric. Franklin.

1710. Christopher Webb.
       Thomas Talwyn.
1711. Thomas Clayton.
       Thomas Scott.
       Christopher Webb.
       William Sworder.
1712. Mr. Edward Bangham.
       Mr. John Rose.
1713. Roger Boultwood.
       Joseph Reeve.
1714. Richard Franklin.
       Anthony Appleby.
1715. Mr. Thomas Howle (?).
       Mr. Nath Jones.
1716. Henry Barnes.
       John Ramsey.
1717. Jeff Archer.
       William Speciall.
1718. Abraham Smith.
       Mr. John Adams.
1719. Mr. James Moor.
       Mr. Thos. Bowyer.
1720. Mr. Jonathan Carter.
       Mr. Joseph Phillips.
1721. John Reynolds.
       Sheffield Warren.
1722. W^m. Mahew.
       Rich^d. Haws.
1723. Mr. Thomas Rankin.
       Mr. Saml. Taylor.
1724. John Ramsey.
       Mr. Thomas Scott.
1725. Thomas Mott.
       John Ramsey (deputy for W^m. Speering.)
1726. Arthur Wankford.
       William Hutchin.
1727. Samuel Tayler.
       John Boultwood.
1728. William Hutchin.
       Henry Robinson.
1729. W^m. Wyberd.
       John Wood.
1730. Edward Jubey.
       John Heyden.

1731. Thomas Hayden.
       John Cole.
1732. Joseph Haws.
       Affable Yardley.
1733. Samuel Bayford.
       John Freshwater.
1734. John Bush.
       Thomas Cook.
1735. W^m. Fairchild.
       John Gyver.
1736. W^m. Clark.
       W^m. Palmer.
1737. Thomas Drane.
       Robt. Battell.
1738. Peter Sadler.
       Jonas Reynolds.
1739. Mr. John Bangham.
       Mr. John Rous, junr.
1740. W^m. Baines.
       Thos. Page.
1741. Mathew Palmer.
       John Robinson.
1742. Robt. Lumpkin.
       Francis Jones.
1743. John Dellow.
       Wm. Mills.
1744. John Edwards.
       Daniel Dugard.
1745. Edward Bangham.
       John Phillips.
1746. William Westwood.
       William Wankford.
1747. William Westwood.
       W^m. Wankford.
1748. Joseph Smith.
       Saml. Scott.
1749. Thomas Nash.
       Thomas Dugood.
1750. John Boultwood.
       Benjamin Talwyn.
1751. John Searl.
       Samuel Warner.
1752. John Clark.
       Thomas Nash.
1753. Thomas Houghton.
       Collis Nunn.

- 1754. Thomas Scott.
  John Smith.
- 1755. Fitch Lea Wood.
  John Jones.
- 1756. Thomas Campin.
  William Beaumont.
- 1757. Jonathan Browne.
  William Speciall.
- 1758. Robert Searle.
  Affable Yardley.
- 1759. Mr. Thos. Nash.
  Mr. Matthew Palmer.
- 1760. Mr. Wm. Bird.
  Mr. Isaac Edwards.
- 1761. Henry Marshall.
  Wm. Andrews.
- 1762. Henry Marshall.
- 1763. Abraham Thurgood.
  John Carter.
- 1764. William Palmer.
  Michael Edridge.
- 1765. Mr. Wm. Clark.
  Mr. Joseph Smith.
- 1766. Henry Wade.
  Roger Bolton.
- 1767. Mr. Thomas Palmer.
  Mr. George Patmore.
- 1768. Mr. Saml. Scott.
  Mr. Edwd. Johns.
- 1769. Trimer Robinson.
  Christopher Glasswell.
- 1770. Mr. Wm. Patmore.
  Mr. John Jones.
- 1771. Mr. John Clarke.
  Mr. John Boultwood.
- 1772. Mr. Thos. Scott.
  Mr. Daniel Warner.
- 1773. John Clark.
  Affable Yardley.
- 1774. William Stallybrass.
  Thomas Campin.
- 1775. John Ralph.
  John Searl.
- 1776. Richard Stubbing.
  Thomas Archer.
- 1777. George Juby.
  Wm. Woodham.
- 1778. Thomas Bird.
  Wm. Burton.
- 1779. Peter Ramsey.
  Thomas Houghton.
- 1780. Thomas Dugard.
  James Pavitt.
- 1781. Benjamin Day.
  Thomas Scott.
- 1782. Wm. Palmer.
  Roger Bolton.
- 1783. John Coote.
  Affable Yardley.
- 1784. James Patmer.
  Arthur Mountford.
- 1785. Reginald Jennings.
  Edward Johns.
- 1786. John Boultwood.
  John Campin.
- 1787. Thomas Scott, junr.
  Thomas Clough.
- 1788. William Beaumont.
  John Quilter.
- 1789. John Clark.
  William Lord.
- 1790. William Stallibrass.
  Isaac Livermore.
- 1791. William Hawkes.
  Joseph Speciall.
- 1792. Isaac Emery.
  William Nash.
- 1793. William Francis.
  William Machin.
- 1794. Benjamin Cotton.
  John Perry.
- 1795. Francis Cotsford.
  John Jones.
- 1796. Thomas Nash.
  William Yardley.
- 1797. William Daniels.
  George Starkins.
- 1798. Peter Norris.
  William Johnstone.
- 1799. John Taylor.
  Thomas Tyler.

- 1800. James Summers.
  Richd. Lawrence.
  Wm. Pavitt.
  Wm. Bayford.
- 1801. Thos. Clough.
  Val{tn}. Beldam.
  Benjn. Day.
  James Jones.
- 1802. Thomas Scott.
  Thomas Patmore.
- 1803. Reginald Jennings.
  William Stacey.
- 1804. George Perry.
  Nathl. Smith Machin.
- 1805. Zach{h}. Jolly.
  John Baynes.
- 1806. Thomas Sparling.
  Robert Hawke.
- 1807. James Clements.
  John Wyles.
- 1808. Samuel Francis.
  Thomas Glasscock.
- 1809. Fred{k}. John Nash.
  Robert Cole.
- 1810. Joseph Heath.
  Francis Robson.
- 1811. William Barber.
  Thomas Edridge.
- 1812. Pearson Till.
  John Rolfe.
  James Dodd.
- 1813. James Jones.
  William Daniels.
- 1814. Thomas Scott.
  Thomas Patmore.
- 1815. George Starkins.
  A. M. Ashby. (¹)
  Joseph Taylor.
- 1816. Robert Emson.
  Reginald Jennings, junr.
- 1817. William Stacey.
  William Johnstone.
- 1818. Richard Lawrence.
  John Scott.
- 1819. James Patmore.
  Thomas Buck.
- 1820. Joseph Glasscock.
  Robert Smith.
- 1821. Thomas Clifford.
  Samuel Francis.
- 1822. Joseph Fairman.
  James Summers.
- 1823. Samuel Emson.
  Joshua Cheffins.
- 1824. John Slater.
  William Tyler.
- 1825. John Stone Allen.
  Richard Patmore.
- 1826. Thomas Bird.
  Frederick Chaplin.
- 1827. William Beaumont.
  George Seymour.
- 1828. James Clements.
  S. T. Stubbing. (²)
  Joseph Heath.
- 1829. William Bird.
  Isaac Denning.
- 1830. George Chambers.
  George Perry, junr.
- 1831. Joseph Fairman.
  Richard Patmore.
- 1832. Thomas Glasscock, senr.
  John Cater Canning.
- 1833. John S. Eddy.
  John Tucker.
- 1834. William Taylor.
  William Palmer.
- 1835. Thomas Waterman.
  James Bean.
- 1836. John Morse Mullinger.
  Thomas Coote.
- 1837. John Miller.
  John Newton Nind.
- 1838. Joshua Miller.
  James Phillips.
- 1839. Thomas Quilter.
  Charles Hawke.

[1] Arthur Mumford Ashby was overseer from 1815 to 1827.
[2] Samuel Tiffen Stubbing was overseer from 1828 to 1834.

1840. John Carter Cornwell.
Burton Mumford.
1841. Richard Perry.
Thomas Beard.
1842. John Smith.
James Sanders.
1843. Joseph Thomas Johnson.
1844. Edward Beldam Johns.
Joseph Heath.
1845. Jones Gifford Nash.
James Odams.
1846. George Beadle.
John Barber.
1847. William Jolly.
Henry W^m. Young.
1848. Edward Harvey.
John Barnard Glascock.
1849. Joseph Hunt.
George Sworder.
1850. Henry Glasscock.
Peter Yardley.
1851. Mynot Titchmarsh.
John Henry Snow.
1852. George Field Grounds.
James Watts.
1853. Robert Cole.
Charles Portway.
1854. James Haiden.
Charles Scarfe.
1855. John Slater.
Joseph Duncombe Conquest.
1856. Benjn. Perry.
James Patmore.
1857. William Hughes.
Henry Patmore.
1858. George Perry.
Thomas Slater.
1859. George Edward Pritchett.
John Laybank Glascock.
1860. Thomas Bradfield.
James Amos Ashwell.

1861. William March.
James Everard.
1862. Henry Tucker.
William Harvey.
1863. Henry Soole.
William Barnard.
1864. Benjn. Nind Beard.
Henry Phillips.
1865. George Speechley.
James Sapsford.
1866. George Green.
John Pittock.
1867. John Miller.
Robert Lock.
1868. John Stubbing.
Henry Parish.
1869. Charles Dodd.
Frederick Miller.
1870. James Harvey.
William Fowler.
1871. James Burls.
William Smith.
1872. William Pavitt.
Henry Collings.
1873. Arthur Boardman.
Francis Richard Crick.
1874. Robert W. Cowell.
Benjn. Perry.
1875. Alfred Rushall.
Henry S. Wilton.
1876. Thomas Lee.
James Woolston.
1877. John Hardy.
George Pasfield.
1878. Rowland R. Pratt.
William Cornwell.
1879. William Holland.
George Stocker.
1880. Joseph Crisp.
Abraham Haselgrove.
1881. Frederick Jones Nash.
William James Waylett.

THE FINDINGS OF THE COMMISSION APPOINTED TO INQUIRE INTO THE SEVERAL CHARITIES BELONGING TO THE CHURCH AND POOR OF STORTFORD, 1692.

Transcribed from the vellum bound book.

Mr. Gibbs' gift of 20s. yearely.

IT is found that William Gibbs sometyme of Bishopp Stortford in ye said county, gent., by his last will did devise or appoint that soe much land should be bought as should bee worth to be lett att twenty shillings by ye yeare to ye intent that ye Rents and proffitts thereof should yearely for ever be distributed on St. Thomas day to and amongst the poore of the said towne of Stortford att ye discretion of ye minister and Churchwardens for ye tyme being, and by a deed of ffeoffment dated ye nineteenth day of Aprill in ye sixth yeare of King Charles ye first, made betwixt Thomas Barnard of th'one parte and John Matthew and others of th'other parte, did for ye consideration of Eighteene pounds tenne shillings purchase to them and their heires all that peice of land lying in Stortford aforesaid, in a feild called Sheephoe als Windlefeild and called Long hedge peece, conteyneing by estimation two acres more or lesse to such uses as is above expressed. And that Edward Maplesden and Robert Lay, being Churchwardens of ye said towne of Stortford, did by their Lease dated the Second of ffebruary, 1682, lett ye said peece of ground to Thomas Barnard of Stortford aforeseid for one and twenty yeares from the first day of January next before ye day of ye date of the seid Lease att the rent of Twenty shillings by the yeare, and that att ye tyme of makeing the seid Lease the Inheritance of ye seid two acres of land by vertue of one Indenture of ffeoffment, dated the 16th of August, 1680, was settled in Edward Denny, gent., Thomas Leigh Clerke, George Holgate, Ralph Manister, Samuell Ailmer, William Saunders, Richard Ffeast, senr., Nathaniel Jones, Thomas Jones, Matthew Ramsey, Robert Lay, John Barron, William Bayford, and others, for ye use and benefitt of ye poore of Stortford aforeseid. And that for about one yeare last past the seid premisses have been letten by ye seid Thomas Barnard his ex^{ors} admin^{ors} or assignes to one John Boltwood att ye rent of Twenty sixe shillings and eight pence by ye yeare, which is more by sixe shillings and eight pence by ye yeare than was reserved to the use of the poore by the seid Lease :—

And that in or about ye twenty first day of July in the yeare of our Lord God 1630 Thomas Newcomen and others, inhabitants of Stortford aforeseid, were in the right and for the behalfe and benefitt of ye poore of the said towne seised of a parcell of ground taken out of a greate yard belonging to John Dane with a Tenement thereon built, and halfe part of a Well lying in Hockerill Streete as appeareth by the said deed of purchase made betwixt the said John Dane of the one parte and the said Thomas Newcomen and others of ye other parte, and itt is found by ye said Inquisition that George Barnes the present owner hath Stopt upp ye said Well to the damage of ye poore inhabiting in ye said tenement.

Two pieces of land in Comon Downe.

And wee doe find that there are divers other Charityes belonging to ye poore of Bishop Stortford, some of which were settled in Trustees by severall deeds of ffeoffment, and others are now managed by the Overseers of ye poore, viz., two pieces of land lying in a Comon feild called Comon Downe in Stortford aforesaid. One piece conteyneth by estimacion three Roods and the other three Acres, and are lying as by deed of feoffment dated the Eleaventh of Aprill in ye yeare of our Lord God 1634 doth appeare.

40s. per a^m out of ye Mannor of Walkers in Farnham.

And that there is fforty shillings by ye yeare paid to ye Overseers for ye poore of the said parish of Stortford out of ye mannor of Walkers in Ffarneham in Essex att Christmas yearely, given by the last will of Mr. Rowland Elliott, and acknowledged to be due by Mr. Meade the present owner of the said mannor.

Hoys Gift.

And that there is sixe Shillings and Eight pence paid as aforesaid out of the Holy Bush Inn, as appeareth by a deed dated the 15th day of July, 1686, made betweene Henry Hoy of Albury in ye County of Hertford of the one parte, and Samuel Snoden,

Gent., and Thomas Barnard, Scrivener, both of Bishopp Stortford in ye same county of the other part, pursuant to the last will and Testament of Thomas Hoy of little Hallingbury in ye said County of Essex, deceased.

Ellis' Gift, 20s. per an^m.

And that there is twenty shillings by ye yeare paid as aforesaid out of a messuage and lands in Southstreete bought of William Thorne by William Ellis, and given by his last will, beareing date the 5th day of July, 1636.

£5 per an^m p^d from Ironmongers Hall.

And that there is five Pounds by the yeare paid by the master and wardens of Ironmongers Hall in London halfe yearely, viz., att Lady day and Michaelmas, and was given by Mr. Dane for ye use of ye poore till there should be a ffree Schoole settled in the said towne of Bishopp Stortford, and then to goe towards ye maintenance of the said Schoolemaster.

Dr. Harvey's Gift of £3.

And the said Jurors doe further find that Henry Harvey, doctor of Laws, did by his will, dated the 1st day of November in ye yeare 1584, give and devise the sume of three Pounds by ye yeare for ever to ye poore of Stortford aforesaid, to bee paid and issueing out of an Estate belonging to Trinity Hall in Cambridge.

£17 at Interest.

And the said Jurors doe further find that there is the sume of Seaventeene Pounds att Interest att Seaventeen Shillings by ye yeare now in ye hands of John Burling of Bishop Stortford, being a Stock for ye use of ye poore of ye said Parish.

And it is found by the said Inquisition that there is halfe an acre of land lying in Apton al^s Appletonfeild in Stortford, and that ye same was lett by ye said Edward Maplesden and Robert Ley to the said Thomas Barnard by Lease made in ye yeare 1682 without the consent of ye Parish att ye rent of sixe shillings and eight pence by ye yeare and noe more. And that the said Thomas Barnard did lease out ye premisses to one John Boltwood att twenty shillings by the yeare, and that Mary Barnard widdow is his Relict and Executrix, and the said Thomas, and Mary his wife, Successively have received the sume of twenty shillings by ye yeare for ye said peice of ground for foure yeares ending at

Michælmas last past, and that it is a Charity belonging to yᵉ said Parish Church of Bishopp Stortford.

Barnestraw house and Stable in Water Lane.

And that there is one barnestraw house and stable with a yard, Orchard, and backside thereto belonging, situate in Watery Lane in the towne of Bishopp Stortford, and conteyneth in breadth from yᵉ gatehouse of the said Edward Denny to the dwelling house of Richard Osborne Thirty five feete, and att the other end next yᵉ River Twenty five feete, And yᵉ said ground extendeth from yᵉ said lane called Watery Lane to Stortford River, and that it is a Charity belonging to the said Parish Church of Stortford and of yᵉ vallue of three pounds by yᵉ yeare, And that yᵉ said Edward Maplesden and Robert Ley did demise yᵉ said premisses to ye said Edward Denny by Lease dated yᵉ seaventh day of January in the thirty fourth yeare of our late Sovereigne of blessed memory King Charles yᵉ second without yᵉ consent of the Parishoners of yᵉ said Parish att yᵉ yearely Rent of fforty shillings payable to them and their successors for thirty yeares. And that yᵉ said Lease was Altered since yᵉ sealing, and the word Thirty putt into Habendum instead of Twenty, as it was sworne by one Osborne, a witness to yᵉ same, who said he heard the same read just before the sealing, and that itt was read twenty and not Thirty as itt now standeth partly written in the said Lease where the Parchment was Rased, and that yᵉ same hath beene for tenn yeares last past att Twenty shillings by yᵉ yeare lesse than yᵉ same was truely worth and might have been lett for.

4d. per An^m out of Shortlands.

And itt did appeare by severall Rentalls to the said Jury produced, and by a witness that swore the same, that there was anciently paid out of halfe an acre of land called Shortlands, lying in a feild called halfe acres, the sume of foure pence by yᵉ yeare, and that yᵉ said land is now in yᵉ occupation of one Mary Miller, or her assignes, and that it is in arrears for Thirty one yeares or thereabouts.

The Library att Schoole.

And itt is found for severall yeares last past divers Bookes of greate vallue have been given by Schollers of and Benefactors to yᵉ Gramar Schoole of Stortford aforesaid, which together amount in value to Three hundred pounds and upwards, and that yᵉ same were given and designed as well for the perusall and benefit of the present Schoolmaster from tyme to tyme, and such persons of quality and others as have been or shall bee Schollers of or benefactors to the said Schoole and Library as for y⁀e greater Reputation and improvement of the said Schoole, and such as should be Masters and Schollers thereof, Soe as the said bookes should not be diminished or any wayes dampnified thereby, and that there never was any person or persons appointed for the preservation and safe keeping of the said bookes or Library other than such as were given by Mr. Thomas Leigh late vicar of Stortford aforesaid. And it is found that there is a house called the Gramer schoole house and Library Roome thereunto adjoyneing and y⁀e tenements and grounds to the same belonging as they are now in the possession of Mr. Tooke y⁀e present Schoolemaster and some other Tennants.

Houses and lands belonging to the Church.

Which last mentioned houses, tenements, and grounds, as well as all other the messuages or tenements here after named, are and ought to bee imployed to and for y⁀e reparation and ornament of y⁀e said Parish Church of Stortford, viz., That messuage or tenement neare Tainter Hill with the Outhouses and[1] appurtenances in Stortford now in y⁀e occupation of Edward Jobinson, situate by the tenement now of Thomas Appleby, North, John Reade, South, Potters Streete, West, and the River, East. And all that little peice of ground or standing for stalls in the ffishmarket, whereon a fixed stall or shopp lately stood, conteyneing in length about twelve feete, and in breadth aboute tenn feete, abutting on the High Streete, North, upon a Shopp new built in the tenure of John Reade, South.

And all that peice of ground, conteyneing by estimation two acres lying in a comon feild called Aptonfeild, abutting on the Highway leading from Stortford to Thorley East.

And all that peice of ground lying in Hockerell feild conteyneing by estimation halfe an acre, lying by the land of John Reynolds, West, and one other peice of land lying in y⁀e same feild, conteyneing by estimation three Roods, lying by y⁀e land of William Read on the West.

And that peice of Meadow called Sextons mead conteyneing by estimation three Roods, lying by the River on the South, formerly held by Henry Balaam, now in y⁀e tenure of Thomas Clayton.

[1] This house was formerly known as "The Green Dragon." It was a few years ago occupied by Messrs. Perry and Son, and now forms part of Mr. Lock's carpet warehouse.

And all that messuage called the Church house, wherein John Wybert and Anne Vinteman now dwelleth, situate neare North Streate in Stortford aforesaid.

And all that messuage or tenement called the Roundhouse with the appurtenances, in which the widow Chandler now dwelleth. Situate on Poultry Hill, alias Leather Markett, in Stortford aforesaid.

And all that messuage with the appurtenances thereto belonging, situate in and ffronting upon South Streete in ye tenure of Henry Wallis.

And one other messuage now in ye tenure of one John Dugard, lying in and fronting upon South Streete aforesaid West, and the River, East. Samuel Taylor's tenement North, and a house called the Catherine Wheele, South.

And also one Butcher's Stall, holden by Stephen   in the Butcher Rowe, conteyneing in breadth ffive feete and a halfe, and in length sixe feete and a halfe.

And all that Croft or close of pasture conteyneing by estimation an acre and halfe, and now in the tenure of Thomas Jones, sometyme parcell of a feild called Chalke Croft, now inclosed with hedge and ditch, lying by a lane or way leadeing from Wickham Hall, West, and by a tenement of John Crabb or his Assignes, East, and upon land in ye tenure of Henry Aley, South, and ye Highway, North.

And one peice of ground and a messuage now holden by George White and Richard Hanchett, abutting on ye highway leading from Stortford to Sabridgeworth, East, and a feild called Sandpitt feild, West.

And those two tenements situate att ye bottome of South Streete with their appurtenances, now in the tenure of Richard Harman, John Greene, and widdow Patmore, abutting on South Streete, West, and ye River, East.

And all that peice of land lying in a Comon feild called Comon Downe, by the land late of William Read, in ye tenure of ffrancis Patmore, South, ye lands of William Mills, North, the lands of William Holgate, West, and ye highway leading from Stortford to Manuden, East.

And also all that peice of ground called Horsemans ditch, now in the occupation of John Gill, Gentleman, lying next y^e

Viccaridge Yard towards yᵉ East, and yᵉ Churchyard towards the north, conteyneing by estimation one Rood more or lesse.

Quit Rents 26s. 6d.

And that there is issueing out of divers lands and tenements in Stortford aforesaid the sume of Twenty six Shillings and sixe pence, which last mentioned lands, tenements, and Rents now are, and for divers yeares last past have been, in yᵉ hands, custody, or power of yᵉ Churchwardens, as appeareth by divers leases thereof by them made to the present occupiers or tenants, or their Assignees, and by their accounts by them annually passed to which Relation being had may appeare.

£27 15s. 0d.

And whereas itt is found by yᵉ said Inquisition that Edward Maplesden and William Rochill were churchwardens in 1679, and they then had in their hands of yᵉ said Parishioners yᵉ sume of twenty seaven pounds ffifteene shillings, which they were to pay att yᵉ goeing off of their Office to the said Parishioners againe, And that they are since dead, and that att the tyme of their death neither they or either of them had paid backe yᵉ said sume of Twenty seaven pounds and ffifteene shillings, and that nyne pounds three shillings and fourpence of itt doth belong to the poore, And Eighteene pounds sixe shillings and eight pence to the Church, and that neither itt nor any parte of itt since yᵉ same tyme hath been imployed to and for yᵉ said uses, but hath remained unaccounted for in yᵉ hands of yᵉ said Edward Maplesden or William Rochill, or their Executrixes, who are Mary, yᵉ widow of Edward Maplesden, and Judith, the widow of William Rochill, and that with ye Interest thereof yᵉ said sume att five pounds per cent since yᵉ yeare 1679, doeth amount to fforty three pounds nyneteene shillings and upwards :—

The Order and Decree of the Court which follows the above finding is not sufficiently interesting to transcribe here, but it may be summarised as follows :

The Commissioners being "satisfied that parte of yᵉ said charityes hath been imbezilled or misemployed," and " that there is a greate want of Trustees," proceed to make the following orders and decrees :

Thomas Barnard's lease of 2 acres of land near "Windlefeild" was made void and widdow Barnard had to pay up £3, " which att sixe shillings and eight pence by the yeare for nyne yeares amounts to soe much, and is the increase of rent over and above what hath been hitherto paid."

George Barnes was ordered to "lay open ye said well and make itt in as good repaire as formerly itt was, soe that itt may be usefull to ye poore people dwelling in ye said house."

Thomas Barnard's lease of half an acre of land in Aptonfield and Mr. Denny's lease of the Bark Barn in Water Lane were made void. The Commissioners considered the land in Aptonfield worth 20s p^r an^m, and they therefore ordered Widow Barnard to pay the sum of £6, "which att Thirteene shillings and four pence by ye yeare amounts to soe much and is for the arrears of ye said land to make ye full vallue for the same."

Mr. Edward Denny was ordered to pay £10 "being the sume due for arreares of rent, and to make the said rent of 4os. by the yeare amount to £3 by the yeare," he had also to pay 37s. "for and by reason he hath not duely and sufficiently kept the said premises in repair."

Mrs. Sarah Eve, the daughter and heiress of Mary Miller, had to pay 10s. 4d. "being due for one and thirty yeares arreares of Rent," and was ordered in future to pay 4d. per an^m to the Churchwardens.

The Commissioners finding "that they haveing assets of their husbands sufficient in their hands," ordered Mary Maplesden and Judith Rochill to pay the sum of £43 19s. 0d.

The Commissioners further found that some of the charities had been "soe miserably managed that if some due care be not taken the said charityes will come to decay and ruine," they therefore appointed as Trustees of the charities belonging to the Church and Poor of Stortford the following gentlemen:

Sir Edward Turner of Great Hallingbury, Kn^t.

Sir Thomas Middleton of Stansted Mountfichet, Kn^t.

William Kendall of Takely, Esquire.

William Allen, Thomas Paske, William Newce, all of Much Hadham, Thomas Bonest of Hornemead, Matthew Blucke of Hunsdon, "William Calverd of ffurnix Pelham," John Yardley of Stortford, Esquires.

Michael Altham of Latton, Clerk.

Matthew Wolley, Samuel Snoden, William Cason, Thomas Hastler, all of Stortford, Gentlemen.

William Saunders, Apothecary, Richard Osborne, Tanner, Samuel Jocelyne, Grocer, William Bayford, Currier, all of Stortford.

The Vicar of Stortford for the time being (then Christopher Cooper), The Master of the Grammar School for the time being (then Thomas Tooke).

The Commissioners then proceed to lay down rules for the guidance of the Trustees, the Churchwardens, and the Overseers, after which they make the following additional orders and decrees.

Edward Denny was ordered to pay the sum of £6 "in respect of yᵉ greate charge and extraordinary trouble by his delayes and otherwise he hath put yᵉ prosecutors to in obteyneing this decree as aforesaid."

George Barnes had to pay 20s. "for and in respect hee stopped upp yᵉ said well to the wrong and damage of yᵉ poore people that Inhabitt therein."

Mary Miller had to pay the sum of 10s. "for and in respect shee kept in her hands money belonging to the Church and refused to pay yᵉ same though shee was civilly required soe to doe."

The monies thus obtained were to go towards paying the costs of the decree, and if this was found insufficient to meet the charges then the remainder was to be paid out of the monies recovered for Interest and Arrears of Rents.

Some of the persons mentioned in the above orders and decrees being at the time of the Inquisition dead, their arrears had to be paid up by their heirs, executors, or administrators.

On the next page are the minutes of a meeting of the trustees, held on April 19th, 1693, from which the following items are extracts :

Item.

It is ordered that yᵉ Churchwardens shall buy a Booke to keepe accounts, and a Chest to keepe yᵉ writeings Relateing to yᵉ Church.

Item.

It is ordered that Whereas Mrs. Judith Rochill and Mrs. Mary Maplesden, who were decreed to pay yᵉ sume of £43 19s. 0d., have this day and before been ffrendly desired to pay yᵉ same, and were this day summoned to appeare before yᵉ said Trustees, and refused soe to doe or pay yᵉ said sume. It is ordered that Mr. James Altham do serve them with a coppy of yᵉ Writt of Execution and presente them persuant to yᵉ direction of yᵉ decree.

Item.

It is ordered that Mr. William Bayford, one of the Churchwardens, do demand of Mr. Richard Carr and John Burling yᵉ seaventeene pounds with Interestt due on a Bond dated 26th day of June A.D. 1684, And upon nonpayment to deliver yᵉ Bond to Mr. James Altham to be sued.

THE FINDINGS OF THE CHARITIES' COMMISSION, 1692.

There are no other minutes of meetings in this book, but on the next page is copied in an additional order of the High Court of Chancery, 1716.

This was a case heard before the Lord High Chancellor on July 6th 1716, between Sir Edward Turner, Knight, William Calvert, Esq., John Sandford, Esq., William Bayford, and others, the Trustees of the Charities of Stortford, Exceptants, and Thomas Clayton and Thomas Scott, Churchwardens of the said Parish, Respondents. After a recapitulation of the decree of the Commissioners for Charitable Uses, dated June 3rd, 1692, we come to the exceptions taken by the Trustees to this decree, and as these may be considered interesting, I transcribe them in full as follows :

"And the Exceptants' first exception to the Decree being for that the said Trustees, their Heires and Successors were from time to time to suffer the said Churchwardens for the time being to receive so much of the Profits of the Premisses as belongs to the Church, and the Overseers such of the profits as should become due to the Poor, and to lay out the same according to the Wills and appointments of the Donors. By vertue of which power the Churchwardens and Overseers may and some of them have taken upon them to lay out the Charity money contrary to the Direction of the Donors, and without the consent of the Trustees, and particularly the Respondents, the present Churchwardens, or one of them, hath without any directions of the Trustees (the least of the Bells of the Church being crackt) taken upon him or themselves to employ a Founder who hath melted three of the largest Bells, and made six into eight, and caused new Frames to be made, and agreed for chimes, and insist to have the Charity mony employed in defraying the charge ; and the Respondents to cover such Proceedings have called a vestry and proposed they would put the Parish to no charge, but would find another way to do it, which the major part (there being about thirty present) refusing, the Respondents, after most of the vestry were gone, prevailed on eight of the meanest Inhabitants to sign an order that the Respondents should Receive what mony was in the Trustees or any former Churchwardens' hands to defray such charge of Bells, Frames, and Chimes, which Abuse would have been prevented if the Trustees had been impowered by the Decree to order how the mony should be laid out, and no part of the mony ought (as the Exceptants are advised) to be disposed by the Churchwardens or Overseers without the direction of the Trustees, nor ought the Charities to be subject to orders of Vestry, but be divided by the Trustees according to the Wills, Directions, and Appointments of the Donors.

"And the Charity mony, or so much as was requisite, was intended to be applyed in repairing severall Houses part of the Estate given to the Charity, and which, unless repaired, will be left by the Tenants, whereby the Income of the Charity will be much lessened.

"And the second Exception being for that the decree hath not impowered the Trustees to appoint fitting persons to collect the rents of and let the lands and Houses belonging to the Charity and to Repair the Houses for want of which the Charities are misapplied.

"And the third Exception being for that the Decree appointing the Trustees, or seven of them, to meet yearly on the first Munday of August to take the accounts of the Churchwardens and Overseers, which happening to be in Harvest time, they come generally unprovided in their Accounts, and excuse themselves on account of its being Harvest Time; neither is there any Penalty on the Churchwardens or Overseers in case they do not meet at that time.

"And the Fourth exception being for that the Quorum of the Trustees are to be seven, whereas the chiefe of them live at some distance from the said Parish, and in case the Quorum consisted of Five only the Charity would be as well taken care of and more effectually dispatcht, it being a difficulty to get so many together as seven of the Trustees.

"And the Fifth Exception being for that the said Decree doth not sufficiently set forth the Particulars of the Lands and other things subject to the Payment of the Charities, nor which of them are charged for payment of the one Charity, nor which to the other, as the Exceptants are advised it ought to be, Whereto the Respondents Councell alleged That they by their answer confess there was such Decree, and that they were Churchwardens of Bishops Stortford for the years 1713 and 1714, and received the Rents of so much of the Premisses as did belong to the Church for the Reparations and Ornaments thereof except such as were yet in arrear, and have set forth an Account of what their Receipts and Disbursements amounted unto, by which it appears they are in disburse £3 0s. 5¾d., and are ready to produce an account of the particulars and to accompt for what monies are come to their hands as Churchwardens, having all just allowances either before a sufficient number of Trustees or otherwise as the Court shall direct. Confess that in 1713 one of the Bells called the Treble being crackt, and the canons of the Tenor Bell broke, and another Bell being out of order, insomuch that the said Bells were useless, the Respondents did without the direction of the Trustees employ a Founder to melt three of the largest Bells and made six Bells into Eight, and caused new Wheels to be made, but whether the same was contrary to the intent of the Donors they submit to the Court, but insist that what they did to the Bells was a real Reparation and Ornament to the Church, and conceive they were not by the said Decree obliged to consult the Trustees about employing the Bell-founder.

"Confess there was such order of Vestry made as in the first Exception, which order was signed by about eight of the Parishioners, of whom the Respondents were two, and believe the major part of the Parishioners present did not agree to it, and therefore the Respondents have not nor do intend to contract for making of Chimes or to employ any of the Charity money for that purpose without the consent of the Trustees or a sufficient number of them. Believe severall of the Houses are out of repair and untenanted, and the repairing them hath been omitted for the want of mony the Respondents being in disburse as aforesaid.

"Whereupon and upon long debate of the matter and hearing the Decree of the Commissioners for Charitable Uses read, and what could be alledged by councel on either side, His Lordship doth think fit and so order and Decree, That the Churchwardens and Overseers of the Poor of the said Parish do continue respectively to receive the Rents and Profits of the Respective Charity Estates according to the Decree of the Commissioners, but the Churchwardens are not to issue any of the Charity monies to make any Ornaments of the Church without the consent of the major part of the said Trustees first had in writing. The number of the Quorum of Trustees who are by the said Decree to act touching the Charities are to be reduced from seven to Five, which Five are to act in all respects as the Seven were by the said Decree to do.

"And it being suggested that the first   of August, which is by the Decree appointed for the Trustees annually to meet on to take the Accounts of the said Charities, is an inconvenient time by reason of the Harvest and otherwise, His Lordship doth order that such time of meeting be changed to the Monday in the Whitsun week yearly.

"And it is hereby referred to Sir Thomas Gerey, one of the Masters of this Court, to Tax the Respondents their costs of this Suite, which are to be paid them out of the Charity mony in question."

SUBSCRIBERS TO THE SCHOOL-HOUSE.

The following list of subscribers to the School-House and Market Place is with the papers in the church. It is written on parchment but is not dated.

"Those whose names are heare unto subscribed being sencible that the former subscriptions towards building of the school-house and Market plase of Bishop Stortford will not finish the necessary aworke, wee therefor have made a new subscription upon condition that the inhabitants of the Town for whose Benefit and interest the school was built doe subscribe a new towards finishing that worke."

	£	s.	d.
Chas. Barrington	5	0	0
Thos. Brograve	5	0	0
R^a. freman	5	0	0
Edwd. Turner	5	0	0
Will Stanley	2	10	0
Henry Gore	5	0	0
Thos. Middleton (?)	5	0	0
Will Bernes	5	0	0
Robt Elwes	5	0	0
Will Calvert	5	0	0
Charles Turner	5	0	0
Samuel Robinson	5	0	0
John Cheveley	2	10	0
Sir Dudley Cullum of Hawks in Suffolk Baron	5	0	0
Robert Oxwyth	1	0	0
Francis Flyer (?)	3	4	6
William Dyer	3	4	6
Tho. Ren			
John Stone	1	1	6
Henry Twistleton	1	1	6
John Chauncy (?)	2	0	0

SUBSCRIBERS TO THE SCHOOL-HOUSE.

	£	s.	d.
Edward Sebright	5	0	0
Edward Sayer	2	3	0
Geo. Draper	1	1	6
C. Cæsar	5	0	0
John Buxton	1	1	6
Joseph Chaplin of London	3	4	6
John Wright of London	2	3	0
Mr. Millington of Kensington	1	1	6
Mr. English Clerk	2	0	0
Mr. John Hill of London	1	1	6
Mr. George Sayer of London	2	3	6

The names of the inhabitants of Stortford who have subscribed a second time towards the building a school and library there (they have ?) subscribed (as ?) follows in concurrence with a second subscription of the Gentlemen:

	£	s.	d.		£	s.	d.
Mr. Bounds				Thos. Howe, senr. (?)		10	0
Mr. Took		5	0	Samewell Mountford		10	0
„ Wolley		2	3	John Boultwood			
„ Gill				Nath¹ Jones, senr.			
„ Denney		4	0	Nath¹ Jones, junr.		10	0
„ Sandford		2	3	John Green		10	0
„ Cason		5	0	George Bass			
„ Snowden				Edward Bayford			
„ Ely		2	0	Will Spesichall			
„ Saunders		3	0	francis fann		5	0
„ Barnard				francis Willow (?)		11	6
„ Manister		2	10	Mr. Stafford			
„ Hyde		2	0	Thos Cooke		5	0
„ Scott		1	0	Mr. Hellmes (?)	1	0	0
„ Jennens		2	0	Mr. Claton, senr.		10	0
„ Wick		2	0	David Joyce			
„ Wankford		1	0	Will Barnes Hock			
„ Hastler (?)		1	0	Nickolas Tyler		10	0
„ furgusson				Mr. Joslin	1	0	0
„ Lay		3	0	„ Osborne		10	0
„ Browen		1	0	„ Dixon, sen.	3	0	0
„ Game		2	0	„ Dixon, jun.			
Samuel Bayford		1	0	„ Dimsdel	2	0	0
Will Barnes		1	0	„ Reighnolds (?)	1	0	0
John Tavenour		1	0	„ Ruttland (?)			
Mr. Will Bayford		1	1	6	„ Banson			
Zackurey Blower		10	0	Thos Roberts	2	0	0

John Barwick (?)	.		11	6	Mr. Will Denny	.	3	0	0
Goodman Schooling	.				Mr. Cradock	.	1	1	6
George Burrell	.	1	0	0	Rich. Feast	.	1	0	0
John Reeve	.		10	0	Tobias Staines	.	1	0	0
John Baront Baker	.	1	0	0	James Hunter	.		10	0
Edward Johnson	.		10	0	Henry Archer, Shoe-				
Thos Appleby	.	1	0	0	maker	.		10	0
Thos Grove, jun.	.		10	0	Rowland Griggs	.		10	0
George Jollyman	.				Edw. Juby	.		5	0
Thos Clayton, jun.	.				Mr. Will Holgate	.	2	0	0
Mr. Archer (?)	.	1	1	6	Mr. Polhill	.	2	0	0
Edward Ashby	.	1	10	0	Edw. Wood	.		10	0

FROM THE MISCELLANEOUS PAPERS.

169½. A bill for yᵉ Comˢ and Jurymens diners att yᵉ Inquisⁿ about yᵉ charity of Stortford heid at yᵉ Crown Inn Jan. 18.

	£	s.	d.
A dish of Stewed Beefe		4	6
A Shoulder and neck of muton		4	8
ffor pickles		1	0
ffor a sur loyne of Beefe		15	0
ffor a goose		4	0
ffor a Turkey		4	6
ffor fowles and 2 dishes of Larckes		9	0
ffor Lemons		1	0
ffor frute and cheese		2	0
ffor puddens		2	0
ffor ffire		10	0
ffor Bread and Beere	1	1	0
ffor Wine	2	2	6
Layed out to Sumens Mr. Muray		1	6
The Jury mens diner.			
ffor a legge of muton and caper sase		3	6
ffor Porcke and Tornops		3	0
ffor pudens		1	6
ffor 5 Ribes of Roast Beefe		12	0
ffor a Goose		4	0
ffor Bread and Beere		18	6
Wine		12	0
ffor fire		5	0
	£9	3	2

MONUMENTAL INSCRIPTIONS.

As nearly all the Inscriptions within St. Michael's Church have already been printed in full by Sir H. Chauncy in 1700 (reprinted at Bishop Stortford, 1826), Mr. Salmon in 1728, Mr. Clutterbuck in 1829, or by Mr. Cussans in 1870, I did not consider it necessary to give them in full again here, as most readers of this book will probably have access to one or more of the above mentioned County Histories. I have therefore contented myself with noting the position of the Inscriptions as they now stand in the church, giving a list of those which were formerly to be seen in the church, but which have now disappeared, and a full copy of those which appear hitherto to have escaped notice.

Nearly all the Inscriptions remain in their original positions, with the exception of those that were, previous to the restoration of the church in 1869, attached to the columns in the north and south aisles, and to the north wall of the chancel. These are now to be found upon the north and south walls and upon the south wall of the chancel. The different positions assigned to a few others may readily be seen by comparing my list (No. 1) with that of either of the above named county historians. I may here add that Mr. Cussans' account was written previous to the removal of the Inscriptions from the columns and north wall of the chancel, but I cannot understand why he omitted those given in list No. 3, unless they happened at that time to be hidden from view by the old pews.

No. 1.

On the South Wall of the Chancel.

Name.	Date of Death.	Remarks.
Peter Mark Sparke, M.D.	1675	
Edward Denny	1720	Descended from the Dennys of Waltham Abbey, Co. Essex.
Mrs. Cordelia Denny	1698	Dau. of Adam Hill, Esq., of Spaldwick, Co. Huntingdon.

Sir George Duckett, Bart.	1822	Sir George Duckett, Bart., formerly Sir George Jackson, Bart., Judge Advocate of the Fleet. He was a Secretary of the Admiralty and an M.P. for Weymouth, Melcombe Regis, and Colchester. In 1769 he made the River Stort navigable to this town.
John Sandford	. 1743	
Mrs. Ann Sandford	. 1747	
Mrs. Martha Brome	. 1759	Dau. of Thomas Osborne of St. Andrew's, London, Gent.
John Brome	. 1783	
Edward Brome	. 1770	Many years a merchant of distinguished reputation in Lisbon.
John Brome	. 1813	
Elizabeth Henrietta Brome	1777	Dau. of William Bearsley, Esq., of Oporto.

On the Floor of the Chancel.

Lady Margaret Denny	. 1648	Descended from the ancient family of the Edgecombes of Mount Edgecombe in Co. Cornwall.
Charles Denny, M.A.	. 1635	Grandson of the Rt. Hon. Sir Anthony Denny, Knt.
Thomas Edgecombe	. 1614	Inf.
Rowland Hill	. 1693	Descended from the Hills of Fernhill, Co. Shropshire.
Anthony Denny	. 1662	
Mary Denny	. 1666	She was an Aldriche of Swardiston in Co. Norfolk.
Denny Sandford	. 1700	Inf.
Hester Sandford	. 1705	Inf. The inscription on this stone is now nearly obliterated.
John Denny Brome	. 1715	
William Brome	. 1718	On three stones (one of which is broken) in the chancel floor.
William Brome	. 1722	
Anna Maria Brome	. 1722	
Mary Brome	. 1715	
Mary Jenoure	. 1724	Dau. to Joseph Jenoure, Esq. The inscription is nearly obliterated.
Robert Strachie, M.D.	. 1704	

192   MONUMENTAL INSCRIPTIONS.

John Gill, Gent.	. 1711	
Dorothy Gill	. 1700	
Mrs. Sarah Thayn	. 1736	Dau. of the Rev. Thos. Leigh of Bishop Stortford. (In Mr. Cussans "Hist. of Herts" this name is misspelt Thayer.)
Cordelia Brome	. 1727	On a broken stone in floor of chancel.
Cordelia Brome	. 1732	Inscriptions almost obliterated.
Rev. Philip Pipon, M.A.	1734	Master of Stortford School.
John Brome	. 1734	Linen draper and citizen of London; he was descended from a very ancient family, of whom William de Brome was standard bearer to King Edward III. This stone is now partially covered by the seats in the chancel, which have lately been moved forward to give additional accommodation for the choir.

In the Floor of Nave.

John Yardley, M.D.	. 1697	
William Banson	. 1712	Surgeon.
Ann Gurson	. 1706	Wife of Mr. John Gurson of Stortford.
Rev. John Mall, A.M.	. 1755	Master of Stortford School.
Rev. Joseph Clapp, A.M.	1767	Master of Stortford School.
Mary Clapp	. 1781	
Joseph Clapp, Gent.	. 1790	
Mrs. Ann Smith	. 1785	See list No. 3.
Mr. Nathaniel Smith	. 1786	ditto
Mrs. Deborah Fowle	. 1733	ditto
Sarah Matilda Fairman	. 1830	ditto
Joseph Fairman	. 1848	ditto
John Harris Roberts	. 1818	ditto
James Watson Roberts, M.D.	. 1830	ditto
Joanna Roberts	. 1850	ditto

In the Floor of South Aisle.

Simon Rutland, M.B.	. 1682	
Susanna Taylor	. 1725	
John Huntington	. 1775	See list No. 3.
John Chapman	. 1790	ditto

Thomas Chapman	. 1803	See list, No. 3.
Mrs. Mary Staines	. 1708	ditto
One flat stone.	Inscription entirely obliterated.	

In Floor of North Aisle.

Thomasin Rutland	. 1683	Wife of Simon Rutland.
James Pedley	. 1714	Son of John Pedley of Tetworth, C°. Huntingdon.
William Dalton, Gent.	. 1785	
Thomas Scott	. 1709	See list No. 3.
Elizabeth Scott	. 1708	ditto
John Scott		ditto
A. W.	. 1811	
W. W.	. 1827	
L. W.	. 1832	
W. W. W.	. 1812	
W. H. Wilby	. 1831	
T. W.	. 1847	
Elizabeth Paul	. 1826	

One flat stone. Inscription obliterated; at the left hand upper corner there are traces of letters which look like " J. Jen "—the name may be "Jennings" or "Jenoure."

In Floor of Centre Aisle.

John Wright	. 1707

On South Wall.

Mary Maplesden	. 1684	All died of the small pox. "These were the children of Edward Maplesden, Gent., descended of the ancient family of Maplesdens in Kent, and of Mary his wife, daughter of William Hignell, Clerk, of the family of Hignells in Worcestershire. Hester, the youngest daughter, ætat 4 years, died the first of April, 1686. Edward, the father, died Oct. 22, 1689. Mary, the mother, Nov. 19, 1712."
Edward Maplesden	,,	
William Maplesden	,,	
Gervas Maplesden	,,	
Elizabeth Maplesden	,,	
Sarah Maplesden	,,	
Layston Maplesden	. 1685	
Hester Maplesden	. 1686	
Edward Maplesden	. 1689	
Mary Maplesden	. 1712	
Rev. William Polhill, M.A.	1721	Vicar of St. Michael's, Stortford.
Thomas Tooke	. 1713	Son of Mr. John Tooke, A.M.
Revd. Raymond-Edward Lorance Rogers, A.B.	1816	Vicar of St. Michael's, Stortford.

Thomas Adderley, Esq.	1774	"He first suggested the idea of making the river Stort navigable up to this town."
John Pilkin, Esq.	1806	
Thomas Clough, Esq.	1838	
Susannah Clough	1786	

On South-West Wall.

John Yardley, M.D.	1697	
Alice Yardley	1712	W. of John Yardley.
Susanna Taylor	1725	Dau. of Thos. Leigh, and wife of Robert Taylor of Newhouse, Little Hallingbury, Gent.

On the South-East Wall.

Revd. Edmund Gibson, A.M.	1798	He was Vicar of this parish 33 years. He died in London and was buried at Fulham in the family vault of his grandfather, Bishop Gibson.
Mr. Roger Bolton	1816	See list No. 3.

On the North Wall.

Ralph Winter, Esq.	1802	
Susannah Winter	1813	Dau. of Peter Calvert, Esq., of Much Hadham.
William Wilby	1827	
Lydia Wilby	1832	
Lt-Colonel W. H. Wilby	1831	
Walker William Wilby	1842	
Anne Wilby	1811	
Thomas Wilby	1847	
William Wilby	1866	
Elizabeth Paul	1826	See list No. 3.

On the North-West Wall.

Simon Rutland, M.B.	1682

North Porch.

One stone in the porch bears traces of an inscription not legible now.

South Porch.

John Pilkin	1806	On a flat stone.
Two flat stones. Inscriptions quite obliterated.		
Joseph Bangham	1836	See list No. 3.
Mrs. Elizabeth Jones	1827	ditto

No. 2.

The undermentioned inscriptions formerly to be seen in the church are not visible now (1881).

Thomas Fleming	1436	These Inscriptions are mentioned by Weaver. Sir H. Chauncy (1700) does not notice them, and Salmon (1728) says that both brasses and stones were broken or lost in his time.
Joanna Fleming	1411	
Johannes Algar	1484	
Matilda Algar	1480	
George Elyot	1551	Mentioned by Sir H. Chauncy (1700). They were not legible in Salmon's time, as he says "an old stone *had* lately this inscription."
John Elyot	1557	
Joan Staverd	1614	Mentioned by Sir H. Chauncy, and by Salmon, not noticed by Clutterbuck (1829), nor by Cussans (1870).
Jonathan Payne	1681	
William Milbanke, Gent.	1712	He was the youngest son of Sir Mark Millbanke of Hanalby, Co. York, Bart. This inscription is mentioned by Salmon and Clutterbuck but not by Cussans.
Rebecca Banson	1707	Three children of Mr. William Banson, Surgeon. This inscription is given by Salmon, but not mentioned by Clutterbuck or Cussans
William Banson	1712	
Martha Banson	,,	
Sandford Brome	1736	Mentioned by Clutterbuck but not noticed by Cussans.

No. 3.

The following inscriptions which appear to have escaped the notice both of Mr. Clutterbuck and Mr. Cussans are now to be seen in the church.

In the Nave.

On a stone under the lectern.

Here lieth the body of
MRS. ANN SMITH,
late wife of Mr. Nathaniel Smith
of this Place, Grocer, etc.
(and daughter of Mr. William Lack
Tea-dealer in London),

who died the 27th of March, 1785
aged 62 years.

Likewise of Mr. Nathaniel Smith
late of this Parish, Grocer,
who departed this life
the 13th of November, 1786, aged 66 years.

In a vault beneath this Stone
are deposited the remains of
SARAH MATILDA FAIRMAN,
third daughter of
Joseph and Frances Fairman,
who died June 28th, 1830,
in the 11th year of her age.

Also
the above named
JOSEPH FAIRMAN,
who died
Nov. 16, 1848,
aged 61.

On a flat stone: Coat of arms and inscription nearly obliterated.

Here lieth yᵉ body of MRS. DEBORAH FOWLE
who departed this life March yᵉ 21, 1733,
aged 63.

Here also lieth interred the Body
of MRS. DEBORAH O   late of Hertf
who departed this life the   of May
1734, aged   years.[1]

Towards the west end of nave, on a black stone with brass letters:

Depositum
Præcellentissimi Adolescentuli
JOANNIS HARRIS,
Jacobi Watson Roberts, M.D., Filii
Eximiæ spei
vitæ Ineunti anno ætatis suæ decimo tertio, erepti
die Decembrio vicesimo tertio
anno humanæ salutis MDCCCXVIII

---

[1] This name, now obliterated, I find from an entry in the Burials Register to be Oxinton. Mrs. Deborah Oxinton was the wife of Mr. Isaac Oxinton of Hertford; she was buried on May 15th, 1734.

O Virtus! O Comitas! O animi dotes ingeniique indoles!
O suavissima in amicos officia!
O Tenera erga parentes observantiæ!
O Pietas cultusque Dei!
Vos in Cœlum vestrum reduces.
Eheu! Nobis Nunquam Redituros
Plangimus:
At hic tamen solatium illic perfugium
mœrentibus
non defuturum
necnon
JACOBI WATSON ROBERTS, M.D.
et JOANNÆ uxoris ejus:
ille obiit Julii 1 A.D. MDCCCXXX.
Æt LXV.
Hæc Jan ix A.D. MDCCCL.
Æt LXXIII.
requiescant.

In the South Aisle.

MRS. MARY STAINES,
dyed yᵉ 2nd June,
1708.

In memory of
JOHN HUNTINGTON,
late of the Parish of Winterton
near Yarmouth, in Norfolk,
died the 11th of July, 1775,
aged 32 years.

In memory of
MR. JOHN CHAPMAN,
Citizen and Tallow-Chandler
of London,
who died the 6th of January,
1790, aged 47.
Also
MR. THOMAS CHAPMAN,
Coachmaker
of London,
who died Dec. 18th, 1803
aged 54 years.

In the North Aisle.

Here remains all that was mortal
of THOS. SCOTT and ELIZABETH his wife
who lived together 52 years
in this Parish.
Elizabeth entered into
Eternity on ye 20th Sep., 1708,
aged 72 years, Thomas on
ye 30th of Jan., 1709,
aged 81 years.
Here also was buried ye body
of JNO. SCOTT, the Father of
above^{sd} Thos. Scott.

On the South-East Wall.

In memory of
MR. ROGER BOLTON,
whose remains are deposited
in a vault fronting this pew,
52 years Landlord
of the Crown Inn, Hockrill.
Died 27 day of March, 1816,
in the 92nd year
of his age.
An honest man.

On the North Wall.

Sacred to the
Memory of
ELIZABETH,
relict of the late
Robert Paul, Esq.,
many years President of the
Council in the Island of St. Vincent,
Died 17 of Nov., 1826,
aged 50.

In the South Porch.

Sacred
to the memory of
JOSEPH BANGHAM,
who was formerly the Clerk of this Parish,

and discharged his several duties with propriety
for upwards of 40 years,
who died without pain either of Body or Mind
on the 14th of April, 1836,
and has left a memorial which this tablet
would record,
That the end of the upright is peace : Ps xxxvii. v. 37.
Time was granted to him, and he improved the talent
for 82 years,
And this stone was erected by the Parishioners
To testify and perpetuate
the respect and esteem
which they felt for him
during his life.

Honor to whom Honor : Rom xiii. 7.
This Tablet
was consecrated by the Penny and other
Contributions of the Poor of this Parish
to perpetuate the memory of
MRS. ELIZABETH JONES,
Their friend and benefactress, a pattern to Christians
and an ornament of Christianity :
They cannot recompense thee, but thou shalt be
recompensed at the resurrection of the just : Luke xi. 14.
She died A.D. 1827.
Her remains sleep in the adjacent Burial Ground.
Her Epitaph is written in the list of her Charities
recorded on the stone beneath.
The memory of the just is blessed : Prov. x. 7.
Thy Prayers and thine alms are gone up:
Acts x. 4.

On the other side of the porch window is a tablet giving an account of Mrs. Jones' bequests to the church and poor of Stortford. She was the only surviving daughter of John Jones, Tallow-Chandler, and Elizabeth his wife.

On the East Window.

To the Glory of God this window was presented by Joseph Taylor, Esqr., in memory of his dear wife Charlotte, eldest daughter of the late John Dobede, Esq., of Soham Place, Cambridgeshire.

On the West Window.

This window was presented by the Parishioners as a Memorial of the Ministry of Francis W. Rhodes, M.A., Vicar of this Parish, A.D. 1849—A.D. 1877.

INSCRIPTIONS NOW REMAINING UPON STONES IN THE CHURCHYARD.

For position of the plots see plan facing Title Page.

Plot A.

Name.	Date of Death.	Age.	Remarks.
Ashby, A. M.	Sep. 28, 1833	73	
,, Sarah	Sep. 27, 1836	74	Wife of A. M. Ashby.
Ashford, Edward	Dec. 23, 1806	76	
,, Sarah			
Archer, Thomas	April, 179-(?)		
Archer, Ann (?)	April, 1797	77	
Beverly, Joseph	July 17, 1845	49	
Beaumont, Elizabeth	Mar. 10, 1805	53	
Blackwell, Mary	July 1, 1831	26	Dau. of William and Elizabeth Newman.
Barker, Mary	Dec. 20, 1791	34	
Barker, Isaac	Mar. 8, 1819	61	
Bium, Henry	July 22, 1846	58(?)	This stone formerly stood in the pathway next the wall.
Bium, Mary	Dec. 10, 1830	70	
Bear, James	June 4, 1837	56	
,, Mary	Dec. 21, 1833	67	wife of James Bear.
Burton, Elizabeth	1794	61	
,, William	1794		
,, Elizabeth	July 11, 1842	40	
Bolton, Thomas	July 6, 1839	38	Son of Joseph Roger Bolton.
,, John	Jan. 19, 1832	22	
,, Joseph Roger	Oct. 10, 1803	35	
,, John	Sep. 6, 1794	67	
Barber, Andrew	April 13, 1829	28	
Brown, Sarah	1810		
Canning, Kate	1855	Inf.	
Chopping, Judith	Feb. 1, 1838	52	
,, Samuel	Nov. 18, 1837	18	Son of William and Judith Chopping.

Cheffins, Joshua	Aug. 29, 1832	55		
,, Mary	April 26, 1817	4		
,, Elizabeth	Jan. 18, 1863	82		
Christy, William	Nov. 29, 1854	47		
,, Joseph	Nov. 24, 1834	67		
,, Elizabeth	Jan. 22, 1842	68	Wife of Joseph Christy.	
,, Mary	Jan. 22, 1824	31	Dau. of William and Mary Christy.	
,, William	June 7, 1809	47		
,, Isabella		Inf.		
,, William		,,		
Campin, John	1791			
Cribb, Mrs. Margaret	May 3, 1794		Dau. of Mrs. Elizabeth Davies.	
Cribb, William	1789	Inf.		
Cook, John	Mar. 26, 1799	21		
Chaplin, William	1798	Inf.		
Dresser, William	June 2, 1807	7	Son of John and Ann Dresser.	
Davis, Mary	1801			
Davies, Mrs. Elizabeth	1820	88		
Finch, Sarah	Jan. 30, 1845	39	Wife of Augustine Finch.	
,, Caroline Letitia	Oct. 24, 1844	21	Dau. of above.	
,, George Austin	July 17, 1837	12	Son of above.	
Flindall, Eliza	Mar. 19, 1828	22	Wife of William Flindall.	
Fiske, Samuel	May 8, 1851	76	Son of Samuel Fiske, Esq., late of Clopton Hall, Suffolk.	
Goodwin, Henry	Nov. 16, 1852	50		
,, Elizabeth	Nov. 25, 1839	28		
,, James	Dec. 2, 1831	7		
Greenfield, Thomas	June 21, 1831	81		
Gilbey, Mrs. Elizabeth	Nov. 6, 1821	40	Wife of Joseph Roger Bolton.	
Gilbee, Mary			This name is upon the headstone of Robert Kippage.	
Hamilton, Hannah	May 29, 1851	48		
,, John	Feb. 10, 1855	60		
Henson, George	April 15, 1850	27		
Henerth, Frederic William	Jan. 3, 1854	69	Formerly of Frankfort-on-the-Main, and late of London.	

Name	Date	Age	Notes
Heskin, Harriet Caroline	June 25, 1826	22	Dau. of Thomas and Sarah Heskin.
Heskin, John	April 25, 1816	25	
Horner, George	1796	Inf.	
Hoy, William	April 25, 1832	52	
Hoy, Martha			
Hoy, Judith	Dec. 8, 1834	18	
Hawes, Francis	Feb. 12, 1831	84	
Ingold, Jepthah	July 11, 1840	75	
,, Ann	Aug. 18, 1843		
Kimpton, John	Jan. 21, 1844	63	
Kippage Robert	Mar. 30, 1789	35	
,, Mary	April 30, 1796	42	Wife of Robert Kippage.
,, Ann	Dec. 12, 1819	30	Dau. of ditto.
Luck, W.	Oct. 19, 1852	28	
Lawrence, Daniel	1797		
Liles, Joseph	1791		
Leeder, William	May 2, 1807	41	
Lewin, Ellen	April 25, 1824	20	
Mackenzie, Mary Ann	Jan. 26, 1845	30	Wife of James Mackenzie and dau. of Joseph and Mary Burls.
May, John	Dec. 26, 1811	51	
,, Sebethey	May 21, 1797	35	Wife of John May.
Mackenzie, Frances	Jan. 18, 1855	68	Wife of James Mackenzie.
Martin, Mrs. Letitia	Dec. 4, 1852	82	
Moore, Mrs. Molly	July 24, 1822	53	
,, John	Dec. 16, 1845	70	
,, Sarah	Aug. 17, 1854	67	
,, Eliza	Nov. 22, 1827	Inf.	
Nicholls, Ann	Oct. 19, 1830	38	Wife of John Nicholls.
,, James	May 15, 1821	38	
,, Louisa Ann	Dec. 24, 1835	Inf.	
,, Frederic William	June 23, 1844	8	
Nicholls, Ann	Jan. 5, 1841	Inf.	
Nixon, Dorothy Ann	Mar. 20, 1810		Dau. of Joseph Nixon.
Nunn, Collis	April 24, 1791	56	
Player, William	Mar. 20, 1851	80	
Powter, Mary	June 19, 1836	41	Wife of Thomas Powter.
,, Thomas	Feb. 8, 1851		

Peck, John	April 12, 1834	54	
Porter, Ann	Aug. 16, 1803		
,, Ann	Mar. 25, 1807	55	
Pope, Susannah	May 17, 1799	26	
Percival, Katherine	Sep. 14, 1817	59	Wife of Richard Percival.
,, Richard	Jan. 7, 1823	73	
,, Catherine	Nov. 5, 1828	4	
Page, Charlotte	1849	Inf.	
,, Mary	1854	4	
Rider, George	Oct. 27, 1844	65	
,, Henry	Jan. 17, 1857	28	Son of George and Sarah Rider.
Ruse, Henry Ling	Aug. 27, 1803	34	
Reynolds, Catherine			
Rhodes, Louisa	1873	37	Wife of Rev. F. W. Rhodes.
,, Basil			Children of above.
,, Frederick			
Rawlins, Elizabeth	May 30, 1824	88	
,, John	Sep. 17, 1792	57	
Skipp, William	April 28, 1851	83	
,, Sarah	July 7, 1852	82	
,, William	Oct. 3, 1848	40	Son of William and Sarah Skipp.
Smith, Susan	Mar. 15, 1844	70	
Spencer, John	Jan. 1, 1828	55	
,, Mary Piper	Feb. 28, 1818	38	Wife of John Spencer.
,, Elizabeth	Jan. 31, 1825	86	
Stock, Edward	Sep. 2, 1814	31	
,, Willey		Inf.	
,, Sarah	Aug. 12, 1825		
Sparling, Joannah	Mar. 19, 1844	76	
,, Thomas	May 6, 1851	84	
Stibbard, Mary P.	May 31, 1847	50	
Scarr, John	1802	65	
Titchmarsh Harriot Susanna	Jan. 27, 1855	37	Wife of Mynott Titchmarsh.
Tucker, Clarissa	June 6, 1831	33	Wife of John Tucker, junr.
,, Mary Ann	April 10, 1839	42	
Tillbrook, Mary Ann	April 19, 1854	62	
,, Samuel	Aug. 12, 1838	41	
Tofts, Timothy	Jan. 8, 1842	69	
,, Ann	Oct. 25, 1833	53	Wife of Timothy Tofts.

Tunstall, Mrs. Ellen	July 13, 1797	85
Thompson, Richard	Oct. 10, 1797	67
Thompson, Mary		
" Mrs. Elizabeth	Jan. 22, 1825	25
Thompson, Mary Ann	1825	Inf.
Thompson, William	July 8, 1865	70
" Richard	Feb. 15, 1801	35
Weale, Elizabeth	April 11, 1844	75 — Widow of Robert Weale, and dau. of Thomas and Alice Langton of Leicester.
Weatherley, George	Nov. 4, 1827	37
Woodley, Thomas	Nov. 26, 1832	75
" Susannah	Jan. 5, 1827	69
" Susannah	Oct. 3, 1826	36
" Thomas	Mar. 16, 1827	34
Welsman, John Davis	Dec. 5, 1798	35
Wilkes, Elizabeth	May 12, 1830	68
Webb, John	Feb. 6, 1812	51
Webb, Elizabeth		— Wife of John Webb.

Plot B.

Buckland, Elizabeth	Feb. 14, 1852	29
Baynes, Elizabeth Margaret	Mar. 18, 1843	51
Baynes, John	Mar. 6, 1862	87
" Robert		Inf.
" Emma Wood		"
" Sarah	Feb. 9, 1811	29
Bull, James	Aug. 17, 1819	26
" George	1820	
" George	Aug. 25, 1825	63
" Dorcas	1827	77
Clark, John	June 25, 1788	
" Sarah	Mar. 17, 1799	
Dugard, Sarah	Nov. 1, 1830	81
" William	Dec. 18, 1807	76
" Martha	Aug. 5, 1767	44
" Martha	April 29, 1764	71
" Thomas	Nov. 18, 1777	79
" Thomas	Aug. 7, 1801	72
" John	1809	
" Sarah	Feb. 18, 1775	37

Glasscock, Joseph	Jan. 25,	1845	71
,, Sarah	Nov. 18,	1816	44
,, Rebecca	July 4,	1843	63
Handscomb, Matthew	Oct. 10,	1807	52
,, Bathsheba	Mar. 14,	1841	85
,, Catherine	Nov. 30,	1851	65
,, Mary Ann	July 25,	1848	22
Harrington, Sarah	Nov. 7,	1800	22
,, Ann	June 4,	1821	17
Hawke, Mrs. Elizabeth	April 11,	1816	40
Hawke, Robert	Aug. 5,	1834	61
,, Caroline	July 31,	1834	28
,, Elizabeth			Inf.
,, Edward			,,
Hunt, Sarah	April 26,	1873	73
Johnson Neville Hunt	Dec. 12,	1840	2
,, Emma Goodman	Dec. 25,	1850	15
McLeod, Mrs. Margaret		1800	76
Mott, Matthew		1807	42
Peverell, Ann		1780 (?)	Wife of Robt. Peverell.
Peck, Susanna	Dec. 29,	1827	43
Perry, Mrs. Elizabeth	Mar. 16,	1818	81
,, John	June 16,	1824	84
Radley, Elizabeth	Mar. 10,	1798	62
Rogers, Revd. Raymond E. L., A.B.	Aug. 22,	1816	44
Roome, Mrs. Elizabeth	July 16th	1801	69
Summers, James Hillat	Sep. 20,	1865	70
Summers, Amelia	May 3,	1829	32
,, 5 Infants			
,, James	Feb. 10,	1817	60
,, J. H.	Sep. 29,	1821	33
,, Mary	June 22,	1838	79
Seymour, John	Aug. 15,	1832	71
,, Elizabeth	Nov. 13,	1805	
,, Mary Maria	June 10,	1827	37
,, John	Aug. 15,	1792	58
,, Mary	Dec. 21,	1812	84
,, Mary	Nov. 30,	1819	12

Seymour, Thomas	. April 7,	1835	72
,, Mary	. May 21,	1806	31
,, William } Westwood }	June 13,	1837	33
Seymour, Mary	.		Inf.
,, Mary	. Feb. 20,	1830	43
,, William	. Dec. 11,	1803	41
,, Mrs. Frances	.		
,, George	. Sep. 10,	1860	89
,, Mrs. Fanny	Jan. 30,	1829	57
,, Elizabeth	. July 11,	1831	27
,, John	.	1803	Inf.
Twomlow, Ann	.	1780	

Twomlow, (a daughter of the above, rest obliterated).
Twomlow, John .
,,   Thomas . Nov. 22, 1812   32
Taylor, Mary   .   Dau. of Samuel Taylor, Malster.
Taylor, Samuel   .
Watts, Anne .   . April 16, 1848   26
  ,,   Samuel James Feb. 14 1849   3
One headstone next to Johnson's, inscription quite obliterated.

Plot C.

Choppin, Elizabeth . Mar. 22, 1813   68
Guyver, John .   .   1738 47 (?)
  ,,   George . Sep. 15, 1736 Inf.
  ,,   Mary .   .   5
Machin, Nathaniel } April 16, 1837   64
  Smith   .   . }
Machin, Mary .   . June 16, 1809   27
  ,,   Susan   . Dec. 3, 1816   36
  ,,   4 infant children, of whom two died 1807 and two 1817.
Patmore, Elizabeth . July 13, 1819   40
  ,,   Thomas . Feb. 15, 1847   74
  ,,   Charles   } Mar. 25, 1840   29
  Percival   . }
Patmore, 4 Infants.
Treacher, William } May 9, 1848   22
  Terrell   .   . }

Plot D.

Ayley, Robert .   . Jan. 24, 1762   69
Barnes, Agnes Mary Mar. 16 1850   3
Barber, Thomas   . Nov. 15, 1814   46

Beadle, Elizabeth	Mar. 31, 1828	42	
Clark, Elizabeth	Jan. 8, 1847	46	
Clayton, Edward	Sep. 17, 1835		Innholder.
Chandler, John	July 9, 1837	44	
" William	June 6, 1838	22	
Edwards, Isaac	June 1, 1825	55	Near this spot are buried four of their children.
" Susan	Dec. 31, 1799	29	
Franklin, Henry	Aug. 31, 1838	72	
" Mary	June 10, 1828	67	
Glassborow, Amey	July 16, 1804	41	
" Scrips	May 27, 1825	65	
Hodge, Sarah	July 1, 1854	55	
Hodson, Ann Conquest	April 2, 1845	Inf.	
Hodson, Sarah Mary Goddard	Jan. 3, 1853	79	Widow of Edward Hodson of Hatton Garden and Pierrepoint Row, Islington.
Joyce, William	Jan. 27, 1827	63	
" Abigail	Oct. 26, 1856		
Lloyd, Ann	Feb. 4, 1845	49	Widow of Thomas Palmer Lloyd, Merchant, late of Old Broad Street and Muswell Hill.
Mountford, Arthur	Jan. 3, 1801	73	
" Susanna	Nov. 20, 1804	76	
Nash, Ann			
" Mary	Feb. 3, 1850	63	
" Phillip	Mar. 9, 1853	69	
" Elizabeth	April 28, 1792	46	
Parker, John	Aug. 18, 1789	38	
" Mary	Feb. 7, 1811		
Slater, Ann	June 19, 1844	47	
Spiltimber, James	Jan. 26, 1837	68	
Smith, Mary	Nov. 2, 1825		
Sell, Richard	Nov. 29, 1851	60	
Spencer, Charles	July 7, 1849		Vicar of Stortford.
" Amelia	Oct. 20, 1859		
Surrage, John	no date or age		On the headstone of Robert Ayley.
Taylor, Mary	Jan. 28, 1852	60	
Wood, Thomas	June 6, 1774		

MONUMENTAL INSCRIPTIONS.

Wilson, Ann	June 3, 1829	22	Wife of R. S. Wilson, and dau. of Isaac Edwards.
Webb, William Horsell	Nov. 21, 1822	34	
Warner, Susanna	April 8, 1838	90	
,, John			
,, Mary	April 5, 1816		
,, Daniel	Aug. 7, 1798	88	
,, Elizabeth	Oct. 7, 1803	88	
,, Thomas	Oct. 20, 1817	71	
,, Mary	Mar. 2, 1818		
,, Daniel	Feb. 11, 1819	85	
Ward, Mrs. Sarah	May 28, 1740		
Yardley, William	Aug. 10, 1836	45	
,, Sarah	Nov. 2, 1825	31	
,, Joseph	Sep. 9, 1826		
,, James	1779		
,, Elizabeth	1787		Wife of James Yardley.
,, Sarah			
,, Mary	1799		
,, Joseph	April 3, 1805	52	
,, Ann	Mar. 2, 1812		
,, William	June 2, 1827	71	
,, Ann	Aug. 25, 1832	74	

In this plot there is one wood memorial of which the inscription is entirely obliterated, and one headstone on which only the following can be read :
O . . . . Dec. 2nd, 1752, aged 72.

Plot E.

Bass, Hannah	1776 (?)		
Duckett, Sir George Bart.	Dec. 15, 1822	97	Epitaph within the Church.
Francis, William	1787	100	
,, Sarah	1792	80	
,, William	Oct 19, 1805	7	
Gilbey Henry	Sep. 29, 1842	52	
,, William J. C.	Nov. 2, 1847	20	

Plot F.

Coote, John	Dec. 1, 1787	45	
,, Ann	April 17, 1826	73	

Coote, Mary	Dec. 29, 1803	36
,, Ann	Mar. 9, 1756	39
Cole, Robert	May 24, 1849	65
,, Charlotte	Nov. 29, 1871	87
Coote, James	July 24, 1848	65
,, Sarah	Nov. 13, 1830	14
,, Betsey		Inf.
,, Martha		,,
,, Robert		,,
Jackson, Elizabeth	Jan. 19, 1826	93
,, Thomas	Dec. 27, 1802	65

Near this spot lie seven of their children.

Mills, William	Nov. 30, 1810	83
Newton, George	Aug. 18, 1846	27
,, William	Jan. 10, 1852	48
Norris, Peter	Sep. 15, 1805	37
,, Sarah	May 15, 1838	79
,, Henry		Inf.
,, George		,,
,, Edward		,,
,, Caroline		,,
Newton, William	Feb. 22, 1839	55
Pope, William	Jan. 15, 1801	57
,, Elizabeth	May 24, 1820	75

Plot G.

Edridge, Michael	1789	31
,, Michael	1782	
,, Elizabeth	Aug. 13, 1807	67
L. B.	April 1777	
Machin, William	Dec. 31, 1798	57
,, Mary	Jan. 28, 1823	76

Next to the above stone is another with the name Machin upon it, but everything else quite obliterated. These two stones were originally upright, but are now laid flat close to the vestry wall.

Wallace, Rev. Michael	Mar. 29, 181-		Curate of this parish.
Wallace, Sarah	1815 (?)	22 (?)	
,, Mrs. Ann	June 20, 1780	22	
Warner, John	May 17, 1738	84	On a marble slab built into the church wall.
Wood, Fitch Lea	July 28, 1756	45	Draper and grocer.

Wood, Elizabeth		1756	6	
„ Jane				Wife of Fitch Lea Wood.
„ (On flat stone, Christian name and dates obliterated).				
„ Deborah	Oct. 23, 1738		53	
„ John		1745	Inf.	
„ John	Feb. 11, 1759		76	Draper.
„ John		1768 (?)		
„ Elizabeth		1767 (?)	Inf.	

Plot H.

Glyn, John		1784	62 (?)	Surveyor and engineer.
„ Elizabeth		1795		
„ John				
Wherling, Mary	May 11, 1842		96	

Plot J.

Angus, Abigail	June 24, 1758		Inf.	Daus. of Rev. John Angus.
„ Deborah	July 19, 1801		40	
„ Mrs. Abigail	Sep. 24, 1756		30	First wife of ditto.
„ Mrs. Mary	Sep. 22, 1784		68	Second wife of ditto.
„ John	Feb. 24, 1776		14	
„ Rev. John	Dec. 22, 1801		77	The Rev. John Angus was minister of the Independent Chapel in this town.
Beldam, Valentine	May 26, 1828		85	
„ Sarah	April 2, 1810		67	
„ Hester	Jan. 15, 1837		60	
„ Elizabeth	July 20, 1854		78	
Bolt, Elizabeth	Jan.	1799	76 (?)	
Bayford, John				
Bates, Susannah	Nov. 17, 1813		31	
„ Elizabeth	Jan. 23, 1822		31	
„ Henry Michael	April 8, 1836		17	
Bayford, John	Oct. 5,	1793	62	
„ Elizabeth	Jan. 5,	1802	Inf.	
„ Emma		1806	Inf.	
Buck, Thomas	Feb. 3,	1834	71	Brazier.
„ Sarah	Dec. 5,	1800	40	
„ Mary	June 20, 1838		77	

Cowell, Henry		1802	63
,, Sarah	May 24, 1816		78
Cass, Sarah	Nov. 24, 1848		46
Connell, Mary Ann	May 25, 1837		25
Collis, Edward	June 3, 1831		37 Wheelwright.
Colls, William George	Oct. 19, 1854		27
Collins, William		1790	
,, Richard		1777	76
,, Sarah	April 26, 1801		47
Dellow, John Crane	Dec. 14, 1793		30 Maltster.
,, John		1790	Inf.
Death, Lydia	June 18, 1831		28
,, William	May 2, 1842		41
,, Sarah	July 17, 1832		63
,, William	Nov. 11, 1846		85
,, Anne	Sep. 25, 1831		22
,, Sarah	Jan. 28, 1833		35
Drawbridge, Joseph	Oct. 7, 1811		16
,, Maria	July 7, 1816		22
Fairman, Agnes Rivers			Inf.
Fairman, Joseph	July 5, 1859		38
Feast, Richard	April 7, 1799		61 Butcher.
,, Ann			
Fordham, Mary	Nov. 19, 1830		63
,, Josiah	June 18, 1852		81 Plumber.
Flack, Martha	July 20, 1797		76
Feast, Elizabeth	June 23, 1813		34
,, Thomas Turner	June 16, 1843		42 (?)
Feast, Thomas	Oct. 16, 1835		65
,, Rachel	Mar. 14, 1841		68
George, Ellen	May 8, 1834		27
Hawkes, William Robert	May 10, 1859		74
Hawkes, Elizabeth	Oct. 2, 1839		81
,, William	Feb. 26, 1794		39 Brewer.
Heath, Elizabeth Susan		1839	Inf.
Heath, Elizabeth	Mar. 23, 1847		6
,, Elizabeth	Mar. 30, 1866		59
,, Joseph	Feb. 9, 1873		67
,, Edward Hawke	Nov. 25, 1874		32

Hack, Robert	Feb. 27,	1831	34	Printer.
,, Anne Maria	Mar. 25,	1834	5	
,, Mary Jane	Mar. 2,	1840	13	
,, Elizabeth Chandler	Sep. 26,	1840	17	
Holgate, George		1727	74	
Hayden, William	Oct. 8,	1849	64	
Hughes, Jane	Nov. 7,	1841	42	
Hayden, Mary	Aug. 30,	1841	65	
,, Joseph	Feb. 10,	1842	34	
Hale, John	May 30,	1814	40	
Holmes, Thomas	Mar. 13,	1804	76	Of Long Acre. Son of John and Susanna Holmes.
Holmes, Mary Silvester	Jan. 8,	1817	44	Wife of Thomas Holmes of Sloane Street, Chelsea, the son of Thomas Holmes of Long Acre.
Johns, Edward Beldam, Esq.	Feb. 20,	1866	87	
Jennings, Sarah	Aug. 12,	1779	28	
,, Nathaniel	Dec. 4,	1779		
,, Sarah	Mar. 25,	1756	82	
,, Nathaniel	Mar. 16,	1783	72	Surgeon.
,, Elizabeth	Aug. 7,	1785	12	
,, Sarah	Feb. 16,	1787	12	
Johnson, Elizabeth	Dec. 30,	1851	81	
Jones, John	Oct. 7,	1777	67	
,, Mary	Nov. 28,	1768	26	
,, George	Jan. 24,	1789	72	
,, John	April 2,	1789	8	
,, John	Oct. 8,	1789	49	
,, Elizabeth	Dec. 18,	1830	84	
,, Stephen	Feb. 27,	1790	22	
,, Elizabeth	Feb. 26,	1788	57	
,, Joseph	Dec. 2,(?)	1782		
,, Ann	Nov. 1,	1818	50	
,, James	Feb. 20,	1822	53	Maltster.
,, John	Dec. 30,	1812	61	Tallow-chandler.
,, Elizabeth	May 24,	1827	68	
,, Nathaniel	Dec. 23,	1726	84	Brazier.
Johnstone, Elizabeth	June 10,	1812	39	
,, Alfred	June 19,	1813		

Johnstone, George ⎫ James ⎭	July 2,	1846	29
Johnstone, William	Nov. 16, 1848		38
,, Hannah	Oct. 28, 1864		89
,, John	Dec 7, 1853		42
,, William	Aug. 10, 1857		86
Lewis, Mrs. Mary	1777 (?) 60 (?)		Wife of Thomas Lewis.
Lamb, Joseph	July 31, 1799		54
,, Sarah	Dec. 5, 1816		75
Law, Edmund	Jan. 26, 1810		82
,, Susanna	April 12, 1819		82
Liles, Hannah	Feb. 28, 1800		55
,, Joseph	Dec. 24, 1810		26
,, Elizabeth	Mar. 6, 1854		72
Lee, William	Jan. 9, 1854		35
Liles, John	Dec. 28, 1813		66
,, Samuel	May 28, 1828		53
Miller, John	Aug. 3, 1819		58
,, Susannah	Mar. 5, 1813		82
,, Charlotte	April 2, 1836		49
,, David	May 3, 1845		55
,, Susannah	Feb. 26, 1840		60
Nicholson, Mary	May 17, 1854		78
Nash, Mary	Dec. 29, 1803		Inf.
,, Frederick John	June 16, 1803		Inf.
Newton, Joseph	May 16, 1816		42
,, Millicent	Sep. 3, 1813		30
,, Sarah	Dec. 24, 1809		5
,, Joseph	Nov. 16, 1817		11
Perry, James	July 17, 1844		45
,, Richard	July 27 1843		49
,, Robert	Mar. 25, 1808		53
,, Elizabeth	Mar. 26, 1827		61
,, Ann	Jan. 23, 1807		20
,, Henry			Inf.
,, James			,,
,, Thomas			,,
,, Charlotte			,,
Mary	Dec. 24, 1781		54
Charles	Jan. 24, 1782		57
John	April 22, 1817		55
,, Sarah	Nov. 3, 1854		90
,, Charles	May 9, 1833		Inf.
,, Ann			Inf.
,, George	Oct. 26, 1834		9

Palmer, Henrietta	Sep. 17, 1844	43	
,, William, senr.	Jan. 13, 1796	62	
,, Martha	Mar. 12, 1769	28	
,, Mary	Dec. 7, 1786,	Inf.	
,, William	Aug. 29, 1787	Inf.	
,, Thomas	Mar. 16, 1798	35	
,, Mary	Oct. 7, 1796	35	
Polley, Mary	Aug. 16, 1838	50	
,, John	Mar. 29, 1846	48	
Pettet, Kezia	Aug. 30, 1843	25	
Powter, William	Oct. 19, 1827	31	
,, William		Inf.	
,, Harriot		,,	
,, George	Mar. 29, 1845	48	
,, Esther	Oct. 25, 1852	54	
Rous, John	Dec. 15, 1759	54	
,, Sarah	April 6, 1763	53(?)	
Richardson, John	Dec. 1798	65	
Rankin, Thomas	Dec. 27, 1751	59	Grocer.
,, Elizabeth	Nov. 30, 1743	52	
Reynolds, Thomas	Sep. 1795	89	
Shipman, Sophia	Aug. 10, 1821	33	
Sumpner, Abigail	Dec. 17, 1752	85	
Serjeant, John	May 24, 1839	73	
,, Ann	Oct. 22, 1841	67	
Stubbing, Richard	June 10, 1789	70	
,, John	May 7, 1798	32	
,, Martha	April 17, 1802	79	
Stallybrass, Sarah	Dec. 22, 1819	59	
Scarr, Ann	April 27, 1853	64	
,, Renforth Thomas	Dec. 8, 1854	74	
Tucker, Sarah	Oct. 15, 1840	62	
,, Elizabeth	Oct. 24, 1852	53	
,, Henry George	Oct. 30, 1847	16	
Tucker, Susanna	April 15, 1805	53	
,, Joseph	Nov. 4, 1829	83 (?)	
Tice, John	Aug. 17, 1817	67	
Tweed, Robert	April 21, 1844	84	
Thurgood, Thomas	Jan. 31, 1855	84	
Turner, William	1762		
Tyrrel, Catherine	1851	Inf.	
Tipler, Mary	May 22, 1844	24	

Tipler, John	Feb. 13, 1821	73	Yeoman.
,, Mary	Mar. 25, 1844	17	
Taylor, Elizabeth	Mar. 3, 1853	41	
,, Charlotte	Feb. 15, 1830	43	
,, Joseph	June 10, 1864	79	
,, George	Dec. 17, 1850	62	
,, John	Dec. 26, 1826	63	
,, Charlotte	Jan. 26, 1820	63	
,, John Dobede	April 6, 1880	68	
,, Frederick	Mar. 26, 1848	Inf.	
Usher, Barbary	April 26, 1780	64	
,, John	April 2, 1793	75	
,, James			Children of the above.
,, Mary			
,, Gwillam			
,, Gerald			
Woolston, Jeffrey	Aug. 7, 1815	43	
,, Jeffrey	May 9, 1831	32	
,, Mary	June 12, 1850	78	
,, John	Oct. 24, 1785	47	
,, Mary	Mar. 30, 1804	62	
,, James	May 10, 1854	51	
Wilkinson, Catherine	Feb. 15, 1825	63	
,, Jane	Sep. 6, 1852	64	
Woolston, Jeffrey	Aug. 27, 1842	19	
Winter, Ralph, Esq.	July 8, 1802	63	
,, Elizabeth	April 22, 1804	71	
,, Susanna	Sep. 9, 1813	74	
Ware, John	July 20, 1838	36	
,, Ann		Inf.	
,, Matthew		,,	
Wyles, John	April 8, 1823	62	
,, Mary	April 16, 1824		
Wilby, Lydia	Oct. 9, 1820	15	

The inscriptions on the following six stones in Plot J are now illegible or altogether obliterated.

Two flat stones near the tomb of Ralph Winter, Esq.
One flat stone near the tombstone of Sarah Cass.
One ,, ,, ,, ,, Joseph Lamb.
Two curiously carved headstones near the south porch.

Plot K.

Bird, Thomas	Nov. 12, 1859	67
,, Clara Beldam	Mar. 16, 1833	6
,, Charlotte	Oct. 28, 1858	26
,, Mary Lord	Oct. 7, 1864	42
,, Elizabeth	June 19, 1800	42
,, John Bangham	Dec. 12, 1849	53
,, Thomas	Mar. 25, 1811	65
,, Rebecca Bangham	Jan. 29, 1839	16
Bird, William	Jan. 31, 1867	76
,, Sophia	July 26, 1881	87

Widow of Thomas Bird, and dau. of John Dobede, of The Place, Soham, Cambs.

Boultwood, Ann	1779	
,, Martha	1778 (?)	
,, John	1782 (?)	
Bull, Charles	April 22, 1836	51
,, Susan	May 25, 1840	63
Boultwood, John	Aug. 29, 1801	56
,, Ann	1800	47
Bradford, Henry	1824	
,, Jane	Dec. 23, 1824	56
,, John	1828	35
Clark, William	Feb. 7, 1772	73
,, Martha	Mar. 28, 1819	23
,, Martha	May 21, 1819	4
Cooper, Henry	Dec. 20, 1843	46
,, Henry	Mar. 7, 1836	16
,, Mary Ann	Jan. 17, 1837	37
Dimsdale, Robert, M.D.	Dec. 29, 1814	81
Dimsdale, Elizabeth	Sep. 18, 1814	74
,, William	June 25, 1832	61

Son of Robert Dimsdale.

Driver, Rev. John	April 18, 1831	68
,, Elizabeth	Mar. 25, 1802	36
Gee, Robert	Mar. 14, 1806	35
,, William	April 13, 1850	73
,, Harriet	Mar. 19, 1879	82
,, Maria	Jan. 24, 1820	45

Of Cambridge.

Glasscock Thomas	April 16, 1847	45	
,, Sarah	Mar. 29, 1857	53	
,, Thomas	April 6, 1850	18	
Hodgkin, John	July 2, 1823	66	
,, obliterated.			
Johns, Mary	Oct. 6, 1788	53	
,, Edward	Dec. 28, 1797	57	
Johns, Mary Lord	Mar. 13, 1854	94	Dau. of Mrs. Mary Johns.
Jones, Mrs. Mary	Nov. 17, 1779		
,, Francis	1782 (?)		
Ley, Thomas	Aug. 12, 1840	57	
,, Ellen Margaret		Inf.	
Lord, John Searle	Feb. 28, 1796	Inf.	
,, William	Dec. 21, 1802	15	
,, William	Dec. 19, 1818	59	
,, Rebecca	Nov. 26, 1827	24	
,, Mary	Mar. 7, 1850	86	
Lee, George			
Mead, Elizabeth } Morris	Oct. 18, 1855	15	
Nottage, John	Dec. 24, 1830	52	Butcher.
,, Ann	July 8, 1828	46	
Parish, John	Oct. 9, 1838	41	
,, Mary Jane	Nov. 8, 1837	11	
Patmore, Henry	April 20, 1839	5	
Percival, Joseph } Roger	Dec. 19, 1802	Inf.	
Percival, Thomas	Dec. 29, 1802	3	
Porter (see Quilter).			
Pavitt, Fanny	Oct. 24, 1831	32	
Quilter, Thomas	April 15, 1823	6	
,, Elizabeth	Aug. 19, 1840	60	
,, Thomas	Jan. 29, 1845	54	
,, Marianne	Mar. 30, 1847	24	Wife of E. E. Porter.
Rosendall (or Rosingdale) Jane }	May 24, 1768	41	
Rosendall, Joseph	April 16, 1793	66	

The inscriptions on this stone are almost obliterated; the dates of the months and ages I took from the Parish Register.

Simson, Felix, Esq.	May 21, 1823	77	Collector of Excise.
Smoothy, Abraham	Feb. 2, 1850	57	
,, Sarah	July 18, 1863		
Swallow, William	June 14, 1852	47	
,, Elizabeth	Nov. 11, 1853	51	

Searle, Elizabeth	July 29,	1777	36
,, John	Feb. 16,	1786	53
Smith, Charles	Aug. 18,	1814	68
,, Mary	June 12,	1832	75
Tofts, Sophia	Aug. 8,	1829	25
,, John	Mar. 25,	1845	41
Turner, John		1831	26
Wilkinson, Benjamin	April 7,	1834	34
Willson, Edward	Nov. 22,	1853	20
Wood, Ann	Feb. 11,	1805	53
,, William	Dec. 30,	1822	75

Plot L.

Ashby, Ann	Feb. 16,	1845	75	
Allen, Hannah		1821	Inf.	
Blamire (?) Edward		1817		The first figure of the age is 6.
,, Mrs. Martha		1819 (?)	69	
Brown, Thomas	Feb. 16,	1835	78	
,, Elizabeth	June 2,	1811	64	
,, Charlotte	Mar. 6,	1825	48	
,, Henry		1789	56	
,, Elizabeth		1780	69	
Bygrave, Elizabeth		17-7 (?)		Wife of Mr. Nathaniel Bygrave.
Coote, Susanna	July 3,	1848	44	
Clough, Mrs. Susanna		1786	75	Wife of Thomas Clough.
Colley, John	May 25,	1836	35	
Emson, Elizabeth				Wife of Robert Emson.
Franklin, Sabina	Dec. 24,	1842	2	
,, Martha Mary	Nov. 19,	1853	6	
Fitch, Samuel Haiden	Sep. 21,	1834	73	
Folks, Mary Chapman	May 8,	1841	34	
Griffiths, Mary	Feb. 12,	1835	69	
,, Sarah	Oct. 13,	1838	70	
Game, Thomas	April 7,	1815	18	
,, Samuel	Aug. 4,	1843	44	
Gorsuch, Elizabeth	Nov. 26,	1773	49	
Glasscock, Sarah	Aug. 18	1844	38	
,, John	Sep. 25,	1847	36	
Handscomb, John	Mar. 4,	1830	72	
,, Hannah	April 11,	1834	83	
,, James	Oct. 10,	1843	39	

Hanchett, John	Dec. 21, 1805	55	
,, Frances	April 30, 1809	56	
King, Mrs. Mary	Feb. 7, 1841	73	
,, William	Mar. 20, 1855	83	
Lovett, William	Dec. 27, 1841	58	
,, Elizabeth	Mar. 2, 1843	73	
Moore, James	Feb. 8, 1729	36	
Martin, William	May 20, 1851	2	
,, Millicent	1774		Wife of Robert Martin.
Powterell, Samuel	Dec. 5, 1812	26 (?)	
Pouterell, Joseph	April 13, 1794	47	
,, Mary Ann	May 12, 1839	27	
Patmore, Ann	May 11, 1817	20	
Robson, Frances	Feb. 25, 1829	68	
,, Sarah	Dec. 14, 1811	70	
Sayers, John	1789	36	
Springle, Daniel	June 25, 1838	48	
Siggs, Ann			Wife of Charles Siggs.
Swan, Wm. Francis	Mar. 23, 1814	Inf.	
T. I.	1817		
T. M.	1830		
Tyler, John			
,, William	Sep. 23, 1853	79	
,, Elizabeth	Nov. 15, 1813	41	
,, Mrs. Sarah	Sep. 15, 1821	69	
,, Thomas	Oct. 17, 1822	78	
,, Charles L.	Oct. 30, 1832	32	
,, Arthur	1824 (?)		
Walker, Robert	1785		
,, Robert	1758		
,, M.	1779		
Welch, John	Mar. 26, 1855	60	

On a flat stone next the stone of Hannah Allen a name beginning with B (? Bull), all the rest obliterated.

Plot M.

Campin, Richard	July 17, 1792	22	The inscriptions on these two stones are nearly obliterated; the dates of the month and ages I took from the Parish Register.
,, Thomas	Dec. 22, 1779	61	

Handscomb, Kezia	Feb. 11, 1841	52	
,, Joshua	Dec. 9, 1854	60	
Lee, Mary	Aug. 7, 1833		
Scott, Joseph	June 24, 1735	77	
Sadler, Peter	Oct. 1747	66	Woollen Draper.
,, Ann	July 6, 1716	27	
,, Peter	Dec. 1747	24 (?)	

INDEX OF NAMES.

The Index includes all names of persons mentioned in the book, except those contained in the following sections, which are not indexed, viz.:

Notes to the Churchwardens' Accounts   *pp.* 89—109.
Names of the Vicars and Churchwardens of St. Michael's pp. 110—117.
Names of the Overseers   *pp.* 168—173.
Names of Persons buried in the Churchyard   *pp.* 200—220.

As the pages are full, and the names difficult to find, it has been thought well to indicate their position in the page by the letters a, b, c, d, which refer roughly to the four quarters of the page.

Abbat, 54 a.
Abbott, 61 c, 160 d.
Abell, 66 d, 69 c.
Acastre, 142 b.
Adams, George, 78 b.
Adderley, 194.
Ailmer, Samuell, 174 d.
Akastr', Thomas, 20 b.
Albert, John, 54 a.
Albert, 72 d.
Aldriche, 191.
Alese, Mother, 161 c.
Aley, 67 c.
Aley, Henry, 179 c.
Algar, 195.
Algood, John, 14 d.
Algore, John, 27 b, 118 c, 141 a.
Allen, Mother, 60 c; 62 c.
Allen, Justice, 80 c.
Allen, William, 181 c.
Allis, Thomas, 70 c.
Almon, William, 146 d.
Alsopp, 58.

Alsoppe, 61 c.
Altham, Mr. James, 84 c, 85 a, 182 d.
Altham, Michael, of Latton, clerk, 181 d.
Andrew, Thomas, 6 b, 15 d, 17 b. 140 c.
Andrewes, Wy., 149 c.
Angell, Gabr., 150 c.
Angell, Thos., 149 c.
Angell, William, 148 a.
Appleby, Thomas, 178 c, 188.
Ap-Rice, 33, 36.
Arch, James, 146 c.
Archer, Thomas, 147 a.
Archer, Timothy, 64 c.
Archer, Henry, shoemaker, 188.
Archer, 72, 73, 75, 188.
Ardent, John, 17 b.
Arkebald (or Archibald), 139.
Ashbie, Ed., 149 a.
Ashbie, Thos., 147 b, 155 b.
Ashbye, Mrs., 77 c.

INDEX

Ashby, Edward, 78 b, 166 a, 188
Ashlocke, Thos., 146 c.
Assewelle, 25 c.
Atte-Lee, 10.
Atwood, Thomas, 146 c.
Auncell, Tho., 151 c.
Ayle, ffather, 161 b.
Aylett, John, 151 c.
Ayley, 67 c.
Ayley, Nicholas, 85 b.
Aylie, 72 c.
Aylie, Ezechiell, 73 c.
Aylmer, Justinian, 147 b.
Aylmer, 77.
Ayrie, Ezechiell, 146 b.
Aynsworth Mrs., 78 d, 79, 80, 82 b.

Baduley, Tho., 151 c, 153 d.
Baker, John 166 a.
Balaam, Henry, 178 d.
Balaam, Thos., 77 c.
Balam, Thos., 144 a, 162 b, 164 a.
Balam, Wm., 50 a, 56 a.
Baldewyn, 30 c, 40.
Baldewyn, Reynolde, 31 c, 33 b.
Baldewyn, Reginald, 22 b.
Baldok, 43 d.
Baldwin, Victor, 118 b, 121 d, 123.
Baldwin, Sir Rafe, 40.
Baldwin, 121, 123, and note.
Bancks, 146, 149.
Banckes, 153 a.
Bangham, 194, 198.
Banks, Roger, 78 a.
Banson, 192, 195.
Banson, Mr., 187 d.
Banson, Mrs., 77 d.
Banstret, 41 d.
Barbor, Thoms., 14 a, 53 d, 11 d., 12b d, 13 c.
Barbour, 14
Barbour, William, 17 a.
Barbore, Thomas, 52 c.
Bardeney, Robert, 27 b, 141 d.
Bardeney, William, 37 b.
Bardeney, 38.
Barell, John, 41 c.
Bargayn, John, 6 a b.
Barges, Richard, 61 b.
Barlee, 120 c, 121, 132.
Barlee, Wm., 128 c.
Barley, Mr., 51 c, 56 d.
Barnard, 53 d, 60 c, 62 d, 70 c, 74 b, 75 c, 77, 78, 79 a, 83 d, 137 b, 145, 147 c d, 153 c, 155 a, 159, 161 b,
162 c, 174, 175, 176, 180, 181, 187 c.
Barnes, 54, 63 c, 78, 81, 153, 175, 181.
Barnes, George, 182 b.
Barnes, Henry, 86 a.
Barnes, John, 146 d.
Barnes, Matt, 56 b, 69 c. 160 a, 159 b.
Barnes, Will., 80 b, 187 d.
Barnese, Matthewe, 161 a.
Baron, Peter, 36 b.
Baront, 188.
Barre, Willm., 161 a.
Barret, 42 a.
Barrington, Esqre., 167 d.
Barrington, Charles, 186 c.
Barron, 174.
Barron, John, 77 d.
Barwick, 188.
Baryngton, Sir Nicolas, 33 d.
Bass, George, 187 b.
Bate, 34.
Bat's Wyfe, 142 d.
Bawcock, Rich., 78 c.
Bawcock, 150.
Bawdwin, Victor, 120 b.
Bawdwin, 26.
Bayer, 76.
Bayford, 54, 56, 57, 58.
Bayford, Mr., 62 b, 187 c.
Bayford, Geo., 148 b.
Bayford, John, 55 d, 132 a.
Bayford, Samuel, 187 d.
Bayford, Will., 84 b, 181 d, 187 d.
Bayford, William, 149 b, 182 d, 183 b.
Bayforde, 161 b.
Bayfourde, 52.
Bayley, 132, 135, 136.
Bayley, Mary, 80 c.
Bayly, Mr., 43 a, 49 a.
Baynes, 152.
Baynes, Thos., 146 b.
Beamond, John, 155 b.
Bearsley, 191.
Bedwell, 49, 53, 61.
Belheme, 16.
Belheme, John, 14 c.
Belhos, Will., 16 d.
Bell, Will., 148 b.
Bendish, 69.
Bendish, Mrs., 147 d, 153 c.
Bennett, Jo., 148 b.
Bennett, 66, 146, 149 a.
Bennett, Willm., 76 b.
Bernes, Will., 186 c.
Ber, Thomas, 15 d.
Best, Roger, 147 c, 154 b.

Best, Toby, 150, 154 b.
Best, Widow, 149 a.
Best, 61.
Best, William, 143 c.
Bett, Father, 161 c.
Betts, Mr., 82, c.
Beveris, 17 a.
Beverley, 6.
Bevis, Robard, 161 a.
Billams, Mr., 71 c.
Billam, 144 a, 154.
Bingham, Wid., 77 c.
Bingham, 150 d.
Bird, George, 64 b.
Bird, John, 151 d.
Bishop of London, 23 a.
Bishop, Mr., 167 a.
Blackwell, Mr., 67 d.
Blank, Walter, 10 c, 68 b.
Blankes, 17.
Blankes, Walter, 18 b.
Blancheflower, 38.
Blaunchflower, T., 139 b.
Blossmes, 121 d.
Blower, Zacharey, 187 d.
Blucke, Matthew, 181 c.
Blythewyn, 17 c.
Bolton, 194, 198.
Boltwood, 176.
Boltwood, John, 175 a.
Boltwood, Wido., 148 b.
Boly, 54 b.
Bolyngton, Wylliam, 142 b.
Bolyngton, John, 33 c, 29 c, 142 b.
Bolyngton, Nicolas, 141 c.
Bolyngton, 5..
Bolyngton, George, 28 d.
Bond, 160 b.
Bond, Tho., 148 a.
Bonest, Robert, 85 d.
Bonest, Thomas, 181 c.
Boukker, John, 118 d.
Bonns, Robert, 79 a, 80 c, 81 a, 82 a, 83 b, 85 b.
Bore, 61, 65.
Bore, Mother 160 b.
Boteler, Sir Ed., 70 d.
Boultwood, T., 187 b.
Bounds, Mr., 187 b.
Bowntyngfourde, 50 d.
Bowyer, 54, 68.
Bowyer, John, 160 b, d.
Bowyere, John, 62 b.
Bowyere, Thomas, 145 c, 61 d.
Bowyere, Harry, 68 a d.
Bowyere, Will., 148 c, 161 d.

Bowyere, Robert, 68 a.
Brancheflower, 40, 41 b.
Brand, Andrew, 148 c.
Brand, James, 164 a.
Braugwyn, 61 a, 65 c.
Brawghing, Mr., 26 d.
Brett, Giles, 161 b.
Brett, Will., 161 b, 162 c.
Bretten, Richard, 148 d.
Bretten, 64 b.
Bretton, Robert, 142 d.
Bregge, Richard, 18 b.
Bridges, 61.
Brograve, Thos., 186 c.
Brooks, Jo., 150 a.
Brooke, 67 a, 148 a.
Brome, 191, 192, 195.
Browen, Mr., 187 c.
Brown, John, 15 c, 160 b.
Brown, 59 b, 77 b, 123, 151, 163.
Browne, Edmond, 53 d.
Browne, 45 a, 62 a, 121 b, 163 b.
Bryan, Richard, 36 c.
Bryd, John, 3 b.
Bryon, 17.
Bryson, John, 17 c.
Bukberd, 5, 13, 14, 15, 16.
Bull, James, 54 b, 161 c, 162 d.
Bull, 77, 144 a.
Bull, John, 70 d, 149 c, 163
Bull, Ralfe, 74 b, 145 b, 154 d.
Burch, Jo., bookbynder, 147 c.
Burges, 61, 151, 153 b, 161 c.
Burle, 47 c, 48 a, 52.
Burling, Elias, 145 c.
Burling, 176 c, 182 d.
Burlse, 162 c.
Burrell, 188.
Busch, John, 16 c, 18 c.
Busch, 3, 6, 9, 13, 19.
Busch, Hugo, 17 c.
Busch, Matthew, 149 d, 154 c.
Bush, Danyell, 152 a.
Bush, John, 19 a, 19 d, 30 d.
Bush, Tho., 149 d.
Bush, 61, 152.
Bush, William, 145 c, d.
Bushe, Philologus, 65 b.
Bushe, 161 b.
Bushe, John, 148 b.
Bushe, Matthew, 154 b.
Bushe, old John, 71 c.
Bussh, John, 29 d.
Busshe, John, 142 d.
Busshe, 53.
Butler, Mr., 74 d.

Butler, Mrs., 72 c.
Butler, 32, 79.
Butler, Wylliam, 40 b d, 143 c.
Buxton, John, 187 a.
Byllam, 61 d.
Byngham, Dr., 63 a.
Bysmer, William, 16 c.

Cæsar, C., 187 a.
Calidaye, 161 a, 160 c, 162 d.
Callidaye, 62.
Calton, 152 d.
Calton, Andrewe, 66 d.
Calverd, William, Esq., 181 c.
Calvert, Mr., 144 c.
Calvert, Will., 186 c.
Calvert, 182, 194.
Calyday, 43 d, 45.
Calyday, Richard, 54 a, 162 c.
Camp, 153 c.
Campe, Robert, 146 c.
Capell, Mr., 59 b.
Carpenter, 9 b, 22 a.
Carr, Mr., 182 d.
Carrow, Mr., 49 b, 51 a, 62 a, 161 b.
Carrowe, 44, 45.
Carter, 87.
Carter, John, 144 c.
Carton, Oswald, 62 b.
Cason, Mr., 181 d, 187 c.
Cater, Alese, 162 a.
Can(? w)ton, 55c.
Cawbeck, 61 b.
Cawlton, Andrewe, 64 c.
Cawton, 54 a, 61 a, 161 a.
Chalk, John, 78 a.
Chambar, Robard, 161 b.
Chamber, Thomas, 160 d.
Chambers, 78.
Chamberlayne, Thomas, 142 d.
Chamberlein, 148 c.
Chamberleyn, Thomas, 32 c, 153 c.
Chambre, John, 17 c.
Chancey, Mr., 79 c.
Chandler, Edward, 70 c.
Chandler, Sara, 71 a.
Chandler, George, 78 c.
Chandler, Robt., 153 c, 154 d, 155 b.
Chandler, Wido., 148.
Chandler, John, 149 c, 152 a.
Chandler, Katherin, 151 a.
Chandler, 179.
Chandler, Willm., 79 a.
Chandlere, Goodman, 51 d.
Chandlers, Widow, 146 c.
Chandlers, Robert, 146 c.

Chandlers, Ed., 147 b.
Chaplin, Joseph, 187 b.
Chaplin, Mr. Frederic, 88 a.
Chapman, 192, 193, 197.
Chapman, Widow, 144 b.
Chatirton, Mr., 120 c.
Chauncy, 190, 195.
Chauncey, John, 186 d.
Chaundeler, old, 130 d.
Chaundeler, Thomas, 55 b, 58 a, 61 b, 62 c, 134 c.
Chaundeler, William, 33 a, 34 d b.
Chaundeler, 33, 36, 49, 53, 65, 128, 131, 136, 137.
Chaundlere, Robert, 53 d.
Chaynye, 54 b.
Cheany, George, 69 b.
Cheny, 61,
Chepe, 141.
Cheveley, John, 186 c.
Cheyne, John, 134 d.
Cheyne, 136.
Chirche, 20, 22.
Chirche, Reginald, Bellfounder, 23 a.
Chrichlowe, 147.
Churchwardens of St. Michael's, 111-117.
Clanford, 152.
Clapp, 192.
Clapton, 6.
Clapton, John, 3 b.
Clare, 44 d.
Clarke, 49, 50 b, 52.
Clarke, Good-wife, 161 b.
Clark, Persy, 51 a, d.
Clarke, Ralfe, 56 b.
Clarke, Rayffe, 51 a.
Clarke, Tho., 151 b.
Clarvyce, John, 120.
Claton, Mr., 187 c.
Clayden, 88 c.
Clayton, Thomas, 77 b, 84 a, 164, 183 b.
Clayton, 78, 178, 188.
Clee, John, 19 b.
Clerk, 30, 31, 121, 122.
Clerk, John, 6 c, 68 b.
Clerk, Willm., 28 b.
Clerk, Thomas, his bonfyer, 40 b.
Clerke, 36 b.
Clerke, John, 26 a, 141 a, 142 b.
Clerke, Thomas, 142 b.
Clough, 194.
Clutterbuck, Sir Thos., 79 c.
Clutterbuck, Mr., 190, 195.

Clyfton, 140 d.
Clyfton, Andrew, 36 a, 41 a, 143.
Cok, John, 29 d.
Cokeyn, William, 14 a, 15 c.
Coks, Gylbert, 139 b.
Cole, Mr. Robert, 88 b.
Colburne, 54 b.
Colle, John Halle, 118 d.
Coller, 61 b, 152 d.
Coller, Wido, 149 b.
Colt, 152 d.
Colt, Robt., 68 c.
Colt, Richard, 64 c.
Colte, James, 146 a.
Coltie, Wid., 152 c.
Colyn, 6, 14.
Colyn, John, 12 d.
Colyn, William, 20 b.
Comfret, 60.
Cook, John, 7 b, 16 d, 17 a, 67 d, 154 b.
Cooke, widow, 160 c.
Cooke, 22 a, 77 b, 147 c, 148 c, 152 b, 187 c.
Cooper, Christopher, vicar of Stortford, 181 d.
Cooper, 80.
Corear, Mother, 161 c.
Cornelys, 50 b.
Cornelyus, 54 c.
Cortney, ffrances, 76 a.
Cory, Mr., 60 c.
Cosyn, John, 28 b c.
Cotiller, John, 10 b.
Cotterotte, 26.
Courtney, Mrs. Penelope, 82 a.
Covill, 153 c.
Cowell, 151 b.
Cowley, 45.
Cowley, the capper, 41 b.
Crab, 45.
Crab, Henry, 146 a, 149 b.
Crabb, 54 c, 56 c, 179 c.
Crabbe, good-man, 159 a.
Crabbe, Widow, 160 c.
Crabbe, Thomas, 54 b, 62 a, 143 a, 160 d.
Crabbe, John, 161 a.
Crabbe, Margaret, 162 b.
Crabbe, 38, 46 c, 47 a, 48 c, 63 c.
Crabs, Henry, 154 a.
Cradock, 188.
Cramphorne, Good-man, 77 a.
Cramphorne, ffr., 147 d.
Crappes, 161 b.
Crawthorne, Mr., 54 c, 140 c.

Crawthorne, Mrs., 61 b.
Cripps, 151 c.
Cromwell, 124 b.
Crowch, 149.
Crowcheman, 38 b.
Crowe, Margerie, 119 d.
Crowe, 61.
Crowe, Wm., 29 d, 141 a.
Cullum, Sir Dudley, 186 c.
Culverhowse, 62 b.
Curtes, Mother, 161 d.
Cussans, Mr., 190, 195.
Cuttercote, Richard, 7 b.
Curtis, 77 c, 143 d.
Curtis, Ralfe, 146 b, 153 b.

Dalton, 193.
Dane, 6, 23 b, 30 d, 31, 62, 140, 141, 175 a, 176 b.
Dane, Mrs., 62 c.
Dane, Old, 160 b.
Dane, John, smith, 10 c, 36 d, 37 a c.
Dane, Thomas, 26 b.
Danyell, 141 d.
Darling, Edward, 145 d.
Darnell, Edward, 77 d.
Davie, Robert, 151 c.
Davy, Edward, 54 b.
Davy, John, 54 b.
Davy, Edmund, 27 b.
Davy, Edmond, 32 c.
Davy, Edmonde, 29 c.
Davys, John, 143 a.
Dayne, 71, 139.
Daw, Peter, 54 b.
De Brome, 192.
Denison, John, 161 a.
Denison, George, 164 b.
Deny, Lady, 151 d.
Denney, Mr., 182 a, 187 b.
Denny, Mr., 78 c, 144 b.
Denny, Edward, 174 d, 83 d, 181 b.
Denny, Mr. Antony, 74 c, 145 c.
Denny, William, 188 a.
Denny, Henry, 154 a.
Denny, 177, 182, 190, 191.
Dennyes, the Lady, 73 c.
Denys, 27.
Denyson, 152.
Denyson, John, 61 c.
Denyson, George, 146 c, 152 d, 155 c.
Depon, or Depom, William, 118 c d, 119 a.
Derrington, 148.
Devenish, 149, 150 b.

Dewgard (*see* Dugard and Dugood), 34 c, 137.
Dimsdel, 187 d.
Dixon, Mr., 78 b, 187 d.
Dixon, Humfrey, 76 c.
Dixon, William, 147 c, 153 d.
Dobede, 199.
Dorington, George, 167 d.
Dorrington, James, 74 c.
Dorrington, John, 86 a, b.
Dorrington, Widow, 87 a.
Dowsede, John, 46 c.
Dowsehed, John, 46 a.
Drakelowe, Ada, 6 c, 7 c, 9 a, 10 b.
Drakelowe, S.
Draper, Geo., 187 a.
Duckett, Sir George, 191.
Duddesbury, Richd., 37 b.
Dugard, John, 179 b.
Dugood, 78 d.
Duning, Samuell, 147 a.
Duke, Mr., 163 b.
Dyer, 186.
Dyker, Roberd, 143 b.

Earle, Ralfe, 148 b, 155 a.
Ederiche, 42 c.
Edgecombe, 191.
Elkin, Edward, 166 c.
Eliot, Mr., 54 b, 161 c.
Elliot, Mr. Rowland, 175 c.
Eliott, 61.
Ellis, Widow, 146 c.
Ellis, Mr., 78 c, 176 b.
Elwes, Robt., 186 c.
Ely, Mr., 187 c.
Ely, Mr. Samuel (Apothecary), 167 b.
Elyatt, John, 128 b, 137 c.
Elyot, Mr. 49 b, 55 a.
Elyot, John, 54 b.
Elyot, 160, 195.
Emerson, Robt., 149 c.
English, 187.
Erles Bury, Manor of, 122 c.
Esgore, John, 21 b, 27 a.
Eton, 141.
Eton, Julian, 37 b, 140 b.
Etrige, Mother, 161 d, 162 b.
Eve, 62, 74, 77, 153.
Eve, Mrs. Sarah, 181 b.
Eve, John, 73 b, 75 b, 150 c d.
Everard, 5 a, 9 c, 139 b.
Evered, Widow, 58 d.
Everede, 162 b.
Everist, 147.

Fairman, 88 b, 192, 196.
Fann, Francis, 187 c.
Farnham, 34 b.
Feld, Thomas, 22 d.
Feaste, Richard, 161 a.
Fleming, John, 3 b.
Fleming, 195.
Flemyng, 17.
Flyer, Francis, 186 c.
Foster, John, 161 c.
Fountayne, 59 d.
Fowle, 192, 196.
Francis, Mother, 160 b.
Fraunces, John, 23 a.
Fraunces, 61.
Frengle (?), 160 b.
Freman, Richard, 186 b.
Freeman, Robert, 163 b.
Frere, Alicia, 19 a.
Frere, John, 19 a.
Frier, Tabita, 162 b.
Furgusson, Mr., 187 c.
ffabyan, Symon, 148 c.
ffeast, Richard, 77 a, 174 d, 188 b.
ffeast, Thomas, 147 a, 153 b.
ffeild, Sir Thomas, 79 c.
ffitch, Mr., 150 a, 153 a.
ffoster, 151.
ffreeman, 78.
ffrench, 145.
ffuller, 28.
ffleccher, Robert, 29 c.
ffinshe, John, 79 b.
ffletcher, W. J., **148** c.
ffletcher, Old, 153 c.
ffoxe, 151 b.
ffranklin, Symon, 80 d.
ffreeman, Robert, 149 d, 152 d.
ffreshwater, Geo., 148 b.
ffreshwater, Lawr., 149 d.
ffreshwater, W., 150 c.
ffullere, John, 118 d, 119 b c.
ffullere, Roberd, 32 d, 143 c

Gace, High Constable, 65 c.
Gace, W., 153 b.
Game, Mr., 187 d.
Gardiner, Robert, 151 d.
Gardiner, John, 151 d.
Gardner, Edward, 81 a.
Gardner, 78 c.
Garnett, Mr., 148 c.
Garole, Mergit, 119 d.
Gary, Nath., 147 b.
Gary, Wid., 147 b.
Garye's man, 66 c.

INDEX. 227

Gase, 167.
Gates, John, 62 c.
Gaze, 161.
Gerey, Sir Thomas, 185 d.
Gennyngs, 60 b.
Gib, Richard, 42.
Gibbe, 161 c.
Gibbs, Mr. William, 174 b.
Gibson, 160 d, 194.
Gibson, Rev. Mr., 87 b, 144 b.
Gill, 85, 192.
Gill, John, 179 d.
Gill, Mr., 86 d, 187 b.
Gilson, Jean, 162 b.
Gilson, Annes, 161 c.
Gladwin, Thomas, 145 d.
Gladwin, Richard, 145 d, 153 c.
Gladwyn, Wm., 78 d., 148 a., 154 c.
Glascock, 144 a, 153 b.
Glascock, Henry, 71 c.
Glascock, Phill., 87 a.
Glascocke, John, 151 d.
Glascok, 24, 141 d.
Glascok, Grace, 45 c, 53 d.
Glascok, Mysteris, 53 b.
Glascok, John, 73 c.
Glascok, Mostres, 44 c, 45 b.
Glascok, Richard, 37 b.
Glascoke, Maistris, 161 b
Godfrey, H., 153 b.
Godfrey, Mr. and Mrs., 77 d c.
Gold, 164.
Goldsmith, 75 d.
Goldsmith, Ed., 152 a.
Gooday, 132, 134.
Goodday, Robert, 54 b.
Goodday, 138 a, 160 d.
Goodman, Dr., 82 b.
Goos, John, 6 a.
Gore, Henry, 186 b.
Gornard, 160 b.
Gost-lyn, 159 d.
Gostelyn, 61.
Gower, 62 a.
Grace, 22, 120.
Grace, John, 21 c, 119 b, 121 b c, 139 c.
Grathorne, Mr., 161 b.
Graunt, 160 b.
Grave, Richard, 54 b, 161 b.
Grave, John, 79 b, 164 d.
Graves, John, 79 b.
Gray, Edward, 151 c.
Gray, John, 80 d.
Gray, John, 76 a, 145 d.
Gray, Peter, 123 c.

Gray, William, 149 a.
Gray, 36, 54.
Graye, 160 b.
Graye, John 39.
Grene, 161 d.
Grene, John, 54 a.
Grene, Nicolas, 142 d.
Green, 155.
Green, John, 179 d, 187 c.
Green, Henry, 61 d.
Grey, Roberd, 33 b.
Grice, Henry, 154 b.
Griggs, Widow, 148 b.
Griggs, Rowland, 188.
Grigges, Thom, 65 b.
Groome, Anne, 155 c.
Grounds, George F., 88 c.
Grove, Thos., 188.
Growte, Ed., 161 b.
Gryce, Henry, 149 d.
Gryce, 71.
Gurnard, 73, 147 d.
Gurson, 192.
Gybbe, Mr., 159 a.
Gybbe, Richard, 37 d, 143 b.
Gybbe, John, 143 b,
Gybson, Edward, 54 a.
Gybson, Edward, 54 c, 61 b.
Gylsby, 160.
Gyva, Thomas, 20 b, 27 c.

Hale, 84.
Hales, Wid, 62 c.
Hales, 82 c.
Halese, 161 d.
Halton, Mr., 154 d.
Halshed, Mr., 57 a.
Hall, Isabell, 142 a.
Halle, 118.
Hamond, Ed., 146 b.
Hanchett, 82 d., 179 c.
Hannyng, 142 a.
Hanscombe, Matt., 86 d.
Harlow, 54 b, 151 d, 152 a, 161 b.
Harman, 79 b, 179 c.
Hart, Wm., 140 b.
Hart, 75.
Hartley, 80 d.
Harrington, 139 c.
Harris, Robert, 21 d.
Harrison, 159 c.
Harryes, Mother, 35 c.
Harvey, Henry, 176 c.
Harvie, 59 c.
Hastler, 73 b, 78 d, 79 d, 146 b, 181 d, 187 c.

15—2

Haward, 33.
Hawkyn, 38 c, 40 b, 53 d, 61 b, 62, 63 a, 69.
Hawkins, 53, 147 b, 153 b, 154 c, 160 d.
Hayes, 64.
Haynes, 72 c.
Haynes, Mr., 68 b, 146 c.
Hayward, Sir Ed., 92 b.
Heath, Joseph, 88 b.
Helgay, Thomas, 143 c.
Helgay, Agnes, 160 b.
Hellmes, Mr., 187 c.
Helyat, Mr., 51 c.
Hemyng, John, 161 b.
Heritage, W., 146 a.
Hignall, Mrs., 76 d.
Hignell, 193.
Hill, 190, 191.
Hille, John, 57 b, 187 b.
Hilletam', 54.
Hills, 57 c, 160 b, 161.
Hitcherson, Thos., 146 a.
Hoath, 148 c, 153 b, 154 b.
Hock, Will. Barnes, 187 d.
Hodgkin, 61 d, 148 c, 154 a.
Hodge, John, 152 b.
Hogate, Richard, 160 d.
Hogan, John, 140 a.
Hogon, John, 16 c.
Hokley, 44.
Holgate, 78 c, 147 b, 152 b, 163 b, 164, 174 d, 179 d, 188 a.
Hoothe, 61 b, 62 b.
Hopkyn, John, 34 d, 143 b.
Horwood, Mother, 161 d.
Host, Thomas, 120 c.
Host, 121.
Host, Joone, 142 c.
Hothe, 36 d, 37 d, 40 c, 45 b, 54 a, 142 d.
How, Allen, 82 b.
Howe, Mr., 64 d, 151 b, 153 b, 187 b.
Hoy, Mr., 85 d, 175 d, 176 a.
Hubberd, Mr., 134 b d, 135 a.
Hughes, William, 87 c.
Humfrey, 150 d, 153 a, 77 d.
Hunsdon, 181 c.
Hunt, Willm., 10.
Hunter, James, 188 a.
Huntington, 192, 197.
Husband, Sir Samuel, 82 b.
Hutt, John, 145 d, 164 c.
Hychcok, Perce, 140 a.
Hyde, 84, 146 c, 187 c.

Hyll, 61.
Hylls, 58 c.

Ingram, 70.
Ingrame, Joone, 142 b.
Inscriptions, Monumental, 190—220.
Isaac, Wid., 150 c.
Ive, Henry, 146 d.

Jackson, 191,
Jackson, Thos., 87 b.
Jackson, Mary, 68 d.
Jacklyn, Jo., 148 c.
Janyn, John, 10 b.
Jacob, John, 44 b, 138 a, 141 c.
Jacob, 122, 150, 161.
Jacobbe, John, 49 b, 50 c.
Jacobbe, George, 61 c, 54 b.
Jacobs, Mr., 153 b.
Jakeleyn, 141 c.
Jarfeld, Richard, 140 a.
Jardefeld, 36 d, 136.
Jardefeld, John, 140 d.
Jardefeld, Richard, 37 d, 46 c, 41 d, 134 b, 135 a, 141 d, 143 c.
Jardfeald, 54.
Jardfeld, 59 b.
Jardfeld, Rychard, 31 d.
Jardfeld, Richard, 32 c, 62 b.
Jardevill, John, 25 c, 118 c, 119 a b.
Jardevill, 120, 121.
Jardvilde, Jone, 27 c.
Jardvilde, John, 161 b.
Jardivylde, 50.
Jaxon, 61 a.
Jaxon, Eliazer, 75 d.
Jeffery, John, 63 c.
Jegon, 143.
Jegon, Thomas, 35 c, 143 a c.
Jegyn, 36.
Jegyns, 36 b.
Jenegan, 63.
Jenyn, Roger, 45 c.
Jenyn, William, 37 a.
Jenyn, Mrs., 140 d.
Jenyns, John, 27 c.
Jennens, Mr., 187 c.
Jennens, John, 166 a.
Jenning, Roger, 61 b.
Jennings, 193.
Jenyns, 31.
Jennyngs, Thos., 149 c, 153 b.
Jennyngs, John, 160 b.
Jenoure, 191, 193.
Jernegan, Mr., 61 c, 64 c, 70 c.
Jobinson, Edward, 178 b.

Jocelyne, Samuel, 181 d.
John, John, 38 b, 141 c, 143 b.
Johnson, 165 b.
Johnson, John, 80 b.
Johnson, Edward, 188.
Jollyman, Geo., 188 a.
Jone ap Rice, 33 d, 36 b.
Jones, John, 74 c.
Jones, 144, 146, 149, 187, 194, 199.
Jones, Nath., 79 a, 174 d, 187 b.
Jones, Thos., 78 d, 174 d, 179 c.
Joob-e, 41 a.
Jordan, 80.
Jordan, William, 79 d.
Joslin, Mr., 187 d.
Josselyn, Mr., 121 a.
Josselyn, 36, 44 c.
Josselyn, Thomas, 32 a.
Josselyn, John, 37 a.
Josselyn, John, 35 c, 142 b.
Joyce, David, 187 c.
Jurnegan, Mr., 64 c.
Jurningham, Thomas, 54 a.
Juby, Edward, 188 a.
Jurniman, 161 a.
Just, 150 c.
Just, Richard, 150 b.
Jynninges, John, 65 b.

Keats, 149.
Kemp, John, 39 a.
Kensey, John, 67 d.
Kendall, William, Esq., 181 c.
Kensey, 67.
Keper, Mr. Lowesse, 26 c.
Keteryng, John, 11 b c.
Killett, John, 152 c.
King, 64, 149.
Kinge, Thomas, 147 b.
Kings, Thos., 152 d.
Kirbye, 149.
Knight, 153 d.
Knight, 78, 151 a.
Knight, Mary, 83 c.
Knight, John, 79 a.
Knight, Sam, 75 b, 76 d, 77 a.
Knight, Wid., 151 a.
Knyghtton, Master, 36 b.
Kokyn, Kateyn, 29 c.
Kyng, John, 58 b, 64 c.
Kyng, 159 c.

Lack, 195.
Lamberde, 160 c.
Lambert, 159 c.
Langham, 77, 153.

Langham, William, 33 c, 77 d.
Langhame, William, 140 d.
Lapwood, 150 d.
Laxsame, 50 d.
Laxton, John, 47 d.
Lay, Mr., 77 c, 187 d.
Lay, Robert, 174 c.
Laycock, Widow, 77 c.
Laye, 41.
Leiffe, Ezechias, jun., 148 d.
Leiffe, Ezechias, sen., 149 a.
Leigh, 174, 192.
Leigh, Mr., 80 a, 148 a.
Leigh, Mrs., 72 c, 78 b.
Leigh, Mr. Thomas, 178 b.
Leventhorp, John, 16 c.
Leventhorp, 62.
Lewes, Sir, 30 c.
Lewis, Widow, 151 b.
Lewis, Robert, 55 d.
Ley, 176, 177.
Ley, Mr. W. M., 88 c.
Little, Goodwife, 162 a.
Little, 160.
Lock, Mr., 178, note.
Lockier, Mother, 159 b.
London, My Lord of, 31 c, 56 d, 57 a, 140 b.
London, Sir John, 29 c, 30, 33 d.
Low, 160 b.
Luck, 78.
Luke, 37.
Luckis, W., 149 d.
Lumkin, Robt., 87 d.
Lumly, Mary, 80 c.
Lyndsell, 153.
Lynne, John, 140 b.
Lyster, 137 b.
Lytell, John, 141 d.
Lytill, Wyllam, 136 b.

Machin, 148 b, 154 c.
Mall, 192.
Mallowe, Mr., 139 b.
Manchester, Earl of, 74 d.
Manister, 78 a, 81 b, 187 c, 174 d.
Manistyes, 164 b.
Mannsewell, John 162 c.
Mannyng, 149 b, 154 c.
Maplesden, 77 d, 84 a, 174 c, 176, 177, 180 c, 181 c, 182 c, 193.
Marcha, J., 120 b.
Marchalle, Phillippe, 53 d.
Marchaunt, 10 c, 24 d, 25 b, 26, 29, 31 b, 119 b, 120 a b, 141 b, 142 d.
Marden, 78 b, 149 b c, 161.

Mardon, 54 b.
Margaret, Atte-Lee, 10.
Marion, John, 28 b, 54 b, 160 d.
Marion, 51, 54.
Markall, 146 b.
Marks, 121 b.
Markwell, Thos., 77 d.
Marryon, John, 30 d. 61 b, 143 a, 139 d.
Marshall, 149 c.
Marshall, 154.
Marvell, Harry, 47 a.
Maryon, 32, 33.
Maryone, Old, 51 d.
Masen, Wylliam, 29 b.
Mason, Jone, 27 c.
Mason, 141.
Mason, John, 5 b, 28 c.
Masson, 24 c, 25 a.
Massum, W., 145 c.
Master, Richard, 54 b.
Mathew, 27 a, 53 c, 54 b, 81 c, 145 c, 146, 147, 148, 153, 158, 161 b, 174.
Mathewe, 57 a.
Mathewes, 153.
Mayden, Olive, 24 b.
Meade, 54 b, 61 c, 81 c, 148 d, 153 c, 175 d.
Mede, 141.
Mede, Mr., 41 d, 161 c.
Melborne, or Wellborne, 123 c.
Meller, John, 55 a.
Mendam, 62 c.
Michell, 63 c.
Middleton, 181 c, 186 c.
Milbanke, 195.
Miller, 61 b, 62, 68 b, 71, 83 d, 146 b d, 147 d, 150 c, 152 b c, 153 b, 160 c d, 161 b, 163 a, 177 d, 181, 182 a.
Mills, Wm., 164 c, 179 d.
Mills, 150, 152.
Milton, John, 151 a.
Milton, Widow, 151 a.
Milton, Thomas, 70 c.
Millington, Mr., 187 b.
Molton, 64.
Momford, 60 d, 61, 72 d, 161 c.
Monchow, ffather, 162 a.
Moncke, 147 b c.
Monk, John, 27 c.
Monke, Willm., 28 b.
Monkes, 5.
Monshoe, 159 b.
Monumental Inscriptions, 190—220.
More, Robert and Mary, 81 d.
Morgayne, 160 b.
Morley, 65, 132, 145 c, 159, 160 a c.

Morley, Lord Henry, 48 d, 56 c.
Morrice, Willm., 80 b.
Morse, William, 20 b.
Morton, 20 b.
Morwyl, Henry, 50 a.
Moulton, widdowe, 64 d.
Mountford, Samewell, 187 b.
Mowten, 69 a.
Mowton, 50 b, 151 d.
Mulmore, Duke of, 81 d.
Munday, John, 24 d, 25 b.
Murray.
Musgrave, Henry, 40 a.
Myller, 42 d, 54 b, 162 d.
Myles, 139.
Mynot, Thomas, 8 a, 19 a.

Naylor, 61.
Nayler, Thos., 61 c, 146 a.
Newce, William, 181 c.
Newcomen, Mr., 146 d.
Newcomen, Thomas, 175 b.
Newland, Jethro, 86 a.
Newland, Jeff., 86 b.
Newman, Mr., 64 b, 161 b.
Newman, John, 28 b, 54 b, 137 a
Newman, William, 20 a, 53 c.
Newman, Richard, 31 b.
Nicholls, John, 147 b.
Nicholls, Widow, 79 a.
Nicholls, 85.
Noble, 29 b.
Nobill, John, 27 b, 140 c.
Nobse, Thomas, 161 a.
Noke, 62 b.
Noke, ffather, 161 b.
Noone, Henry, 146 d.
Noone, George, 151 b.
Norfolk, 140.
Norfolk, John, 140 a.
Norfolke, Wylliam, 45 c.
Norman, Thomas, 28 d, 30 b.
Northach, Wylliam, 25 c.
Northsocke, William, 54 b.

Oates, William, 146 c.
Olyve, Mayden, 24 b.
Olyver, Thos., 149 b.
Ombler, John, 10 b, 19 b.
Ormysby, Mr., 120 d.
Ormysby, John, 140 b.
Orringe, Prince of, 83 c.
Osborne, 77 b, 79 b, 164 b, 177, 187 d, 191.
Osborne, Richard, 86 c, 181 d.
Osborne, Laur., 148 a.

Osborne, George, **148 d, 154 b**.
Osborne, Alex., **152 b**.
Oswald, George, **147 b, 160 b**.
Overseers and Collectors, Names of, 168—274.
Oxford, Earl of, **122**.
Oxinton, 196.
Oxwyth, Robert, **186 d**.

Page, John, **139 d**.
Palmer, **27 c, 61 c, 77, 78, 146 b, 148 c, 152**.
Palmer, Isaac, **150 b, 154 b**.
Palsgrave, **73 a**.
Pamflyn, **160 c**.
Panfeld, **19 b**.
Papes, An, **162 b**.
Papis, Thomas, **142 a**.
Papys, **45 d**.
Papworth, John, **120 a**.
Parcely, 136.
Parceley, Herry, **133 c**.
Parkare, Sir Henry, **50 c**.
Parker, John, **7 d**.
Parker, Henry, **123 c**.
Parker, Sir Henry, **48 d, 128 c, 132 b**.
Parle, 29.
Parseley, Henry, **54 b, 61 c**.
Parsmith, John, **56 a, 61 c**.
Parsons, **60 a, 64 d, 154, 160 d**.
Parsons, Mr. Edmund, **66 a**.
Parsons, Thomas, **54 a, 133 a**.
Parys, 37.
Partrich, 16.
Pasfield, **160 b**.
Pasfield, ffr., **146 b**.
Paske, 181.
Patmer, **49 a, 51 c, 128, 133 a, 134 b, 135, 136 b, 137 a**.
Patmore, **179 d**.
Patryk, John, **47 a**.
Paul, 193, 194, 198.
Payn, **3 b**.
Payne, **76 c, 195**.
Payne, John, **23 b, 30 d, 78 b**.
Payne, William, **62 c**.
Payne, Henry, **151 c**.
Payne, Richard, **150 b**.
Pecocke, **62 a**.
Pedley, 193.
Peercy, **45 a**.
Peerson, **149 d, 160 c**.
Pegrome, John, **75 d, 149 b**.
Pelham, 29 d, 140.
Percye, **62 c**.
Perselay, Henry, **160 d**.

Peresmith, **160 d**.
Pernell, 120.
Perse, **161 c**.
Perry, 178, note.
Perry, Widow, **86 b**.
Perry, Mrs., **150 d**.
Perry, Charles and Robert, **87 b c**.
Perry, Thomas, **160 b**.
Petche, John, **41 b**.
Pettford, John, **24 d**.
Pettitt, Geo., **152 c**.
Peyn, John, **41 b, 143 c**.
Philippa, Queen, **123 b**.
Philippe of Haseley, **53 d, 66 d**.
Philpot, Mr., **121 a**.
Phillipps, John, **146 d**.
Phillips, Eliz., **77 d**.
Picke, John, **53 d**.
Pickering, Peter, **149 b**.
Pigott, Thos., **150 b**.
Pilkin, 194.
Pilesdon, **160 d**.
Pilleston, John, **35 c**.
Pilston, **54 a, 58 a**.
Pinton, Widow, **151 a**.
Pipon, 192.
Pitts, **152 a**.
Playle, **162 a**.
Plomer, **62 d, 161 b**.
Plum, Edward, **151 d**.
Polhill, **188 a, 193**.
Pond, John, **147 a**.
Popeley, Mr., **87 b**.
Potter, **45 a**.
Poulter, John, **87 b**.
Powell, Mr., **147 d**.
Prene, 33.
Prenties, **160 b**.
Preslond, **57 c**.
Prior, 151.
Prior, Richard, **27 c**.
Prior, William, **140 b**.
Prior, ffr., **152 b**.
Priour, William, **17 d**.
Pryce, Henry, **68 d**.
Pryor, Thomas, **79 b, 164 b**.
Pye, 40.
Pye, Edward, **142 c**.
Pygeon, Thomas, **3 b, 5 c, 17 d**.
Pygeon, Richard, **19 a**.
Pygott, William, **46 c**.
Pygott, William, **51 c, 128 b**.
Pykat, Thomas, **50 d**.
Pylston, Willm., **54 b, 160 b**.
Pylston, Richard, **51 a**.
Pyllestone, Mr., **42 c, 53 b**.

Pylleston, John, 142 b.
Pynn, John, 77 c.

Rafe, John, 42 c.
Rafe, 46 d.
Rafe, the Sexton, 33 b.
Ramsay, Mr., 147 a, 161 b.
Ramsey, 54, 61, 77 c, 87 c, 151 b, 153 d, 154 d, 167, 174 d.
Ramshaw, Edw., 79 a.
Rannum, Thos., 146 d.
Ransewold, 46 d.
Rawlyn, 152 b.
Ray, Mr., 79 b.
Rayment, 160 b.
Raynold, Nic., 54 b, 151 a.
Raynolds, John, 147 b.
Read, 75, 147, 164.
Read, Mr., 77 c, 153 c, 179 d.
Reade, 63 d, 148, 174 a, 178 d, 184 b.
Rede, William, 7 d, 8 b.
Rede, 65.
Reding, 140 b.
Redontone, Wyllium, 139 d.
Redwood, Nicolas, 34 a, 37 a, 141 b.
Redyington, Herry, 137 d.
Redyngton, 119, 139.
Reeve, John, 166 c, 188.
Reighnolds, Mr., 187 d.
Ren, Thos., 186 d.
Renyngton, Wylm., 142 c.
Renyngton, Herry, 142 c.
Reynold, 26 d, 27 a, 42 c.
Reynolds, John, 167 c.
Reynolds, Mr., 78 b, 178 b.
Rhodes, 200.
Ricard, John, 9 d.
Richardson, Nick., 85 c.
Risby, 85 c.
Roberd, 26 a, 121 c.
Roberds, Ric., 138 a.
Roberdes, Mother, 161 c.
Robert, little Robyn, 21 c, 24 a.
Roberts, 192, 196, 197.
Roberts, Mr., 49 b d, 187 d.
Robinson, Samuel, 186 c.
Robson, 160 c.
Robyn, Little, 21 c, 24 a.
Roce, Thomas, 147 a.
Rochell, Mrs. Judeth, 84 b.
Rochill, Mrs. Judeth, 182 a.
Rochill, 181.
Rochill, William, 180 b.
Rodlon, William, 18 a.
Rogers, 193.
Roose, William, 22 b.

Roper of Stansted, 60 a.
Rose, John, 8 c.
Rosy, Raff, 139 c.
Rottor, 26.
Rowe, Mr., 146 a.
Rowell, Edward, 150 c.
Rowell, John, 150 a.
Rowell, Gyles, 147 c.
Rushe Anne, 141 b.
Russell, 70 b, 119 b, 148 d, 155 b, 160 b.
Rutland, Mr., 83 b, 187 d.
Rutland, 192, 193, 194.
Rutland, Simon, 164 c.
Rutter, Thomas, 141 c.
Ryce, John, 152 a.
Rynger, Wyllm., 141 c.

Sabbisford, Margaret, 20 b.
Sabyn, ffr., 148 b.
Sadd, 71, 139, 140, 141, 152.
Sadde, 22.
Sale, Roberd, 38 d.
Salmon, 190, 195.
Samford, Wm., 76 a.
Sanders, 83 c, 86 b, 146 c, 153.
Sanders, Wido, 151 b.
Sandford, 78 c, 183 b, 187 c, 191.
Sandye, Mr., 65 b.
Saunder, ffather, 161 c.
Saunders, Mr., 85 b c, 187 c, 174 d, 181 d.
Santon, George, 62 a.
Savell, Robert, 140 b.
Savell, 61.
Savell, Edward, 151 b.
Savill, Robert, 33 c.
Savyll, Roberd, 34 c, 35 c.
Savyll, John, 53 a.
Sawyer, 159.
Sawyere, Richard, 145 d, 155 a.
Sawyere, Michell, 160 c.
Say, Sir William, 20 a, 40 b.
Sayer, Ed., 187 a b.
Sayling, 120 d.
Scharpe, 44 b, 125 a.
Schepperd, Willm., 25 c, 26 a, 38 b.
Schooling, Goodman, 188 a.
Schropis, 121.
Schrymp, John, 53 b.
Sckeppe, Herry, 24 d.
Sckyngle, 65 b.
Scrubie, James, 147 b.
Scrybe, 52 c.
Scott, 79 a, 152 b, 164 c, 165, 183 b, 187 c, 193, 198.

Sebright, Ed., 187 a.
Sedgwick, Mr., 78 b.
Seynden, Willm., 119 a.
Shepherd, 61.
Shepperd, 33 c, 64 c, 121 b, 163 a, 168.
Sherwood, John, 54 a.
Short, Thomas, 21 d.
Shrimpe, Robt., 62 b.
Silvers, Isaac, 150 c.
Skepper, 141 d.
Skingle, John, 54 a, 57 a.
Skyngell, John, 60 c, 61 b, 160 b.
Skyllingham, 45 c.
Skynner, Harman, 139 c, 146 c.
Slater, Mr., 71 a, 149 c, 152 d.
Smallwood, 85 d.
Smith, 57 d, 62 c, 69 c, 147 c, 149 a, 150 b, 192, 195, 196.
Smithe, 153.
Smyth, John, 26 b, 27 b, 42 d, 54 b, 61 a, 133 d, 134 c, 139 d.
Smyth, Rafe, 133 b d, 134 c, 136 c, 138 b.
Smyth, 135.
Smyth, Rado, 138 b.
Smythe, Raphe, 49 c.
Smythe, Warren, 49 c.
Smythers, John, 141 a.
Snoden, Samuel, 175 d, 181 d.
Snow, 128.
Snowe, 54 b, 61 c, 130 d, 131, 133 d, 134 d, 135, 136 c, 161.
Snowdon, Mr., 187 c.
Soles, John, 54 b.
Solese, ffather, 161 b.
South, 152.
Southe, Thomas, 43 d.
Sowthe, John, 54 a. 160 d.
Sparke, Dothe, 146 b.
Sparke, 190.
Sparks, Dr., 78 b.
Sparow, Elizabeth, 32 a.
Sparwe, John, 7 c.
Speciall, 165.
Speller, John, 152 c.
Spencer, 20 d, 31 c.
Spencer, Herry, 38 a, 142 a.
Spencer, Rev. Charles, 38 a.
Spenser, Henry, 23 c.
Spesichall, Wm., 187 c.
Spicer, 119.
Spicer, Elizabeth, 24 c.
Spryngholt, John, 6 c d, 7 c, 8 b.
Spryg, John, 55 a.
Sprygge, John, 53 d.

Spycer, 37.
Stacie, John, 151 c.
Stacy, 24 a.
Stafford, 84 d.
Stafford, Thos., 166 c.
Stafford, 187.
Staines, 188, 193, 197.
Standhoop, Dr., 67 b.
Stanes, 145 c, 150 c, 160 b, 162 a.
Stanley, Dr., 86 d.
Stanley, William, 186 b.
Stanley, Rev. Mr., 144 b.
Starford, Mr., 86 b.
Starkyn, Raffe, 53 d.
Staverd, Mrs., 71 b.
Staverd, 195.
Sterdy, Thomas, 139 d.
Stevens, 147 a, 164 b.
Stocke, 151.
Stok, Thomas, 49 a.
Stoke, 29 b.
Stonard, 43 b.
Stokes, 150.
Stonard, 43.
Stone, John, 22 b, 25 b, 186 d.
Stone, 27.
Stonhard, John, 8 b.
Strachie, 191.
Stracy, James, 57 b.
Stracy, of Reyston, 33 c.
Strase, John, 161 b.
Stratford, Ralph de, 123 b.
Stringer, Walter, 148 d.
Strong, 25 a c, 152 c, 154 d.
Sturdy, 32 c, 119 b, 121, 140 a.
Sturdy, Margytt, 142 c.
Summers, James Hillat, 88 b.
Sumpner, Raynold, 61 d.
Swafeham, William, 23 d.
Sweting, Mother, 162 b.
Sweting, Nath., 167 d.
Sweeting, 69.
Sybthorpe, 29 b, 43 a, 141 c.
Symsone, Thomas, 51 c.
Symson, 123 a.
Symson, Thomas, 128 b.

Tailor, 27 c.
Talbott, Mrs. Margaret, 82 a.
Talwyn, 170 a d.
Tanner, 139.
Tanner, John Hilse, 161 c.
Tavenour, John, 187 d.
Tayler, John Cok., 29 d.
Tayler, William, 20 b, 67 d, 68 a, 150 b, 152 d, 160 c.

Taylor, Richard, 63 b, 64 a.
Taylor, 60, 65 d, 143 d, 192, 194, 199.
Taylor, Samuel, 179 a.
Teasor, 67 a.
Tebold, Richard, 37 a.
Tedsewell, Mother, 162 b.
Tendring, Mrs., 146 b.
Teybole, Richard, 143 b.
Thayer, 192.
Thayn, 192.
Theabalds, Willm., 85 a.
Thomas, 50.
Thomas, Rafe, 36 c.
Thompson, 128.
Thomson, George, 40 c, 51 c.
Thorne, Tho., 152 c, 176.
Thresher, 18.
Throssher, 141 d.
Thurkeld, 3 b, 14.
Thurgood, Gyfferey, 40 a.
Thurgood, Wid., 155 c.
Thurgood, 20 b, 42 c, 77 d, 119 d, 141 a, 148.
Thurgood, Thos., 150 c.
Thurkill, 21.
Tidie, 154.
Tingie, George, 152 c.
Tinker, John, 25 a.
Thredcoab, Bennett, 164 b.
Tolson, Widow, 148 c.
Tomsone, Mr., 51 d.
Tompsone, John, 140 c.
Tompson, 61, 70, 140.
Took, Rev. Thomas, 166 b, 181 d.
Tooke, 85, 178, 187, 193.
Torner, 53 b.
Tornor, John, 55 a.
Torington, John, 71 c.
Townesend, 56, 64 c, 149 c, 150 b, 160 c.
Trapps, William, 151 b.
Trenham, 46, 134.
Trenham, Roger, 41 a, 43 b, 44 d, 45 b, 133 d.
Trigg, John, 147 d, 153 c.
Trotte, 18 c.
Trotte, John, 8 a, 28 a.
Turk, Steven, 139 d.
Turner, Sir Edward, 181 c, 183 a.
Turnor, 20 b, 29 d, 30 d, 47 d, 52, 186 c.
Twistleton, Henry, 186 d.
Tydie, Wido., 149 b
Tydie, Thos., 150 b.
Tyes, Tyse, or Ties, 57 c, 59 b, 60 c.

Tyler, 25 d, 72, 82 b, 86, 151 b, 161 b, 187 c.
Tynker, John, 26 b d.
Tyse, 52, 53.

Underwood, Robert, 85 a.

Vandermeulen, Fred., 88 b.
Venter, Burgess, 151 c.
Veysie, Mrs., 68 c.
Vicars of St. Michael's, List of, 110, 111.
Vicar, Mr., 26 a, 52 b, 121 b.
Victor, Baldwyn, 121 d.
Vinteman, Anne, 179 a.
Vykar, The, 51 a.
Vyker, 42.
Vyker, Master, 36 b.

Wainkfords, Mr., 83 a.
Walchis House, 41 c.
Walker, Thomas, 152 c.
Wall, 61, 71, 147 a, 150 b, 152, 154 a, 155 b.
Waller, 37.
Wallis, John, 152 b.
Wallis, Henry, 78 a, 85 d, 164 d, 179 b.
Walsingham, 150 a.
Wankford, Mr., 87 b, 187 c.
Ward, Mr., 81 c.
Warden, 17.
Waren, Roger, 49 b, 138 a.
Waren, 138 b.
Warman, 86 d, 150 d.
Warman, Thos., 71 a, 72 a b c, 75 c.
Warman, Old, 155 c.
Warner, Ed., 152 b.
Warner, 151 b, 166.
Warner, William, 21 d.
Waren, 49.
Warren, 159.
Water, 50 b.
Water, Roberd, 33 c, 42 c, 44 a, 137 b.
Water, Thomas, 59 b.
Waters, 150 a.
Waters, Widow, 78 d.
Waton, 50 d.
Wavell, John, 5 c, 6 a, 7 c, 9 b.
Waylett, John, 86 c.
Waynckfords, Mr., 81 b.
Web, 42 c.
Web, 150 c.
Webbe, Ben, 160 a.
Webb, Edward, 5 c.
Wede, (?) 50 b.
Wecks, Mr., 88 a.

INDEX.

Weldham, John, 14 a.
West, Mr., 148 d., 153 b, 160 b.
Westwood, 136.
Westwoode, 147 c.
Whales, Prince of, 83 b.
Whall, 67 d.
Wheatley, Thos., 77 c.
Whepill, Thomas, 32 b, 141 a.
Wheple, Thomas, 139 c.
Whepyll, Mr., 31 a, 44 c, 49 b.
Whetele, 161 d.
Whippell, 61.
Whippelle, John, 53 d.
White, George, 179 c.
White, 77, 162 b, 163 b.
White, Wid., 151 a.
Whittnow, Mr., 120 c.
Whyte, 41 a.
Wick, 187.
Wifild, John, 161 a.
Wilby, 193, 194.
Willaye, Mr., 161 b.
Willey, 21 c, 54.
Williams, Mother, **159** b.
Williamson, Mary, 75 d.
Willow, Francis, 187 c.
Wilsem, Jo., 147 c.
Wilsemar, Thomas, 160 d.
Wilsemer, 62.
Wilson, John, **151** b.
Wingate, Mr., **151** a.
Winter, 194.
Wolley, 164, 165, 181, 187 b.
Wolverston, John, 19 d.
Wolverston, 3.
Wood, 31, 61, 64 c, 150 d, 188 a.

Wood, Widow, 160 b.
Woode, Richard, 32 d, 53 d, 141 a, 143 b, 146 d.
Wooley, 164 b.
Woolley, 78, 164.
Woolly, 143 d, 144 b.
Wright, John, 5 d, 6 d, 7 b, 8 b, 9 d, 16 b, 187 a.
Wright, 150 b, 193.
Wright, W., 78 c, 152 d.
Write, Mother, **162** b.
Wryght, 142 c.
Wulman, 47 d.
Wyberd, John, 81 c, 146 d.
Wyberd, Tho., 150 b.
Wybert, John, 179 a.
Wylcoks, Mr., 51 d.
Wyldechery, My Lady of, 29 a.
Wylde, Richard, 118 c.
Wilkinson, John, 23 d, 24 c.
Wyllay, John, 51 d.
Wylley, 54, 62, 131, 136.
Wylley, Edward, 48 a, 50 d, 51 c, 128 b, 130 d, 132 a, 133 c, 134 b, 135 a b, 137 a, 156 a.
Wylley, John, 33 d, 140 b.
Wylley, 40 b.
Wylsemer, Tho., 57 a.
Wynn, ffrancis, 77 d.

Yardley, Dr. 84 c.
Yardley, John, 181 c.
Yardley, 192, 194.
Yve, 20.
Yve, John, 84 c.

THE END.

ELLIOT STOCK, LONDON.

www.ingramcontent.com/pod-product-compliance
Lightning Source LLC
Chambersburg PA
CBHW020807230426
43666CB00007B/903